Ultimate
Auto Workshop
Design & Planning

David Jacobs, Jr.

MBI Publishing
Company

First published in 1997 by MBI Publishing
Company, PO Box 1, 729 Prospect Avenue,
Osceola, WI 54020-0001 USA

The information in this book is true and
complete to the best of our knowledge. All
recommendations are made without any
guarantee on the part of the author or Publisher,
who also disclaim any liability incurred in
connection with the use of this data or specific
details.

We recognize that some words, model names and
designations, for example, mentioned herein are
the property of the trademark holder. We use
them for identification purposes only. This is not
an official publication.

MBI Publishing Company books are also available
at discounts in bulk quantity for industrial or
sales-promotional use. For details write to Special
Sales Manager at Motorbooks International
Wholesalers & Distributors, 729 Prospect Avenue,
PO Box 1,Osceola, WI 54020-0001 USA.

Library of Congress Cataloging-in-Publication
Data

Jacobs, David H.

Ultimate auto workshop design & planning /
David H. Jacobs, Jr.
    p. cm. — (Powerpro series)
Includes bibliographical references and index.
ISBN 0-7603-0213-8 (pbk. : alk. paper)
1. Automobile repair shops—Design and
construction.
2. Workshops—Designs and plans.
3. Workshops—Equipment and supplies.
I. Title. II. Series: MBI Publishing Company
powerpro series.
TL152.J297 1997   96-6563
629.28'7—dc21

On the front cover: A bright, clean, comfortable
garage such as this one is ideal for tuning and
restoring your vehicle. Tools are stored
conveniently in the tool box with larger items
hung on pegboards. Remember to install safety
features such as a fire extinguisher and smoke
alarm. *David Newhardt*

On the back cover: Many auto enthusiasts labor
in unorganized, dark garages, which are cold in
the winter and broiling in the summer. Yet
converting an unsuitable garage into a
comfortable workspace like this one, requires the
same types of mechanical skills you already
possess. *David Gooley* A 12x20 one-stall garage
space is a common size for an automotive
workshop. If pressed for space, the shop vacuum
can be stored under the workbench and the air
compressor housed elsewhere to make room for
more storage or another small workbench.

Printed in the United States of America

CONTENTS

ACKNOWLEDGMENTS

The ideas and plans presented in this book are an accumulation of thoughts and printed materials from a number of different people, companies and organizations. I very much want to thank them all for their time, consideration and participation.

A day was spent with Ron Hoffer shooting pictures of his shop. I thank him for the tours through the shops of Chuck Saydan and Pete Burton, his neighbors and fellow auto enthusiasts.

Bob Shawley, Marv Ottness, John Hubbard, John Gittings, Steve Hayes, Bob Greer, Jim Yocum, Brian Lord, Rick and Ron Weglin, Jeff Myer, Alec Emerson, Todd Jensen and Mike Holiman came up with some great shop ideas. I appreciate their help, input and the opportunity to view their workshops.

Craig Southey, Service Manager for Lynnwood Cycle-Barn, Steve Malland, Parts/Service Director for BMW Seattle, and Garry Allen, owner of Jags Plus in Everett, Washington, were most kind to share their auto workshop ideas with me. I appreciate their insight from the automotive professional's point of view.

Timm Locke, Product Publicity Manager for the Western Wood Products Association, provided an abundant array of plans from the WWPA. Likewise, Maryann Olson, Project Coordinator/Public Relations for the American Plywood Association, made a set of plans available for a handy Car Care Cart. I appreciate their continued support.

I want to thank the following people and the companies they represent for their participation in this book project: Michael F. Watkins, Marketing Manager, Adjustable Clamp Company; Betty Talley, Manager of Marketing Services, and Chris Voss, American Tool Companies, Inc.; Victor Lopez, Technical Service Manager, Behr Process Corporation; Hilarie Meyer, Merchandising Manager, Campbell Hausfeld; Jeff Tenant, Marketing Manager, Crush-Proof Tubing Company; Tom Tracy, Advertising Manager, Eagle Windows and Doors; Curt Strohacker, President and David Bowes, The Eastwood Company; David Martel, Marketing Manager, Central Purchasing, Inc. (Harbor Freight Tools); Peter Fetterer, Director of Public Affairs, Kohler Company; Eileen Heller, Marketing Coordinator, Lasko Metal Products, Inc.; Jack Hori, Senior Vice President and Roy Thompson, Makita USA, Inc.; Bill Cork, Public Relations Manager, Plano Molding Company; Bob McCully, Vice President of Sales and Marketing, Power Products Company (SIMKAR); Robert Suarez, Sales Manager, Quality Doors; Bruce Cantrell, Advertising Manager, Rotary Lift; Rob Guzikowski, Marketing Manager and Jason Liebreich, Simpson Strong-Tie Connector Company, Inc.; Shelley Nehrt, Marketing Manager, Stack-on Products; Francis Hummel, Director of Marketing, The Stanley Works; Jim Richeson, President, Sta-Put Color Pegs; and Douglas L. Hicks, Executive Editor, WoodsmithShop Catalog.

My wife Janna spent a lot of time at the computer putting together numerous plans and diagrams for use as illustrations in this book. I appreciate her efforts and thank her for jobs well done. And, finally, I want to thank Zack Miller, Senior Editor and Anne Mckenna, Editor and all of the folks at Motorbooks International for their continued assistance and support.

INTRODUCTION

Seldom does anyone simply dive headlong into a new hobby. Most of us chance upon areas of interest through family members, friends, magazine articles or television shows. Through time, we develop more and more interest in particular pastimes, and continue to learn more about subjects honing our skills as we go, digging deeper into our interests. Our growing skill and interest eventually creates a need for larger workspaces to house the assortment of tools and equipment required.

Most automotive enthusiasts have been turning wrenches or pounding out dents for some time before deciding to set up viable automotive workshops. Most already have a place where they work on their projects. They have just reached the point of considering a more convenient, comfortable and safe place to carry on with, or enhance, their automotive endeavors.

Understand that there is no universal floor plan or layout for perfect automotive workshops. Regardless of size, avid auto enthusiasts have turned out fabulous work from such workspaces as back yards, basements, carports, and one-car garages. The notion that you must have an elaborate workshop equipped with all the latest gadgets to perform quality auto work is simply not true. Bigger is not always better.

However, even if your current space may be adequate right now, wouldn't it be great to have a space that was set up just the way you wanted it? That had a place for everything and everything in its place? Indeed, automotive repair, alteration and restoration activities are much easier to manage and quicker to complete in a well-designed work area. Designing a workshop with convenience, comfort and safety in mind can create a workshop where folks can really enjoy their automotive hobbies and passions.

Professional automotive technicians are provided with large workshops outfitted with the latest in equipment for good reason. They must turn out quality work in minimal time for businesses to remain profitable. The same is not true for home based auto enthusiasts. Larger workshops and equipment inventories are simply enhancements that help to make their automotive activities more enjoyable, convenient and safer. Get the picture?

This book is designed for automotive enthusiasts. It will not cover such topics as $100,000 paint booths, laser guided frame straighteners or other expensive devices geared toward professionals. Rather, the focus will remain on ideas that will help serious, non-professional auto aficionados learn how to set up home based workshops for maximum comfort, convenience and safety.

Information and plans are included along with floor plans and workshop layouts to help you learn how to build workbenches, storage units and other accessories. Let the text, illustrations and photos show you what can be done. Then, use your imagination to improve upon and expand what is presented. Although the activities carried on inside home based auto workshops may be similar, floor plans, layouts and equipment inventories will vary. Each shop carries the signature of its owner. What may be the single most important attribute for one might appear foolish to another.

Relax. Realize that you will not come up with a perfect workshop floor plan or layout on the first try. You probably won't on the second or third try, either. Eventually, you will discover a perfect blend. All of your workbenches, tools, pieces of equipment, parts, supplies and preferred creature comforts will be located precisely where and how you want them. If you are like most of the automotive enthusiasts I have talked with, that time will come only after you have spent plenty of hours planning, arranging, working in, and then rearranging your shop for maximum convenience, comfort and safety. Have fun creating your new workspace. Understand it will take some trial and error before you get to that magic moment when you have a place for everything and everything in its place.

Chapter 1
GENERATING IDEAS

"Now, why didn't I think of that?"

How many times have you repeated the above statement? Most of us have after we see a new tool, recognize a new workshop accessory, or watch someone perform a time saving repair procedure. Although we may think that it is always someone else who comes up with new ideas, we must understand that we can, too.

Plato once said, *". . .the true creator is necessity, which is the mother of our invention."* In other words, it is the need for something that creates the ambition to fulfill it. The need to have a convenient, comfortable, and safe place to work on automobiles, has led to the creation of thousands of automotive workshops. The desire to accomplish a large variety of automotive repair, alteration and restoration tasks has led to an equally large number of auto workshop floor plans and layouts.

While we know there are thousands of different workshops, we must recognize that each workshop has been designed and outfitted to meet specific needs.

A radiator shop, for example, will be different from a front-end alignment shop, and an autobody shop will be different than a new car dealer's service department. In this way, most home based auto workshops are uniquely different from each other, depending upon the owner's automotive interests, creature comforts, budget, and so on.

What this all boils down to is there are many different ways to set up your automotive workplace. The problem is, how do you find out exactly what you want to do? Start your project with the planning stage. This is where you research the subject to learn what others have done and then start incorporating those ideas into your overall workshop plan. This will take time. You will probably come up with more ideas than you could possibly put into effect. Eventually, you will whittle your wish list down to a reasonable level and be ready to put together a convenient, comfortable and safe automotive workshop that is uniquely yours.

Magazine and newsletter resources

A variety of automotive magazines and newsletters are published each month. While most of them focus upon specific automobile repair, alteration or restoration subjects, you will find some, like *Skinned Knuckles*, that periodically feature articles about workshops. Articles cover workshop accessories, new tools, and creative solutions to storage or other common auto workplace problems. In addition, look closely at the pictures in these magazines and newsletters. Many times, good workshop layouts or creative storage systems are revealed in the background

Most libraries carry good assortments of magazines. Scan the library's microfiche or computer to select those with articles of interest. Look for titles of articles that depict workshop themes. This will help to narrow the sheer number of magazines you may want to look through. At your leisure, look through other magazines in hopes of finding photos with neat workshop backgrounds.

Research home improvement periodicals, too. *The Family Handyman* and *Workbench* frequently carry articles that show how to build workbenches and storage cabinets, install lights, outfit home garages, etc.

Automotive and home improvement magazines are found in supermarkets, convenience stores, and book stores as well. *Hemmings Motor News* regularly carries advertisements for sources that offer automotive books and written material of all kinds. This periodical also features plenty of sources for tools, equipment and other workshop accessories.

Experienced auto professionals

Professional auto mechanics, autobody technicians and others in the trade, set up their workshops for maximum work output. You will not find much in the area of creature comforts and the only "frills" are tools and pieces of equipment set up to make jobs progress with optimum efficiency. Although workshop convenience, comfort and safety are prime focal points for home based auto work sites, as opposed to volume and speed, you may spot a number of handy attributes in professional workshops that can easily be adapted into yours.

Workbenches are a good example. If your automotive interests include working on gauges and other dashboard assemblies, how are the workbenches set up at a local speedometer shop? Are they set a little higher than normal so technicians can

This professional auto repair garage does not have many cupboards or storage cabinets, since there is little need for them. Parts and supplies are delivered to the shop and used right away. Tools are generally out in the open for quick retrieval. This counter serves as a storage depot and paperwork center. Note that it was built at a height to accommodate workers as they stand or sit on stools.

sit on stools while working? Is compressed air piped directly to workbenches? How do they arrange small parts storage and electrical receptacles?

For heavy duty work, how are workbenches set up at the local transmission shop? Are tops made from 2x6 or larger lumber? Are they covered with metal so transmission fluid can be easily wiped up? Are they outfitted with a heavy duty shelf below for large parts storage?

Plan to visit a number of professional automobile repair centers in your area. Bring along a six-pack of soda or a box of doughnuts to sweeten up the service manager and technicians so you can learn about their dream workshop ideas. Be realistic and understand that these people are working for a living and may not have time to spend with you at the moment. If so, politely ask if there is a better time and make an appointment.

Mechanics

You might have the best luck talking with mechanics from privately owned garages, as opposed to those at new car service departments. Owner/operators are responsible for everything in their workplaces. Since they are the ones who must work in their shops and pay for alterations or additions, you should be able to get some great information regarding general workshop convenience and actual cost factors.

Look around these shops to see what has been done to facilitate various automotive endeavors. Are they outfitted with pits or above ground lifts? How high are the ceilings? Are air lines and electrical wires routed inside walls or mounted on the surface of the wall in metal pipe? Is one way better than the other? Ask owners and technicians why lines were run a particular way. What are the benefits and downfalls of each method?

For general auto work, private garages may be filled with a large assortment of tools and equipment. How are these things arranged throughout the shop? Are they easy to access? Does the owner wish the arrangement was different? If so, why? How does the equipment inventory in this shop match up with the things you have or expect to purchase in the future?

Pay attention to storage, especially that for commonly used items. Are power and pneumatic tools stowed in cabinets, or are they readily available on pegboard hooks? Does this mechanic prefer a huge roll-around tool chest, or simply a work cart that is filled with tools and parts for just the jobs at hand? What type of system is used for nut, bolt and washer storage? How does the workshop's layout effect maneuverability and convenience? Should a parts washer be located closer to a "dirty" workbench where parts are routinely taken apart, or near another where units are put back together? Ask the owner and technicians questions like these. You never know when your question might prompt a response like, "Now, why didn't I ever think about that!"

Rick and Ron Weglin, owners of Harrah's Automotive in West Seattle, Washington, work out of a shop that has just one large bay. They perform general repair and maintenance on all types of automobiles. It didn't take long for them to realize that they needed an auto lift. They selected an above ground model.

Once the lift was installed, a problem arose when they went to raise a car while its hood was in the open position. Although the ceiling height could easily accommodate a car, it wasn't quite high enough for the front end of an open hood. To solve the problem, Rick and Ron cut a hole in the ceiling drywall to make room for open hood ends between the ceiling joists. This solution also enabled them to park a car under another that was already raised. Now, while a car is parked on the raised lift while Rick and Ron wait for parts delivery, they can work on another stationed below.

The inner sides and top of holes cut in ceiling drywall must be lined on the inside with new drywall to maintain the fire rated safety protection of drywall ceilings. The same holds true for other holes made in walls and partitions. This is especially important for home based garages. Walls and ceilings that separate garages from home living spaces must be covered with 5/8-inch drywall. This is a requirement of the Fire Code and is truly a safety issue. Should a fire break out in your garage, you will want this measure of protection to keep the fire from extending into your home.

Autobody Technicians

In contrast to a mechanic's repair garage, an autobody technician's shop will generally sport much more in the way of open working room and less in the area of workbenches and equipment units. Autobody technicians require much open space to facilitate their needs to remove and install body panels, doors, trunk lids, hoods, etc. Autobody shops commonly have sets of sawhorses available that are used to support body parts while paint preparation work is done on them. This facet also requires plenty of working room.

Along with plenty of open space, autobody repair and paint shops rely upon organized systems of small parts storage. Units are needed to house nuts, bolts, washers, screws, bumpers, grommets, and other similar small body parts. If these items were scattered around shops in small cardboard boxes, it would be difficult and time consuming for technicians to find what they are looking for.

Many of the small parts storage systems found in active autobody shops are provided by the small parts manufacturers and suppliers themselves. Not only does this help autobody shop technicians by having parts organized and close at hand, it also helps small parts supply representatives by making it easiest for them to determine what amount of inventory needs to be replaced during monthly or routine sales calls.

To locate similar parts bins for your shop, ask an autobody shop manager for the name of the small parts supplier in your area. Contact him or her for information. You can also visit swap meets and look under the classified ad sections of newspapers under used auto parts or tools/machinery.

Autobody shops have specific storage systems for tools and other supplies. Since a large amount of dust is created in these shops from sanding body panels, many tools are stored in cabinets equipped with tight fitting doors. Cabinet door jambs may even be lined with weather-stripping to help keep dust out. If you plan to undertake a number of autobody jobs in your shop, pay strict attention to how professionals keep their stored tools and accessories clean during regular grinding and sanding operations.

Dismantled auto parts storage is another area of concern for autobody repair shop technicians. Where do they store seats, doors, hoods, trunk lids, glass and small parts while main bodies of stripped automobiles are worked on? Do they have special racks or shelves for these things? If so, how are they built? Where are they located in the shop? Are these auto parts storage units practical and convenient, or just something that was thrown together for one job and then used continually ever since? How could you improve upon those storage ideas in front of you? How would the shop manager or technicians improve upon that system if they had the time?

Ron Hoffer built this rack between some 2x6 wall studs on an exterior wall of his shop. The racks are used to store many small plastic trays. This part of his workshop is outfitted for woodworking and the trays are used to store nails. A similar storage system could be used for nuts, bolts, washers and other automotive fasteners and small parts.

Good questions that might result in interesting answers and new ideas.

Some other things you may want to investigate while visiting autobody repair shops are: What types of air filtration systems are used? How do the shops dispose of hazardous materials waste, like solvents, thinners, reducers, and so on? How are flammable liquids stored for maximum safety? What are the best means for storing and dispensing masking materials? What about cloth and paper shop towels?

Naturally, you may not want to spend the kind of money it takes to outfit professional autobody shops, but you should be able to come up with some good ideas that, if altered to your budget, could serve the same basic purpose. For example, instead of a commercial size small parts bin made with sheet metal and roller slides, you may be able to get by with a series of heavy duty plastic storage units available at local hardware or home improvement centers. These units may be secured to walls in a uniform fashion and the box or tray fronts labeled for ease of parts identification.

The same holds true for other shop aspects, like air filtration. Instead of shopping for an expensive commercial grade air filtration system, look for ads in woodworking magazines that display small air filtration units. Most of the air filtration systems advertised in woodworking magazines are designed for small home based workshops about the size of regular two-car garages.

Painters

Autobody repair shops are likely to double as paint shops. Professional auto painters must use special paint booths. They must use them for two reasons: first, to ensure jobs are not marred by airborne debris; and, second, to conform to a number of governmental regulations regarding environmental concerns and air pollution from paint overspray. Top quality spray paint booths cost over $100,000.00.

Because of the restrictions governing use of automotive paint products, you should check with your local autobody paint supply store before planning to paint your vehicle in a home workshop. In some cases, it may be best to pay a professional to do the job in an approved paint booth, or, you might be able to rent time in a booth from a local paint shop.

Other than the paint booth, look around the painters work area to see if you can pick up a few tips for your workshop. How are paint products stored for maximum safety? Large painting facilities are equipped with flammable liquid storage rooms. These areas are protected with fire sprinklers, fire walls and fire doors. In addition, concrete curbs are featured just under the doors. These curbs are designed to hold back fluids that may leak from damaged containers. For smaller shops, look for flammable liquid storage cabinets.

Flammable liquid storage cabinets are made of metal and are equipped with metal doors and self-closing hinges. Each door is held open with a fusible link; a small metal bar hooked to chain at each end with a softer metal holding the bar together in the middle. The soft metal in the bar is designed to melt at a prescribed temperature that will then allow the door to automatically close. This design is incorporated into cabinets to keep flames away from flammable liquids in case of fire. A metal curb at the bottom of cabinets helps to contain liquids that leak from damaged containers.

Paint guns must be cleaned after each use. How do professional painters accomplish this task? Do they have a special paint gun cleaning tub or workbench area? How do they store used solvents and thinners? Can you devise a similar storage system in your shop? Most paint shops store used solvents and thinners in special 50-gallon drums. When drums are full, a hazardous waste disposal company picks them up and drops off empty storage barrels. Maybe you could contact the disposal company and pick up empty 30-gallon barrels for your solvent and thinner waste storage. Once the container is full, you may be able to bring it to the same waste facility and exchange it for an empty barrel.

Professional paint shops must have areas set up for masking removal and parts assembly. How are tools organized in this space? Since this should be a clean area, are they mounted on pegboard? Is there a special workbench used just for small parts assembly? Maybe one covered with carpet that minimizes scratch damage potential to newly painted parts? Do you have enough lighting? Painters require plenty of good illumination to properly apply masking tape, hunt for paint nibs and make final paint flaw repairs. Do they have enough fluorescent light fixtures above and portable incandescent or halogen lights on the shop floor?

What color are the shop walls? White walls reflect the most light but they also highlight dirty smudges much more than other light hues, such as grays or tans. Does the shop floor appear smeared with different paints or oil drops? If it is clean, find out what kind of sealer or two-part epoxy paint was used to seal the concrete floor.

Finally, ask painters what shop attributes they would like to have in a dream shop. You may be surprised to find out what is at the top of their list. It might be a bathroom or sink with running water. If a household bathroom is located on the other side of your garage's wall or above on a second floor, you may be able to install a small bathroom or utility sink in the garage. Water supply and drain pipes could be located in the common wall or ceiling or floor space between the garage and the bathroom to make such an addition quite simple to install.

Detailers

Professional detailers must keep a small assortment of tools on hand to dismantle some auto assemblies that will facilitate overall detailing jobs. Generally, these tools are stored on pegboard above workbenches or in roll-around tool chests. Besides working room, detailers require plenty of supply storage.

Along with degreasers and carpet and upholstery shampoo products, auto detailers need assortments of polish, wax, dressing, engine paint, carpet and upholstery dye, shop towels, brushes, and so on. Since a large amount of shop dust is created through paint buffing processes, most detailers prefer to keep storage items tucked away in cabinets equipped with doors. This not only keeps dust and debris off the general supplies, it goes a long way toward keeping new buffing pads and polishing cloths in clean condition.

As with auto painters, detailers require plenty of fluorescent and incandescent or halogen lighting. You'll find that detailers normally have a few portable hand lights within easy reach. These are used under hoods and in trunk spaces to illuminate out of the way work areas. Since buffers are powered by either electricity or compressed air, most detailers prefer electric and air lines come from ceiling mounted retractable reels. Lines that drop from ceil-

Ron Hoffer's detached garage/workshop measures 26 feet by 36 feet. The area on the right is set up with workbenches and an open work table. His hot rod project sits on the left with plenty of open room and the center bay is saved for the family car. As with most automotive enthusiasts, he soon ran out of room in his workshop and added a lean-to for the travel trailer, a small tractor and other stuff.

ings pose fewer tripping hazards than those strung out all over floors.

In tight quarters, with more than one car in the shop, detailers may use dollies under car wheels to make moving them much easier and convenient. Wheel dollies allow one or two people to move vehicles sideways into otherwise difficult maneuvering spaces. This may be a prime consideration for those with home garages that have two small doors, as opposed to a single large door. Dollies allow you to maneuver your project vehicle sideways into the center of your garage to maximize working room all around it.

Since auto detailers go through plenty of shop towels and cleaning cloths every day, you should check out how they store the soiled ones. Obviously, you are not going to keep rags that are covered with grease or oil, but those used for polishing and waxing may be tossed into washing machines and dryers. Soft cotton towels and cloths seem to get softer the more they are washed.

Look all around detailers' workshops. Notice the handy devices they keep on hand to make their jobs easier. What kind of heating system is in place? Do they use creepers and small "brake job" stools on wheels? How are these units stored when not in use? What kind of wet/dry vacuums do auto detailers prefer? How do they store wet wash mitts, brushes and other car cleaning tools? Don't forget to ask detailers what they would like to see in their dream workshop.

Veteran Auto Enthusiasts

Another excellent source of information regarding home based auto workshops are those veteran auto enthusiasts you may meet at car shows, rallies, swap meets and auctions. Don't be afraid to start up a conversation with people who have their cars on display. They are sitting next to their rides for two reasons: one, to keep an eye on their prized vehicles; and two, to shoot the breeze with other auto enthusiasts. You just never know how much a person might know until you carry on a conversation with him or her.

Car Club Members

One of the best ways to learn about cars, trucks and auto workshops is through members of a quality car club. In the so-called old days, some people viewed car clubs as gangs of young people who just liked to parade around, drag race up and down city streets and just hang out at local hamburger joints.

While some of that may be true, many car clubs' memberships include serious automobile restorers and many white collar professionals. Instead of just hanging out, modern car clubs hold classes and meetings to teach members how to perfect their automotive repair, alteration and restoration skills.

Most car clubs are formed around certain types of vehicles. In your area, you may find one for Mustangs, another for Porsches, a club for hot-rodders, those with original antique auto interests, etc. Plan to attend at least a meeting or two of those car clubs

Mike Holiman extensively planned the construction and outfitting of his detached 24 foot by 36 foot auto workshop. Note the wide center bay door for easy vehicle access and the tire rack above the small door in the back. Workbenches, an open work table, a jib boom and other equipment are located on the right. The center of the shop offers maximum working room and the left side is used for ongoing projects.

that fit within the range of your auto interests. See how well you fit in with the theme of the clubs and the members before joining. You will be expected to pay dues and participate in club functions. Your expectations with any car club should be primarily based upon fun, of course, but don't lose sight of the opportunities to learn from well-seasoned members.

Once you have become a member of a car club, do not be bashful about asking other members their opinions about auto workshops. Once you get three or four members all talking about the same workshop topic, you should have a pencil and pad of paper on hand. This is because the more you all talk about it, the more everyone will come up with ingenious ideas and you'll have a tough time keeping up! This is called brainstorming.

Car Show Exhibitors

Chances are good that people who display nice looking vehicles at car shows or other places have workshops or workspaces set up to their satisfaction. Whether or not their shops are perfect, they may have ideas that will help you. If some live near you, they may be able to point out thrifty places to pick up lights, cabinets, workbench materials, tools, equipment, and other things.

This is not to say every car show winner has an ideal auto workshop. As was said earlier, quality work can be accomplished in the most primitive surroundings. One would surely have to believe that anyone with a nice looking show car or truck would have some great ideas on how they would like to set

up a bona fide workshop. After all, the effort that went into the show vehicle proves that the person has worked hard getting it ready for show time. Those efforts must have generated thoughts of how they could be accomplished with greater convenience, comfort and safety.

Racing Teams

If your interest in automobiles is focused around racing, you should be able to pick up workshop ideas from racing teams. Now, don't waltz into the pits in the middle of a race and expect to carry on an intelligent conversation about workshops with the crew chief whose car is in the top three. However, once the race is over and people are just relaxing before packing up, you might be able to bend a team member's ear for a while.

Serious car racers must have access to viable workshops to maintain their vehicles in top condition. It is not unusual to find these shops equipped with heavy duty machines bolted to the floor. You could also assume that these shops are outfitted for maximum convenience and safety. Comfort, on the other hand, may play second fiddle.

Of grave importance to serious auto racers is flat and even floors. This helps them to set up their race car's suspension. Another important point is accessibility. They must have maneuvering room to work on different parts simultaneously. Tools are an important consideration. They must be easy to get to and easy to put away. Find out if the racers you talk with prefer large roll-around tool chests, open

Brian Lord remodeled his house and added an extra large two-car garage. He was smart in continuing the remodel to include the installation of drywall in the garage. This section on the left side of Lord's garage looks like a new kitchen! It is used for household projects. The counter and cupboards were built with 3/4-inch AC plywood, clear Douglas fir rails and stiles and birch plywood for the doors and drawer fronts. 1/8-inch birch veneer was glued to the end of the counter for appearance. The drawers were made with 1/2-inch AC plywood.

pegboard storage areas or work carts. How do they store wheels and tires? What about spare parts storage; like belts, hoses, gaskets, etc.? You never know what advice someone can offer for outfitting auto workshops until you ask. Once you ask, the worst anyone can say is no.

Friends and acquaintances

Perhaps the most common way people learn things is from friends and acquaintances. This holds true with auto workshops as much as anything else. Mention to your friends that you are planning to outfit your garage or new shop around an automotive theme. As conversation continues,

don't be surprised if you're told about some of their friends who have really nice cars or have just completed similar workshop projects. Ask them to introduce you to their other auto enthusiast friend and go from there.

Those with workshops

It is probably silly to mention this in a book, but if you have friends or acquaintances that already have nice auto workshops, make a point to meet with them to discuss your plans. Don't limit yourself to just auto workshops, either. Many times, people have all-purpose workshops that have a wide variety of attributes and handy accessories.

The front and right side of Lord's garage/workshop feature an L-shaped work counter and cupboards. The units offer a great deal of storage space. Cupboards are 16 inches deep and the counter is 30 inches deep. These dimensions maximized plywood utilization. Since only lightweight auto work will be conducted on the counter, it was covered with a plastic laminate, like Formica.

Just because a friend may be an avid woodworking enthusiast, doesn't mean he or she would never tackle an automotive maintenance task in their workshop. Home based workshops are set up for all sorts of different endeavors. What works for one may work for another. Check out the storage cabinets, how big pieces of equipment are mounted on frames equipped with locking casters and what that people have done to make their shop comfortable.

What kinds of creature comforts do your friends' shops exhibit? Can you incorporate the same types of amenities? Would a secondary doorbell from your home's front door serve you well? Would an intercom to the house be useful? Cable television? Stereo? Refrigerator? Microwave oven? Comfortable chair? Desk? Cordless telephone?

If you haven't realized it yet, home based workshops are not just places for work. Auto enthusiasts regard workshops as their havens away from the rest of the world where they can talk about their hobbies and passions and plan for special endeavors in the future. So we have heard, it used to be that folks would gather around pot bellied stoves in local hardware stores to shoot the breeze and solve the problems of the world. Well, hardware stores are much too busy nowadays and they don't have pot bellied stoves.

While generating ideas for the layout and outfitting of your auto workshop or garage, don't forget the simple pleasures that come with comfortable chairs and coffee pots where friends can gather to visit and talk about stuff. Although you will certainly do plenty of work in your workshop, don't lose sight of why you became interested in automobiles in the first place.

Working on automobiles and bringing them to pristine condition will be challenging and rewarding. Remember that fun can be had along the way in a convenient, comfortable and safe workshop. Plan for practicality, but don't forget compatibility. Home based workshops are places where projects get done and where family members and friends may gather to just visit and enjoy each others' company. Workshops are the hardware stores of yesterday and if you want, they can also sport pot bellied stoves.

Chapter 2
INITIAL PLANNING

Before you start outfitting your garage or workshop with workbenches, storage systems and pieces of equipment, you should have an overall floor plan in mind. This is not always easy, especially for larger garages and workshops. Although you may believe that there will be plenty of room, in practice you may not find this to be true.

Some pieces of equipment, like drill presses or sandblast cabinets, may not fit tightly against walls. They may require a few inches of clearance behind and will push out into the working space of the workshop. You should try to maintain a clearance of about 3-feet in front of workbenches, in front of and on the sides of equipment units and all around open work tables. Clearance for equipment and around work areas will eat up floor space in a hurry. Without planning, you could quickly find yourself cramped for space. The easiest way to begin your planning program is to sit in your garage or workshop with a pad of graph paper, a pencil with a good eraser and a 25 or 30-foot tape measure. Measure the walls and door openings and draw out a diagram of the work space on the graph paper with each square representing 1 foot. Then, draw in workbenches, storage units and everything else you expect to put into that space.

Be realistic and measure things before entering them onto your graph paper plans. Paper is cheap, so make many different drawings until you come up with the perfect plan.

Actual Workspace Dimensions
Drawings on graph paper and life-size dimensions are two different things. On paper, you may think that there is plenty of room for a new sandblast cabinet and floor to ceiling storage unit next to a door opening. In reality, though, you will want to leave a foot or two of clear space next to door frames. This makes it easier to carry large boxes or other things through the door. Be frugal with the space you seem to have on paper and realize that open space for working around cars and maneuvering parts and tools is a premium. Auto workspaces demand plenty of elbow room.

When you measure the inside of your garage or workshop, be sure to take into account the small concrete foundation wall that may be sticking out at the bottom of the wall. This obstruction will cause some

A hydraulic press is stationed in front of a fastener bin and about 4-feet away from a workbench. The bin can be accessed from the open table side or through the press. Although this is not an ideal location for the press, the positioning works well for most projects. Notice that the press can be moved out in the open when needed for large parts. An arrangement like this may be required for cramped workshops.

items to be pushed out into the workspace. Counters and workbenches should be made to fit over foundation protrusions to maximize space utilization.

Be certain to account for other obstructions around the area such as garage door springs, garage door openers, a door that opens into a garage from inside the house, household plumbing pipes, heat registers, and so on. Plumbing pipes and heat regis-

An old kitchen counter is used as a workbench for lightweight jobs. Around 26 inches deep, this unit works well at the front of a 24-foot deep garage. Open room in the front of garages and workshops is important, for automotive engine work.

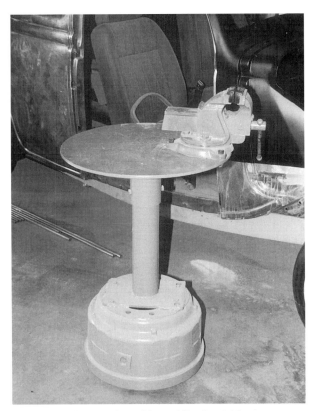

The heavy plate steel on this mobile vise table can withstand a great deal of pounding and other heavy work. The size of the base and weight of the entire unit makes it quite stable. A good heavy duty vise is a necessity for any workshop. Gauge vise size to the base upon which it is secured.

ters are common in home garages that have second floor living spaces above them. These obstructions may require that shelving and other storage units be custom built around them.

Vehicle Size Considerations

Garages and workshops set up for automotive endeavors must offer plenty of maneuvering room. It would be a shame to outfit such workspaces with large workbenches, tools and equipment only to find that a project car can barely squeeze into the area. Therefore, measure your project car, or the biggest family car, and plot that dimension on graph paper in the center of a garage bay or where you plan to park and work on vehicles.

Open a door and measure the distance from the car body to the end of the door. Will there be room in your plans for you to get around an open car door once the shop area is outfitted? If not, you had better plan to leave a wide open space along walls where car doors can open. Instead of leaving that open space blank, maybe you can install a sheet of pegboard on the wall and use it for the storage of smaller tools or packages of supplies.

Is your garage or workshop deep enough to support a nice workbench at the front, accommodate a full size automobile and still provide enough room for maneuvering around the engine compartment? If not, maybe you should locate your workbench on a side wall or at least toward a corner of the shop area.

It is imperative that you take accurate measurements of the equipment items you expect to place in your workshop area. Draw those dimensions onto the graph paper to see how well they fit into different corners or spaces in the garage or workshop. You will want to set up the floor plan to best accommodate your regular work activities. Remember that you might have to sacrifice the convenience of having a certain piece of equipment next to another to efficiently use your available working room.

Ideally, workshop floor plans should feature layouts that enable users to easily move from one function to the next in an orderly manner. This is much like the kitchen triangle floor plan, where the refrigerator, stove and sink or counter are situated in some form of a triangle so chefs can easily move from food storage to food preparation and to the cooking unit in the least amount of steps. In your

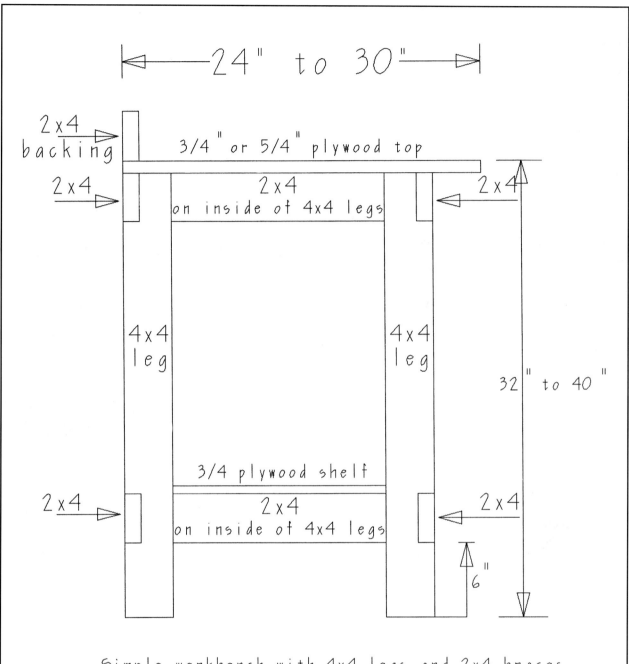

Simple workbench with 4x4 legs and 2x4 braces.
Bottom shelf is 3/4" plywood. Workbench top
can be 3/4" plywood up to 5/4" plywood
depending upon loads to be placed on it.
Workbench height may be from 32" to 40"
depending upon user's size.
An ordinary desk generally sits at 30-1/2".

workshop, such a triangle may include a parts storage unit, workbench and vehicle or, workbench, buffer and vehicle, and so on.

Workbench height and depth

Workbenches and counters should be built to heights that are comfortable for you. Generally, a workbench top should be located about 4 inches below your waist. For a person that stands around 5 feet 8 inches, a workbench top should be built at about 36 inches. For a person that stands 6 feet 4 inches, the workbench top should be about 39 inches.

Workbenches should be built to a height that is most comfortable for you. If you plan to sit on a stool most of the time while at the workbench, you may consider building the top at 40 inches or whatever height will give you about 8 inches clearance between your thighs and the bottom of the workbench top.

About the best way to find out which workbench height is best for you, is to set up a little work area at a kitchen counter. Is that counter height perfect for you? If it is too low, place a bread board on top of a couple of telephone books to see how that working height fits you. Slip books of different thicknesses under the bread board to try out various working heights. Keep at it until you arrive at an ideal height. Then, plan to build your workbench or work counter to that dimension.

Workbench depth is also an important consideration. Those too narrow will be most inconvenient while working on larger assemblies and those too deep will make it difficult to reach things that get knocked toward the back of the workbench. The ideal workbench should range between 30 inches and 24 inches.

The actual layout of your garage or workshop may dictate workbench depth. For example, measure the distance from a wall to the garage door frame located closest to it. For most home garages, this is generally about 24 inches. If you want to install a workbench along that wall, you may want to limit its depth to 24 inches. This way, it will not jut out past the garage door opening and should allow sufficient maneuvering room between the edge of the workbench and any vehicle parked next to it.

While planning for the ideal height and depth for your workbench, take time to determine comfortable

← A simple workbench can be made with 4x4 legs, 2x4 cross members and 3/4 or 5/4-inch AC plywood. Use 16d nails to secure the frame and 8d finishing nails to secure the plywood. Notice that the 2x4 framing members along the front and back are fitted into notches cut in the 4x4 legs. Wooden workbenches should be sealed or painted to prevent them from becoming saturated with oil, grease and other fluids.

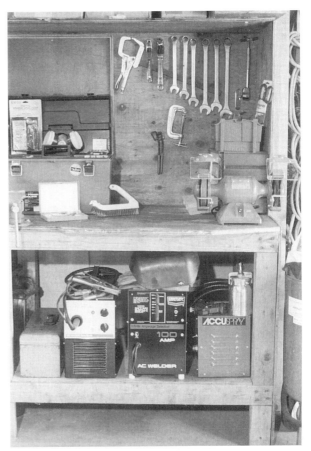

A large shelf on the lower section of this workbench serves as an ideal spot for storing an HVLP spray painting machine, welders, tool boxes and other items. Nails partially driven into the top backing hold hand tools. Pegboard may have been a better backing choice. Notice that the lower workbench shelf is about 10 inches off the floor. This helps to keep moisture away from the equipment when wet cars are parked in the garage after being driven in the rain or snow.

heights for other things such as storage shelves and sawhorses. As a rule, the highest shelves should be located about 12 inches below your highest comfortable reach; a drill press should be adjusted to about the middle of your chest; a lathe should be about waist high; and sawhorses can be made to a height anywhere between your knees and the middle of your thighs, whichever is most comfortable for you.

Required Storage

You should already have a good idea of what kinds of things you will definitely be storing in your auto workshop or garage. These are the required storage items like tools, fasteners, cleaning supplies, and so on. Designate certain spaces on your graph paper plan for the accommodation of such storage.

Attached home garages and basements may already have electrical outlets located close to the floor. To gain access to wall spaces for the installation of outlets higher on walls, tear out just the lower 3 feet of drywall.

A roll-around tool chest will require specific storage space, as will a mobile work cart. Since they will take up valuable floor space, what can you do to maximize the empty space above them? These spaces may be ideal for cabinets or open shelves that are secured to the wall. Consider building and installing cabinets so their tops hang about 12 inches down from the ceiling. This way, you will have an open space to store such things as trim and other long objects that would not normally fit in cabinets or on shelves.

Shelves under workbenches make handy storage spots, as do shelves under open work tables. Pegboard is excellent for storing smaller items and doesn't require a great deal of room. Look at the open areas above doors. Would a small shelf or cabinet serve you well if located there? What about the space directly above the garage door along the header that supports the door opening?

While working room is very important, it is just as important to provide adequate storage space. Too often workbenches, tables and counters are cluttered with parts and supplies. Not only are cluttered workbenches eyesores, they could prove unsafe when you attempt to conduct work on them.

Extra Storage Space

Active auto do-it-yourselfer's can never seem to have enough storage space. This is especially true when it comes to automotive tear down and restoration. Where will you store all the dismantled parts that come off your project vehicle? If your workshop area is part of the home's garage, where do you plan to store all the household stuff that seems to always find its way into the garage? These are important concerns that you must address in your initial plans.

One-story home garages and workshops may provide extra storage space on top of rafters. Be aware

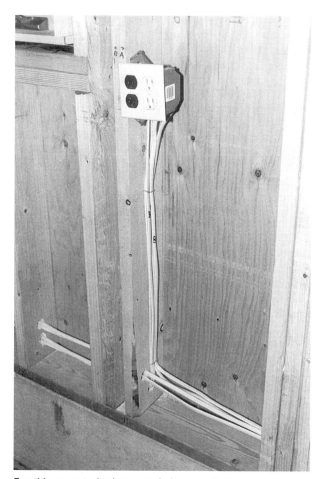

For this soon to be busy workshop, each electrical circuit was outfitted with receptacles of a different color. Here, a duplex outlet houses an ivory receptacle for one circuit and a brown outlet for another circuit. This way, two heavy duty machines can be operated at the same time and users will know that each is on its own separate circuit.

that most common rafters are not designed to hold much weight. Plan to limit storage in those spaces to lightweight items, like auto trim, interior door panels, dashboards, small fenders, etc. Manufactured trusses pose similar weight limitation restrictions.

Some common rafters and trusses can be beefed up to allow them to carry more weight. You will have to consult a truss engineer to determine how to reinforce the rafters or trusses and to figure out just how much weight these reinforced structural members can safely support. Truss companies are listed in the yellow pages under "Trusses - Construction."

Once an attic area above your garage or workshop has been reinforced for storage, consider putting down 1/2 or 3/4-inch plywood to serve as a floor. Then, install drywall over the ceiling to keep lint and dust from falling out of the attic and onto your work. An attic ladder will provide convenient access.

Should there be a second floor living space over your garage or workshop, you might be able to remove the ceiling drywall and then line the spaces between the ceiling joists with drywall to establish a series of storage areas between the joists. The easiest way to support storage in these spaces is to secure 1x4's across the openings every 3 or 4 feet. Or, you might be able to build long narrow boxes that fit into the spaces completely. Hinge them at one end to a block nailed between the joists and secure the other end with chain.

While drawing your initial plans, you must understand that the need for storage always tends to increase. Therefore, attempt to take advantage of empty wall space located above work areas for the installation of shelves and cabinets. You may not need or be able to afford that much storage cabinetry at the moment, but draw such ideas on your plans for later reference.

Basic Utility Considerations

Putting in a new electrical service, water lines, some form of heat and a lighting system is much easier to accomplish before garages or workshops become overloaded with accessories. During the planning stage, be sure to note whether you might ever want to install a bathroom or utility sink in the work area. This way, you may be able to run a water supply and drain pipe to a designated spot before installing drywall or another type of wall covering.

This idea is true for electrical lines and either 220-volt or natural gas lines for heaters. It is much easier to install basic wiring and plumbing before walls are covered even if you consider water and heat to be future extras.

Electricity

Automotive workshops must be outfitted with enough electrical power to support an air compressor, welder, lighting system and any number of power tools. At the least, you should attempt to provide a home garage with a 100-amp service and a detached auto workshop with a 200-amp service.

Mike Holiman outfitted his detached workshop with a 400-amp service because he knew that members of his race car team might all be working with him occasionally. With such a large electrical service, his shop is able to support a number of heavy-duty electrical units all at the same time with no loss of power or safety problems.

Running new electrical service into your garage or workshop service panel will be done by the local power company. Running circuits from the main panel out to the work area should be done by an experienced and licensed electrician.

Although electricians should be hired to run and hook up electrical lines, you are the one to designate where the receptacles and switches are placed. During initial planning, figure out where you will need

220-volt receptacles for your welder, air compressor, plasma cutter, and any other high voltage items. Plan to place 110-volt receptacles in strategic spots, too. Most frequently, garages and workshops are best served with electrical receptacles placed higher on the walls than normal households. About 4-feet from the ground is good. Placed lower, you may find it difficult to plug in a power cord when tools or pieces of equipment are in the way. In addition, plan to install a few outlets in the ceiling. This is a good idea even if your shop has an unusually high ceiling. To make use of ceiling receptacles, simply install retractable cord reels on the ceiling next to the electrical receptacles. Ceiling receptacles and retractable cord reels are handy and help to make workshops safer. This is because power cords are not strung out all over the floor to create tripping hazards. The use of retractable ceiling cords is highly recommended by almost every workshop owner who has them.

Water

Some folks may regard bathrooms or utility sinks as automotive workshop luxuries. A bathroom might be, but a utility sink should be considered a safety item. Working around cars and trucks generally carries with it some use of harsh chemicals like solvents and thinners. Should those liquids get splashed in your eyes, you will need a ready source of clear water to flush them. In addition, utility sinks are very handy for many regular chores; like parts cleaning, mixing up buckets of sudsy solution for car washing, and so on.

On your graph paper planning sheet, make a note as to where an existing bathroom or kitchen may be located next to or above the garage or workshop. Household bathrooms and kitchens must have plumbing pipes somewhere in the wall, ceiling or second floor space. It is in that wall or ceiling space that you should be able to tap into the existing water supply. Although you can run water supply pipes and drains almost anywhere, it may be easiest to locate your shop's utility sink close to the existing source.

The installation of a water supply and drain system for a detached workshop is a completely different story. Water supply pipes must run from a source under the foundation and to the utility or bathroom site in the shop. The drain pipe must run from the bathroom or utility sink to the main sewer or septic line and maintain a 1/4-inch per foot drop along the way. Since the fresh water supply will be under pressure, lines can run in any direction. However, drain pipes rely on gravity to get waste water from a sink or bathroom to the sewer or septic system.

A bathroom or utility sink is an important consideration for any automotive workspace. Unless you have plumbing experience, you may have to hire a licensed plumber to complete the plumbing work before you insulate and cover walls. In most areas, you do not need a permit nor do you have to hire a licensed plumber to add a utility sink to a garage. However, you should practice soldering copper pipe together before starting the job. Use extreme caution while soldering pipes next to studs and any other combustible material.

Lighting

Fluorescent lights offer the greatest amount of shop illumination at the lowest cost. However, they will not light up specific work areas or workbench tops as well as incandescents. Therefore, plan to install plenty of fluorescents in the ceiling and have a few incandescent lamps available to light up equipment work tables and workbench tops.

To take full advantage of all available floor to ceiling height room, consider installing fluorescent ceiling fixtures that fit up into ceiling joist or rafter areas. Having units hang down below ceilings is not always good. You will find that they will get knocked around while you maneuver long pieces of tubing or other items and they will collect dust and other air-borne debris particles.

A wide variety of fluorescent light fixtures are available at lighting outlets and home improvement centers. Many workshop owners prefer using 4-foot two or four bulb models. Using 8-foot fixtures is fine, but it is sometimes difficult to find spaces to store spare 8-foot long bulbs. Fifteen or sixteen 4-foot 2-bulb fluorescent light fixtures should do an excellent job of lighting up a 24x24 workshop. Check with a lighting company for more details on setting up a ceiling lighting system. Companies that manufacture and sell light fixtures have gone to great expense developing formulas for determining proper illumination output for specific lighting tasks. Sketch light fixtures into your plans so that you remember how many light receptacles must be installed and where an electrician needs to run wire.

If your garage or workshop has more than one door, strongly consider installing three-way or four-way light switches. This will allow you to turn the lights on or off at different locations. For example, have one switch at the garage door that comes from the house, another at the door that goes to the back yard and a third next to one of the big garage doors. This way, you should never have to grapple around in the dark looking for a light switch no matter which door you enter into the garage or shop.

For lighting around close-up work, check the catalogs from The Eastwood Company and Harbor Freight Tools. These mail order companies carry a good selection of clamp-on and magnetic incandescent light fixtures. Consider using an articulating desk lamp on workbenches. These are commonly featured on drafting tables. You should find them advertised for around $10.00 in newspaper inserts and other ads for home improvement centers, hardware and other retail stores.

Workshops are well served by sinks with hot and cold running water. Models like this plastic unit are inexpensive and easy to install as long as a water supply and drain line are nearby. This sink is located on a wall that separates the attached garage/workshop from an interior bathroom. Plumbing pipes in that wall were easily tapped into.

Type of work to be done

Another very important aspect to consider while planning your automotive garage or workshop is the type of work you expect to undertake. This will determine many things including how many compressed air lines may be needed, whether workbenches and tables need to be extra heavy-duty and just what other accessories your workspace may require. Those with interests in building engines should make plans for some type of ceiling mounted engine hoist or, at the least, a storage area for a portable engine hoist. Restorers must take into account the amount of dismantled parts storage that will be needed. Auto-body and paint enthusiasts need to realize the amount of sanding dust that will be created and make plans for dealing with it. Each area of automotive interest carries with it special concerns. These factors should be addressed in your plans so that you can continually move forward in your endeavors to set up a perfect home garage or workshop.

The roof trusses in Ron Hoffer's garage/workshop run parallel to this I-beam hoist. He secured 5/8-inch plywood to the underside of the five trusses closest to the hoist and then bolted a metal bar across the five trusses. The I-beam was then secured to the metal bar with box channel. Consult with a truss engineer before installing a hoist or boom to roof trusses or rafters.

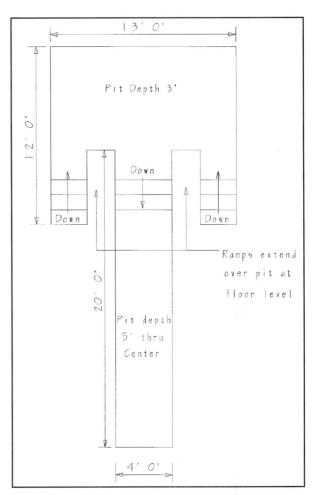

John Gittings discovered this front end pit design at a local tire shop. The 3 foot deep area at the front is ideal for workers when rolling around on little stools with wheels; like those used by brake job technicians. The 5-feet deep by 20-feet long center pit area makes for easy access to undercarriage components.

General Maintenance

On one hand, you may think that setting up a home garage or detached workshop for general auto maintenance would be a snap; a workbench, storage locker, portable air compressor and a few lights. However, an all-purpose work area may need to be set up to handle a wide variety of automotive endeavors. General maintenance tasks may involve brake jobs, transmission service, engine tune-ups, detailing, and any number of other preventive maintenance chores. Therefore, consider the type of storage that will be needed to contain all the materials and supplies that will surely be used as jobs come up. How many specialty tools or pieces of equipment will the work area need to handle? Will a small portable compressor have enough power to support all of your planned pneumatic procedures? What size vehicles are you expecting to place inside your workspace? These are all concerns that you must note on your planning sheets.

Heavy Mechanical

More defined areas of automotive interest make it easier to decide which types of workbenches and other accessories would be most appropriate for the workshop. In the case of heavy mechanical, you can count on the fact that workbenches will require heavy-duty 2x6 or 2x8 dimensional lumber tops to support the weight of engines, transmissions and other heavy assemblies.

In addition, having several compressed air outlets peppered throughout the workshop would prove quite useful. You'll need compressed air for pneumatic wrenches under vehicles, air at workbenches for the dismantling and assembly of mechanical components and air at the entrance to the shop to dry off freshly cleaned engines.

Would a work pit or above ground lift be better for your heavy mechanical endeavors? What about used anti-freeze, engine oil and transmission fluid? How do you plan to store and dispose of these materials? If you expect to store them in 30-gallon barrels,

All kinds of auto workshop activities create dust and other airborne debris. Buffing endeavors are no exception. Plan for these types of dusty jobs by installing plenty of covered storage areas.

where will they be situated in the workshop? How will you get full barrels into the back of your pickup truck for transport? These are all questions that you should investigate and list on your initial planning sheets. The more you can overcome obstacles while planning, the better off you will be when it comes time to set up and outfit your garage or workshop.

Restoration

Those who are planning to restore automobiles in their garage or auto workshop have to plan for the storage of dismantled auto parts. This is one of the biggest factors in frame-off auto restorations. If you have never attempted to restore an automobile before, you must be forewarned that cars and trucks include a tremendous amount of small to medium sized parts and fasteners of all kinds. Along with all the other considerations for setting up a viable auto workspace, auto restorers must make plans for the neat and organized storage of dismantled parts. "Basket case" is a term used to describe autos that were partially dismantled with all the parts just tossed into a basket. Can you imagine what a nightmare it must be to figure out which of those parts go where and how they are assembled? This is truly what you want to avoid with any type of auto restoration.

On your planning sheets, designate a specific area for dismantled parts storage. Then, on another sheet, draw up a plan for the system of organized storage you feel is appropriate for your endeavors. You may want to save one area for dirty parts storage and another for those parts that have been restored and primed. A third storage area may also be required for those parts that have been completely restored and painted.

As important as organized storage is to auto restorers, it is paramount to plan for the safe storage of restored parts. You must realize that restoration of any automobile will entail many tasks that will create sanding dust and other messes. Just imagine how dirty your shop will get while tearing down your project vehicle to the frame. What about all the grinding dust that will be created while you strip paint, remove rust and so on. Safe storage, in this case, refers to the stowing away of pristine parts so that they are protected from dusty atmospheres and other types of debris. Gauges, radio components, upholstery, glass, and many other parts may fall into this category. Along with locating such safe storage areas, you should investigate what means you will use to store the parts. One consideration is cardboard boxes.

Office products outlets offer many different sized boxes that come with lids. These may work out well, especially if they are strong enough to support other boxes stacked on top of them. Use a felt marker to write on box ends what parts are stored in each container.

Optional Considerations

This is where workshop planning can really be fun. Imagine that you have an unlimited budget and let your imagination run wild. Draw in every convenience item you can think of and then more. Look through auto magazines to see what the latest rages in tools and workshop accessories are, and draw them into the overall floor plan. Although your budget and actual workplace dimensions may not support all the goodies you draw on your plans, you never know when a combination of accessories may prompt you to plan for a new addition to your workshop in the future.

Compressed Air Supply

Initially, you may have plans to use a portable air compressor for all of your pneumatic needs. However, you may have drawn in a large upright air compressor during your optional accessories dream planning. If that is the case, and you fully expect to buy such a unit in the future, why not run black pipe compressed air lines through the walls now in preparation for the day when you can buy the compressor of choice? At the same time, run air outlets at convenient locations. With those air lines in place, you can run a flexible air hose from your portable compressor into the inlet for the system and enjoy the convenience of piped in air throughout your shop. Granted, a portable air compressor will not put out as much air as a larger 5 horsepower unit, but the convenience of having outlets all around the shop should be helpful in the interim.

Soundproofing

The use of insulation in walls will lessen the noise that will be generated in your workshop. Soundproofing is a very important factor in garages that are attached to household living spaces. Sounds could also be a problem for detached auto workshops. Banging on fenders and the noise generated by power tools will echo wildly throughout the neighborhood. Before you cover walls with drywall, seriously consider the addition of soundproofing materials. Insulation does a good job of deadening noises but it cannot compare to actual soundproofing board. Installed much like drywall, soundboard can deaden much of your workshop noise. If you are serious about undertaking major auto restoration or alteration jobs in an attached garage, you might consider building a secondary wall next to the existing wall that separates your garage from the house. This is a common practice for deadening sound between

This 5 horsepower air compressor from Campbell Hausfeld is capable of putting out a large amount of compressed air. Most all experienced auto enthusiasts recommend units with at least 5 hp. Consider installing air lines up to the ceiling and then install air hose reels. This will help to keep the hoses off the floor. Pegboard around compressors makes good storage spots for hoses, filters and other compressor accessories.

apartments. A 1-inch air space is maintained between the original wall that separates the garage from the house and the secondary wall. Both walls are filled with appropriate insulation and the new wall is covered with soundproofing board before being covered with drywall. Although more expensive, this setup will prove well worth it to those in the house.

Special Equipment

Accommodations for special equipment must be made on your graph paper drawings. Be sure to draw in the actual dimensions of each piece and the required room around them needed for maneuvering. Special equipment may include any of the following: Sandblast cabinet, parts washing tub, workbench top welding booth, hydraulic press, drill

Sandblasters are required equipment around auto restoration shops. They are also very handy around all purpose shops. Consider a benchtop model, like this one from The Eastwood Company, if your shop is limited on space.

press, metal lathe, buffer, grinder, boring machine, portable engine hoist, engine stand, sawhorses, dollies, creeper, metal bender, welder, plasma cutter, tire changer, air compressor, cut-off saw, horizontal band saw, metal small parts bin, and so on.

Every item that you expect to put into your shop should have a designated storage area. In addition, you must maintain enough room for working around project vehicles. This is not always an easy task. You will have to measure the items and see where they will fit in with your overall plan. Graph paper is cheaper than building materials and time spent planning will save you money in the long run. Although it can be frustrating redrawing your plans, it is much better than rearranging actual shop accessories. Every once in a while, close your eyes and try to envision what your shop would look like if outfitted the way you have it drawn on graph paper. Eventually, you will arrive at a point where everything has its place and you'll have plenty of room for working on your prized project vehicle.

Chuck Saydan spends a large amount of time in his shop. One of his favorite creature comforts is the television set mounted on a swivel base. The boom is used for pulling engines. It is secured to a beefy pole hidden inside the wall. Note the abundant storage cupboards and counter and pegboard over the workbench.

Space above vehicles must be open and free of obstructions when automotive lifts are employed. The open ceiling design of Chuck Saydan's shop provides plenty of room.

Chapter 3
FUNDAMENTAL LAYOUTS

Generating interesting ideas and attempting to put together different workshop designs may quickly cause some auto enthusiasts to become confused and frustrated. Initial eagerness and excitement about the evolution of a typical garage or barren workshop into a convenient, comfortable and safe workplace may result in plans that are so ambitious that the central focus gets lost.

Eventually, your best ideas, actual budget and realistic workshop space must be blended into a legitimate floor plan. First, you must let your imagination run wild. Once you have tried to fit a mountain of accessories into your work area on graph paper plans, take a break and let the plans and ideas float around in your head for a day or two. Then, start up again with a renewed sense of practicality and focus on your essential workshop needs. Begin with a fundamental layout and then gradually insert extras in order of importance.

Central Work Station

If you were to close your eyes and envision yourself working on a project vehicle, you would most likely see yourself repairing or polishing an actual portion of the automobile rather than standing at a workbench. The main focus in designing any auto workplace is to make sure that you have plenty of maneuvering room around your project vehicle. This fundamental objective should be your primary focal point around which all other workshop accessories are designed.

While large workbenches and spacious storage areas are convenient, you must not sacrifice the main purpose of your workshop. Be reasonable and inventive. Compromise on workbench length and depth to maximize actual maneuvering room around the workshop. Be content with a pegboard wall storage unit instead of cabinets. This will enable you to walk around open car doors instead of having to close them each time you need get by.

In some cases, a set of high quality wheel dollies should be made a priority over other pieces of equipment. For example, say you have a shallow two-car home garage, about 20-feet deep and 24-feet wide, and must leave room to park your family car in there each night. With wheel dollies, you could maneuver your project vehicle sideways in the

Ron Hoffer's garage/workshop is set up with a workbench and open table on one side and open space on the other. This provides plenty of maneuvering room around his hot rod project.

garage while you work on it and then simply push it back into its parking stall at the end of the day. Sitting sideways in the garage, you should have ample room to walk all around the vehicle and take advantage of workbenches and storage cabinets along the perimeter of the garage that would not be in the way.

For one-car garages, consider installing pegboard along both side walls for shallow tool storage. With a car on wheel dollies, you could push it over so the passenger side is tight against one wall to make room for working on the driver's side of the vehicle. Later, you can push it over the other way to make room for work that needs to be done on the passenger side.

Another need may be to conduct a large amount of undercarriage work. Your budget and garage may not be able to accommodate an above ground lift. Consider buying a good hydraulic floor jack and a set of jack stands that are easy to operate, adjust and lock securely.

By making these items a priority over other shop accessories, you may be able to complete undercarriage operations early on in your restoration schedule with convenience, comfort and safety. Later, you can focus your budget upon the workshop accessories that were put on the back burner. By

The Rotary Lift raises vehicles to a height that makes working on their lower sections much easier and more comfortable. This model, the MPAL, is portable and capable of lifting up to 6,000 pounds. It will lock in five different height positions.

Restoration Helpers

Maneuverability 'Expands' Your Space
Heavy-duty wheel dollies carry up to 1,000 lbs. each on four casters. Rounded lower section cradles the tire, reducing the chances of tire damage during long storage. Makes maneuvering your car in small spaces easy.
1429 Racing Dollies, set of 2

Wheel dollies, like these from The Eastwood Company, enable car guys to easily roll rigs around workshops for maximum maneuvering room. The ability to move vehicles with wheel dollies may be especially important to those with smaller garages and workshops where actual driving space is severely limited.

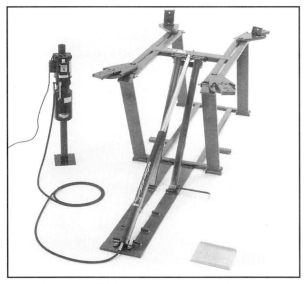

The MR6 Rotary Lift is not portable. It can lift up to 6,000 pounds and has four different height locking positions.

The MPAL is equipped with spring-loaded wheels. Vehicle weight causes them to retract when the unit is in use. A handy handle quickly attaches to the lift for ease of mobility. Rotary Lift also manufactures and sells above ground auto lifts capable of raising automobiles to full undercarriage working heights.

Portable Workbenches

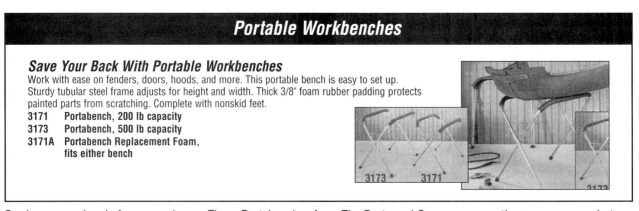

Save Your Back With Portable Workbenches
Work with ease on fenders, doors, hoods, and more. This portable bench is easy to set up. Sturdy tubular steel frame adjusts for height and width. Thick 3/8" foam rubber padding protects painted parts from scratching. Complete with nonskid feet.

3171   Portabench, 200 lb capacity
3173   Portabench, 500 lb capacity
3171A Portabench Replacement Foam,
       fits either bench

Sawhorses are handy for many chores. These Portabenches from The Eastwood Company serve the same purpose but are much easier to store because they fold up. Thick 3/8-inch foam rubber padding protects painted parts against scratches.

focusing in on the fundamental objectives first, you can set priorities that will accomplish the greatest good in the shortest time and with the least expense. Why spend time designing series of workbenches and cabinets when the majority of your efforts won't require much workbench time? Why spend time trying to fit in a large stand-alone sandblast cabinet when a bench top unit will handle the majority of your work? In this situation, the sacrifice of not having the bigger unit will be offset by the benefit of more open working room.

Workbench

A workbench is fundamentally a table. In most cases, workbenches serve as convenient and comfortable shop accessories where you can work on smaller automotive assemblies while standing or sitting on a stool. With the exception of those tasks that require pounding, grinding, welding or other powerful activities, a simple table or fold out ledge might suffice as a workbench. If your auto workshop offers limited working room, consider the use of a folding table or fold-down wall-mount workbench instead of a permanent free-standing unit. With your portable workbench stowed away, you will have open room to work on fenders, seats and other large auto items. You might consider the portability of sawhorses and a sheet of 3/4-inch plywood as a workbench and an open stand for supporting parts. Simply cut a sheet of plywood to the dimensions that will most conveniently fit the workspace and the projects you expect to undertake on it.

Most of the home garages in the Southwest and other warmer climate areas of the country are

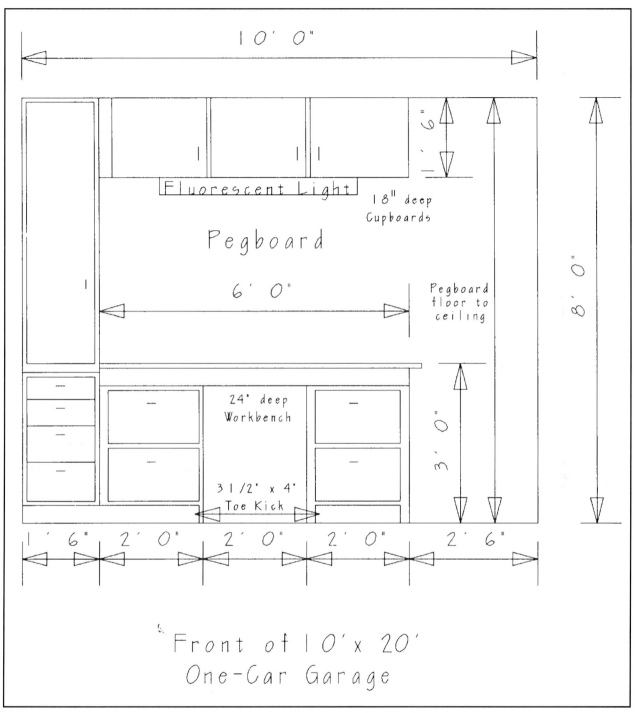

10' 0"

6"

8' 0"

Fluorescent Light

18" deep
Cupboards

Pegboard

6' 0"

Pegboard
floor to
ceiling

24" deep
Workbench

3' 0"

3 1/2" x 4'
Toe Kick

1' 6"   2' 0"   2' 0"   2' 0"   2' 6"

Front of 10'x 20'
One-Car Garage

This is a simple design for a workbench and storage area. A tall cupboard on the left is complemented with drawers below. A fluorescent light hangs from the bottom of upper cupboards and floor to ceiling pegboard on the right provides plenty of storage. The workbench may be outfitted with drawers or shelves, depending upon your preference.

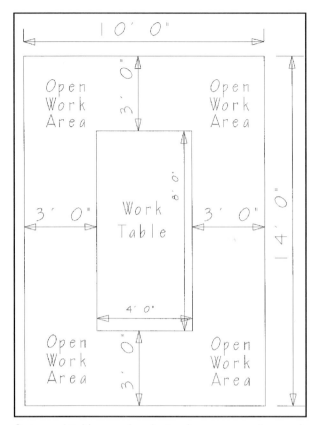

Open work tables require plenty of open room all around. A full 4 feet by 8 feet work table is huge and requires a 10x14 open area. A better size may be 3X8. Consider a shelf under such tables for the storage of large tools and other items.

places where clothes washers and dryers are kept. While many auto enthusiasts may regard this as a waste of otherwise good working room, others have taken advantage of the flat surface provided by these appliances. While working on their project vehicles or performing preventive maintenance chores on their daily drivers, these inventive folks have turned their clothes cleaning appliances into temporary workbenches.

To do this, cut a piece of 1/2- or 3/4-inch plywood to fit over the top of the machines with a 2-inch overlap on the three open sides. Then, secure a section of carpet to the bottom of the plywood with double back tape. Place the plywood on top of the machines with the carpet down. The carpet will not scratch the washer or dryer and you will have a nice wood surface on which to place tools and supplies while working on your car or truck.

In larger auto facilities, like two- or three-car garages and detached shop buildings, you have more leeway to plan for the installation of one or more solid workbenches designed to offer the most in convenience, user comfort and strong support. Home garages seldom offer enough room to justify

more than one heavy-duty workbench. How many heavy-duty workbenches do you really need? Consider the installation of one heavy-duty workhorse workbench supplemented by other countertop-type workbench units. This will give you one workbench to use for heavy pounding, grinding and welding and plenty of additional surface areas that offer protected storage space underneath.

Regardless of your workbench number, size or strength needs, always keep the fundamental purpose of your work area in mind. That is, do not overload the functional area of your workplace with workbenches to the point that maneuvering room around vehicles is compromised. Use graph paper to accurately scale realistic measurements of project vehicles and the amount of preferred open working room you must have around them. If need be, pull a car or pickup truck into your empty garage or workshop. Position it as you expect your project vehicle will be while you work on it. Open the hood, trunk and doors. Walk around the vehicle and observe how much extra room you have between it and the surrounding walls. Squat down next to the car or truck as if you were sanding a body panel or putting on a wheel. Measure the distance between you and the wall. Is there really enough room for a 30-inch workbench? Would a pegboard storage or a fold-down wall-mount workbench be the only way to go?

An excellent way to get a feel for the dimensional realities of a workspace is to use a group of cardboard boxes. Go down to an appliance or furniture store and pick up a few big boxes. Cut and tape them to the dimensions you prefer for workbenches and storage units and to the sizes of those pieces of equipment you expect to house in your shop area. Height is not as important as width and depth. Use a felt marker to identify each box as the workbench, storage unit or piece of equipment it was designed to represent. Position the boxes in the workshop as you would the real accessories. Then, pull a car or truck into the area and park it as if it was a real project vehicle. How does the floor plan work out? Do you have enough working room around the vehicle? Does the layout match your expectations? Do you find the area suddenly cramped and overloaded with shop accessories? Move the boxes around until they are most convenient and comfortable.

Open Heavy-duty Table

Bona fide auto workshops and wide-open basements with adequate room, may be able to support the convenience of a heavy-duty work table. Positioned in an open area, such tables allow users to walk all around them while working on engines, transmissions, differentials, transaxles and other large auto assemblies. Although you might be able to justify a huge work table that measures 4 feet wide by 8 feet long, you may find that 3 feet by 8 feet is much more practical.

Mike Holiman made this jib boom with materials from a local metal salvage yard. The key components are heavy duty truck axle bearings at the top and bottom. The base of the boom is secured in a block of concrete and the top secured to three trusses nailed together. The entire roof structure is tied together with metal strap to help keep the boom and its structure stable. The boom can swivel 360-degrees.

Mike Holiman's shop is 36-feet wide. It could have been built as a three-bay shop, but he decided to install two doors for two bays and keep the area that would have been the third bay separate as a workbench or table area. He built a workbench the length of the outside wall in that enclosed bay and then positioned a heavy-duty work table in the open area away from the workbench and next to the middle bay. Next to the table, he installed a jib boom. This arrangement permits him to pull an engine out of a vehicle with the jib boom and then set the engine down on the table. Open space around the table offers full circle access to the engine for optimum convenience. He has also worked on transmissions and other heavy drive train units as they were supported by the open table. A cribbing system of short 2x4 boards is used to support engines and assemblies while on the table.

Open work tables may be used to accommodate the convenience of working on a host of automotive parts. Along with drive train elements, a clean work table will openly support seats, body panels, trim, wheels and so on. Many meticulous auto enthusiasts outfit their shops with open tables covered with carpet. These are used to support restored and painted auto parts while putting on accessory items or completing other work on them. The soft carpet surface minimizes the potential for scratch hazards and makes a great place for laying out finished parts in preparation for final assembly.

Instead of a heavy-duty work table that can support heavy engines and transmissions, you might consider any of a number of different brands of fold-out tables. You see these all the time at different meeting halls, school cafeterias and business offices. Although they are limited by how much weight they can safely support, folding tables may be perfect for those days when you need to work on long dashboard units, seats, odd-shaped window trim and so on. When not needed, these tables fold up and can be stored against a wall or under a long workbench. The legs used on folding tables may be purchased separately at hardware stores and home improvement centers. Instead of a manufactured table, use 3/4-inch plywood or Melamine to make your own table to any dimension desired. In addition, you might consider using one folding leg on the end of a piece of plywood and building a support at the other end that can be attached to an existing workbench. This will offer an "L" shaped workbench adjunct to assist you while working on odd-shaped auto parts and/or assemblies.

Material and Supply Storage

How many times have you returned to your workshop from a trip to the auto parts store and found that there is no place to set down the stuff you bought? If this sounds familiar, you seriously need to consider an organized system of material and supply storage.

Workplace storage is generally accommodated by open shelves, cabinets with doors, or a combination of the two. Open shelves are easy to get to and the things stored on them are easy to see and retrieve. Unfortunately, open shelves do not offer any means of security nor protection from shop dust and other airborne pollutants. Cabinets with doors, on the other hand, offer good security and will protect contents from shop dust, overspray and other debris. In some cases, locks may be attached to cabinet doors to keep children from getting into hazardous chemicals and thieves away from expensive tools.

Shelves are easy to install. In a garage with open stud walls, you can insert 1x4 or 2x4 boards between studs to make small storage spaces. Alternate the height of each shelf so you can nail through the studs and into the ends of the shelf boards. Larger boards may be used, too. A piece of 2x6, for example, nailed between studs will support one-gallon paint cans. If you are concerned about things falling off these shelves, simply nail a thin board across the front of the shelves to serve as a retainer.

For garages and workshops with finished walls, shop around at local hardware and home center stores. These outlets offer plenty of shelf brackets in all sorts of designs. Some models have upright runners that are screwed to wall studs. The brackets simply fit into slots on these runners. You will have to supply 3/4-inch plywood shelves cut from sheets of plywood or you can buy more expensive shelves already pre-cut.

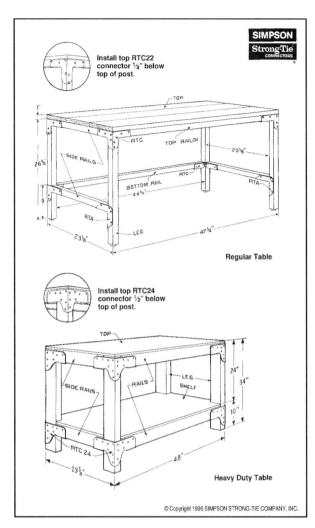

Install top RTC22 connector ⅛″ below top of post.

Regular Table

Install top RTC24 connector ½″ below top of post.

Heavy Duty Table

© Copyright 1996 SIMPSON STRONG-TIE COMPANY, INC.

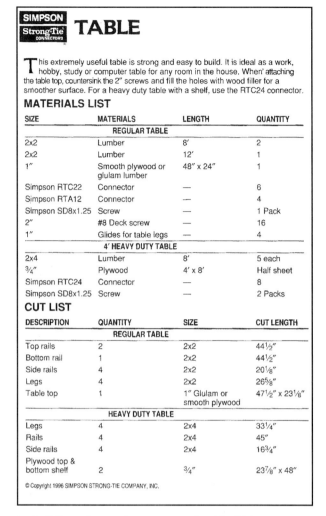

TABLE

This extremely useful table is strong and easy to build. It is ideal as a work, hobby, study or computer table for any room in the house. When' attaching the table top, countersink the 2″ screws and fill the holes with wood filler for a smoother surface. For a heavy duty table with a shelf, use the RTC24 connector.

MATERIALS LIST

SIZE	MATERIALS	LENGTH	QUANTITY
	REGULAR TABLE		
2x2	Lumber	8′	2
2x2	Lumber	12′	1
1″	Smooth plywood or glulam lumber	48″ x 24″	1
Simpson RTC22	Connector	—	6
Simpson RTA12	Connector	—	4
Simpson SD8x1.25	Screw	—	1 Pack
2″	#8 Deck screw	—	16
1″	Glides for table legs	—	4
	4′ HEAVY DUTY TABLE		
2x4	Lumber	8′	5 each
¾″	Plywood	4′ x 8′	Half sheet
Simpson RTC24	Connector	—	8
Simpson SD8x1.25	Screw	—	2 Packs

CUT LIST

DESCRIPTION	QUANTITY	SIZE	CUT LENGTH
	REGULAR TABLE		
Top rails	2	2x2	44½″
Bottom rail	1	2x2	44½″
Side rails	4	2x2	20⅛″
Legs	4	2x2	26⅝″
Table top	1	1″ Glulam or smooth plywood	47½″ x 23⅛″
	HEAVY DUTY TABLE		
Legs	4	2x4	33¼″
Rails	4	2x4	45″
Side rails	4	2x4	16¾″
Plywood top & bottom shelf	2	¾″	23⅞″ x 48″

© Copyright 1996 SIMPSON STRONG-TIE COMPANY, INC.

This is a plan from the Simpson Strong-Tie Connector Company for building a heavy duty open work table. Using Simpson connectors makes the job of building tables quick and easy. The connectors ensure very strong and secure joints. If the floor of your garage or shop is not level, consider installing leg levelers on the bottoms of the legs.

Workshop storage and shop office storage counters and cupboards can be outfitted with good looking doors and drawer fronts from Quality Doors. More visually appealing than hardwood plywood doors, these oak and Melamine doors and door fronts are available in different styles and colors. Quality Doors manufactures doors in custom sizes. All you have to do is give them the measurements and the doors will be delivered directly to your home. (Check the sources section for address and telephone number.)

Instead of store bought shelves, make your own out of 2x4 boards and plywood. Simply nail or screw 2x4 runners vertically along studs. Cut triangles out of plywood to the dimensions you prefer; generally 9 to 12 inch shelf depth is about right. You may find that deeper shelves stick out too far and that getting things from the back of deeper shelves is more difficult. Nail or screw the triangle pieces to the sides of the 2x4 runners and you have shelf brackets ready for shelves. Lighter weight shelves may be made from 2x2 boards and 1/2-inch plywood. When using plywood for shelves, always keep the grain of the plywood in mind. Plywood shelves are strongest when they are cut from the length of the plywood sheet, as opposed to across the 4-foot width. In other words, if you want a 12 inch wide by 3 foot long shelf, measure the 3-foot section along the grain of the plywood (the 8-foot length of the sheet) and the 12 inch section against the grain (along the 4-foot width of the sheet). In addition, 3/4-inch plywood shelves should span no more than 3 feet without a center support. If you make them longer, they will sag. If you plan to place heavy items on these shelves, plan to support the shelves every 2 feet to prevent sags.

Cabinets require more carpentry work and skill than shelves. It will cost more to build them, too. In essence, plan to use 3/4-inch AC plywood for the shelves and 3/4-inch birch or other hardwood plywood for the doors. Doors could be made from regular AC plywood, but this material does not take stain and paint as nicely as hardwood veneer plywood. On the sides of AC plywood cabinets, you can glue on thin (1/8-inch) hardwood veneer for a finished appearance. Rails and stiles for garage or workshop cabinets may be made from clear fir, although most cabinets feature hardwood rails and stiles.

Plan to rabbet the edges of cabinet doors so that they form a seal around cabinet openings. These doors should be cut 5/8 inch longer and wider than cabinet openings. This way, when a 3/8-inch rabbet is made around all four sides of the door, the door will close into the opening by 3/8 inch and there will be 1/8 inch of play between the top and bottom and another 1/8 inch of play from side to side. This will make it easier to adjust doors while attaching hinges and will also prevent doors from sticking when wood swells during damp weather. Rabbet hinges must be used for this type of cabinet door. They are readily available at hardware stores, lumber yards and home improvement centers. Be sure to buy hinges designed for 3/8-inch rabbet edges.

Preventive Maintenance

Workshop storage is best when it is organized. As you plan the layout of your shop, determine which areas will be used the most for specific types of work. This way, you can plan to place storage in those areas for the things you will need the most. For example, cans of oil, filters, belts, lubrication supplies and other preventive maintenance items should be stored close to the front of your shop. This is because you will generally take on oil changes and service chores from the fronts of vehicles when their hoods are open. The front of the shop is also the place to store spark plugs and the tools and equipment you use to conduct auto tune-ups. Most of the items needed for general auto maintenance are small. Therefore, a small cabinet next to a workbench at the front of the shop might be ideal for the storage of general preventive maintenance parts and supplies.

Detailing Supplies

Basic car washing and detailing supplies are best kept next to a utility sink. This way, your wash soap and bucket will be handy next to the sink and hot and cold running water. Waxes and polishes should be stored there, too, as you need to rinse out applicators periodically with clean water. Since brushes, wash mitts and other cleaning cloths must be rinsed out after each use, plan to store them near the sink so they can be quickly put away after they are cleaned.

Some auto enthusiasts prefer to tackle most of their interior and exterior detailing tasks outdoors. If this is the case for you, then maybe a detailing storage locker would be best located next to the workshop or garage bay door. This way, your tools and supplies will be close to the work area and you will not have to walk through the garage or workshop to get to them. A towel rack on the outside of the detail storage cabinet may be nice for hanging up wet towels, wash mitts and other cleaning cloths. Hooks could be installed on the sides of the cabinet for brushes. Plan to keep all of your detailing supplies in this one locker or cabinet. This includes brushes, toothbrushes, towels, cloths, wash mitts, wash soap, polish, wax, tar remover, tire cleaner, rubber and vinyl dressing, window cleaner, and any other detailing supplies. Do not store wet things inside the locker or cabinet. This may result in mold or mildew accumulation. Rather, hang these things out in the open while wet and put them away only after they are dry.

This is a set of plans from the Western Wood Products Association for a complete storage system. You can alter the plans as necessary in order for units to fit your workshop or garage.

ADD-ON STORAGE ROOM

An add-on storage and workroom doesn't have to be expensive. You start with a simple roughed-in structure. Large or small. Then you add your own shelves, cupboards, bins and work areas to make it work for you.

The modular projects described in this Plan Sheet work equally well in your basement or garage, or as starter units in a new storage room.

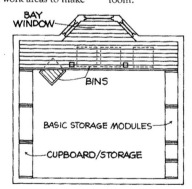

STORAGE PEGS
Cut 1x4 to length and drill 1/4" or 1/2" holes at an angle, evenly spaced, approximately 5" on center. (See Fig. 1 and 2.) Glue 4" dowels in place, then glue/nail 1x4 to storage module, approximately 5' above base.

Materials List for Storage Pegs

Materials List
Storage Pegs
Pegs: 1/4" or 1/2" dowel, 2'
Board: 1x4, 30½"
6d nails
Carpenter's glue

MODULAR STORAGE UNITS

32" WIDE BASIC UNIT
Fig. 1

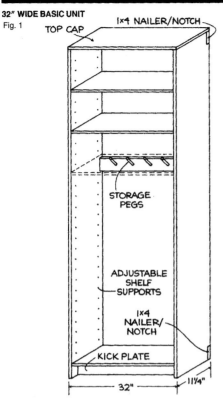

TOP CAP
1x4 NAILER/NOTCH
STORAGE PEGS
ADJUSTABLE SHELF SUPPORTS
1x4 NAILER/ NOTCH
KICK PLATE
32"
11¼"

Fig. 2

Notch for 1x4 Nailer

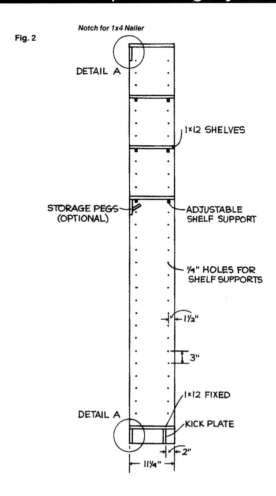

DETAIL A
1x12 SHELVES
STORAGE PEGS (OPTIONAL)
ADJUSTABLE SHELF SUPPORT
¼" HOLES FOR SHELF SUPPORTS
1½"
3"
1x12 FIXED
DETAIL A
KICK PLATE
2"
11¼"

1—Uprights: Measure distance from floor to ceiling. Subtract 1½" from height (for top cap and ease of installation) and cut 1x12 uprights to that length.

2—Notches: Cut a notch 3/4" wide by 3½" long on the back side of both uprights, top and bottom. (See Detail A.)

3—Adjustable shelf supports: Drill two sets of 1/4" holes in each upright, 1½" from edge, as illustrated. Holes are 1/2" deep and 3" on center. See *Woodworking Tips*.

Fig. 2A/Detail

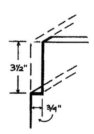

3½"
3/4"

4—1x4 Nailers: Place uprights on edge, face down, 32" apart, outside measurement. (Notches are facing up.) Glue/nail 1x4 nailer into notches at base and top of unit, using two 6d (2") nails each end.
5—Top cap: Glue/nail top cap in place, using five 6d nails each end.
6—Installation: Move storage module(s) into position on wall; attach module by nailing or screwing top and bottom nailers to studs, using 8d nails or 2½" screws. (The use of screws will make the units easier to dismount if you ever decide to move.)

7—Kick plate/bottom shelf: At base of module, position 1x4 kick plate 2" in from front edge of uprights. (See Fig. 2) Glue/nail in place.
Glue/nail bottom shelf to nailer and kick plate.
8—Insert shelf supports and install remaining shelves, as needed.

Materials List for Basic Modular Unit

Uprights: (2) 1x12, ceiling height minus 1½"
Nailers: (2) 1x4, 32"
Top Cap: (1) 1x12, 32"
Kick Plate: (1) 1x4, 30½"
Shelves: (4) 1x12, 30¼" each
Shelf Supports: as needed
Screws: 2½" flathead
Nails: 6d, 8d
Carpenter's glue

CUPBOARD
(For 32" wide modular unit)

Fig. 3

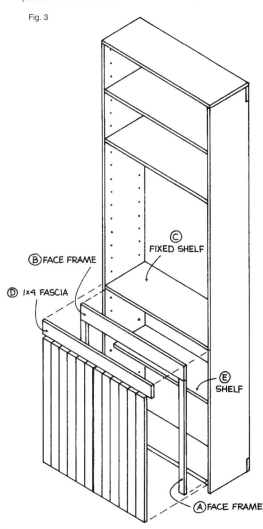

Ⓑ FACE FRAME

Ⓓ 1x4 FASCIA

Ⓒ FIXED SHELF

Ⓔ SHELF

Ⓐ FACE FRAME

1—Build and install modular shelving unit, as described above; drill holes for adjustable shelf supports. Install top cap, kick plate and bottom shelf.

6—After measuring, cut each 2x4 support (G) to length. Toenail 2x4s on edge to 2x4s in front and back, 2' on center; nail supports to posts, as illustrated, using 12d nails.
7—Starting at front edge of workbench, apply 1x4 decking to frame keeping first board flush with edge. Glue/nail decking at each support, using (2) 6d nail per bearing. If decking must be spliced, make certain the joint falls over the center of a support.

NOTE: For a stiffer work surface, edge-glue and clamp 1x4s or use tongue-and-groove material.
For a heavy-duty workbench, or to install vices or other heavy equipment, add 4x4 post and 2x4 support at each end of workbench. (See Detail 8A.) For extra strength, use 2x4 or 2x6 decking instead of 1x4 decking.

8—Glue/nail 1x4 face board (H) to front of workbench, flush with top of decking.

Materials List for Workbench

(12' long, with bay)
Ledgers and Rails (A,B,D,F): 2x4, 65 linear ft.
(If possible, two 2x4s should be full length of workbench)
Supports (C,G): (8) 2x4, 21" (approximately)
Posts (E): (2) 4x4, 35¼" (For heavy duty bench, use (4) posts)
Decking/Face Board: 1x4, 140 linear ft.
(For 2x4 or 2x6 decking): 2x4 or 2x6, 130 linear ft. 1x4, 12 linear ft.
Nails: 6d, 12d, 16d
Carpenter's glue

Fig. 7

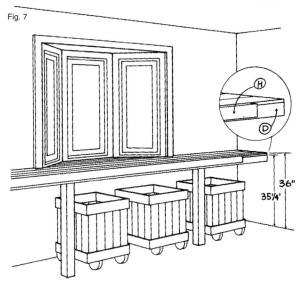

Ⓗ
Ⓓ
36"
35¼'

1—**Ledger:** Using a level, draw a line 35¼" above floor across full length of back wall and first 2' of side walls.

Fig. 8

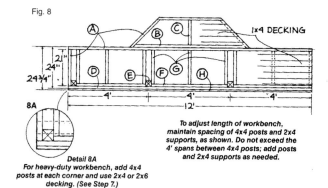

Ⓐ Ⓑ Ⓒ 1x4 DECKING
2¼"
24"
24¾'
Ⓓ Ⓔ Ⓕ Ⓖ Ⓗ
4' 4' 4'
12'

8A

Detail 8A
For heavy-duty workbench, add 4x4 posts at each corner and use 2x4 or 2x6 decking. (See Step 7.)

To adjust length of workbench, maintain spacing of 4x4 posts and 2x4 supports, as shown. Do not exceed the 4' spans between 4x4 posts; add posts and 2x4 supports as needed.

2—Install 2x4 ledger (A) so top is even with mark. Install ledger in window bay first, then apply continuous 2x4 across back wall and bay. Attach 21" ledgers to end walls. Use glue and two 12d (3¼") nails at each stud.
3—Measure width of window bay directly behind ledger; cut 2x4 (B) to length, ends mitered, and glue/ nail to ledgers at ends and sides. At center of span, toenail 2x4 support (C) in place.

4—Cut 2x4 rail (D) to length. (Rail (D) runs full length of workbench.) Before installing rail, glue/nail 4x4 posts to rail 4' on center, as illustrated, flush with top of rail. Secure with (2) 16d (3½") nails per post. Position rail so ends overlap ends of ledger; glue/nail in place, using 12d nails.
5—2x4 (F) fits between posts and between post and ledger. To ensure accuracy, measure actual length of each space before cutting 2x4s; glue/nail to post, ledger and rail.

Fig. 4

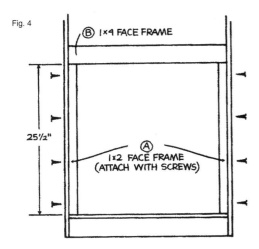

Ⓑ 1x4 FACE FRAME

25½"

Ⓐ 1x2 FACE FRAME
(ATTACH WITH SCREWS)

2—Face frame: From outside of uprights, predrill uprights and vertical 1x2s (A). Glue and screw 1x2s in place, flush with front edge of uprights and bottom shelf. Use four 2" screws each side.

Install horizontal 1x4 face frame (B); glue/nail or screw to uprights, using 6d nails or 2" screws.

Fig. 5

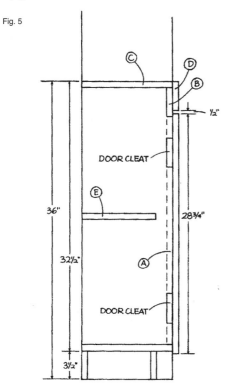

Ⓒ Ⓓ
Ⓑ
½"

DOOR CLEAT

Ⓔ

36" 28¾"

32½" Ⓐ

DOOR CLEAT

3½"

3—Install fixed shelf (C) on top of face frame. Glue/nail to uprights and face frame, using 6d nails. Countersink and fill all nail holes.

4—Apply 1x4 fascia (D) so top edge is flush with shelf.

Fig. 6

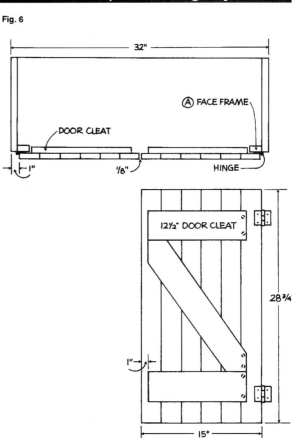

32"

Ⓐ FACE FRAME

DOOR CLEAT

1" 1/8" HINGE

12½" DOOR CLEAT

28¾"

1"

15"

5—Doors: Cut to length and edge-glue six 1x3s for each door. For a tighter joint, clamp until glue sets.

Cut cleats as shown in Fig. 6. Inset 12½" horizontal cleats 1" from inside edge of door. (Make sure cleats clear face frame (A) when door is mounted.) Glue/nail cleats to back of door, using (2) 3d (1½") nails per board. For extra strength, use 1½" screws instead of nails to attach cleats to outside boards. (See Fig. 6.)

Install hinges and mount doors, allowing 1/2" between top of door and lower edge of 1x4 fascia. Allow 1/8" between doors at center. Install door pulls and magnetic or spring catches.

6—Install shelf supports and shelves as needed, including one or more 1x10 shelves (E) in cupboard.

Materials List for Cupboard

Face Frame: (A) (2) 1x2, 25½"
(B) (1) 1x4, 30½"
Fixed Shelf (C): (1) 1x12, 30½"
Fascia (D): (1) 1x4, 32"
Doors (two): (12) 1x3, 28¾"
Cleats: (4) 1x4, 12½" (horizontal)
(2) 1x4, 24"
Inside Shelf (E): (1) 1x10, 30½"
(8) 2" flathead screws
6d, 3d finishing nails
(4) hinges
Magnetic or spring catches
Carpenter's glue

BIN

Fig. 9

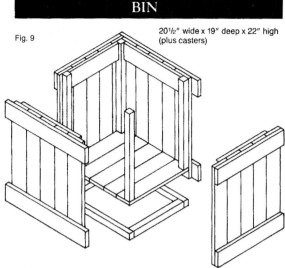

20½" wide x 19" deep x 22" high
(plus casters)

Fig. 11

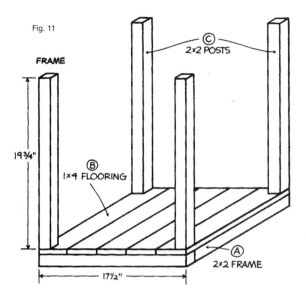

FRAME

© 2x2 POSTS

19¾"

® 1x4 FLOORING

Ⓐ 2x2 FRAME

17½"

Fig. 10

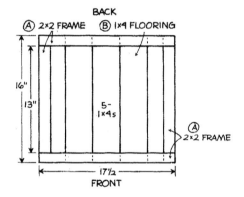

BACK

Ⓐ 2x2 FRAME   ® 1x4 FLOORING

16"
13"
5-
1x4s

Ⓐ
2x2 FRAME

17½

FRONT

2—Posts: Before applying 1x4 flooring to frame, attach the four 2x2 corner posts to outside corners of two 1x4 bottom boards. Glue/nail or screw from the bottom, using (2) 6d nails or 1½" screws per post.

Glue/nail 1x4 flooring to frame, using (2) 6d nails each end.

Instead of attaching from underside of boards, posts may be toe-nailed to base after flooring is in place.

1—Base: Glue/nail 2x2 frame (A) together, using (2) 8d (2½") nails per corner. (Fig. 10) Cut 1x4 flooring (B) to length. Before installing 1x4s, see Step 2.

Fig. 12

Ⓔ 1x4 PANELS

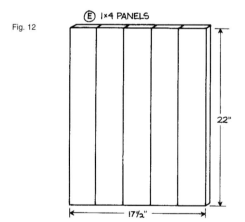

22"

17½"

3—Bin Sides: Cut (20) 1x4 sides (E) to length and assemble the four side panels. (Fig. 12) Each side uses (5) 1x4s, 22" long. (For tighter joints and a more finished appearance, edge-glue and clamp 1x4s until glue sets.)

Fig. 13

SIDE PANELS

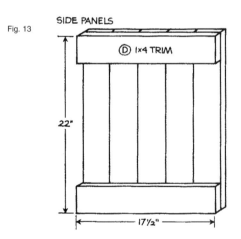

Ⓓ 1x4 TRIM

22"

17½"

For the two side panels: Glue/nail 1x4 trim (D) to top and bottom of panel, flush with edges. Use 3d (1¼") nails. (Or longer nails may be used and clinched on back side.)

FRONT & BACK PANELS

Fig. 14

1½" 1½"

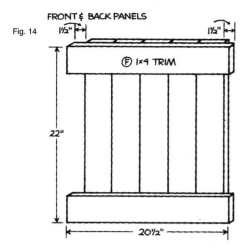

Ⓕ I×4 TRIM

22"

20½"

For front and back panels: Glue/
nail 1x4 trim (F) to panel, flush with
top and bottom edges. Trim extends
1½" on either side of panel. Attach
with 1¼" nails.

Fig. 16

BACK

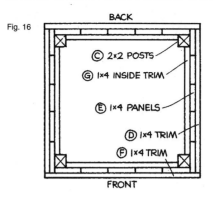

Ⓒ 2×2 POSTS

Ⓖ I×4 INSIDE TRIM

Ⓔ I×4 PANELS

Ⓓ I×4 TRIM

Ⓕ I×4 TRIM

FRONT

6—Inside trim (G): Before cutting
boards, check actual measurement
between posts to ensure accuracy.
(Fig. 16) Glue/nail trim to inside,
flush with top, using 6d (2") nails.
Toenail to posts.

7—Install purchased casters on
2x2 frame.

Fig. 15

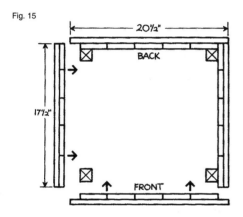

20½"

BACK

17½"

FRONT

4—Position front and back panels
on frame so base of panel is flush
with bottom of frame and top is
even with top of posts. Outside
edges of vertical 1x4 panels are
flush with posts. Turn bin on side
and glue/nail posts to panel, using
8d nails. Glue/nail base to frame.

5—Position side panels so base is
flush with frame and outside edges
are covered by front and back
panels. Glue/nail to posts and
base; nail corners where front and
back panels overlap sides.

Materials List for Bin

Frame: (2) 2x2, 17½" (front
and back)
(2) 2x2, 13" (sides)
Floor (5) 1x4, 16"
Posts: (4) 2x2, 19¾"
Bin sides: (20) 1x4, 22"
Front/back panel trim: (4) 1x4,
20½"
Side panel trim: (4) 1x4, 17½"
Inside trim: (2) 1x4, 14½"
(front/back)
(2) 1x4, 13" (sides)
Nails: 8d, 6d, 4d, 3d
Yellow glue
(4) 2" casters

*CAUTION: Be certain that you
review and understand all steps
of construction and verify all
dimensions before cutting your
material. While every effort has
been made to ensure accuracy in
the design and drawing of WWPA
plans, the possibility of error
always exists and WWPA cannot
accept responsibility for lumber
improperly used or designs not
first verified.*

Fig. A

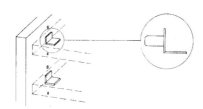

How to install shelf clips
    Shelf clips, which are sold at most lumber and hardware stores, provide an easy, inconspicuous method of mounting shelves. Two clips at each end of the shelf are sufficient to support normal loads.

Clips are installed in holes drilled to match the diameter of the post—usually 1/4".
    You may drill one set of holes for each shelf. Or, to make them adjustable, drill a series of holes, as illustrated.

Fig. B

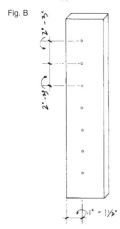

1—One of the simplest ways to help assure a straight hole is to make a drilling jig. Using a scrap of 1x3 or 1x4 two to three feet long (or height of cupboard), draw a line 1½" inside, and parallel to, one edge. Make marks equidistant (usually every 2" to 3") down the length of the line; clamp board to workbench. Select bit the same size as shelf clip post and drill holes as marked, all the way through the board.
2—Clamp jig into position along front edge of end panel and drill first set of holes 1/2" deep. Move jig to back edge, making sure holes are parallel. Drill second set of holes. Repeat steps for other end panel.
3—Insert shelf clips as needed. (Do not glue in place.) Trim 1/8" to 1/4" off length of shelves to accommodate shelf clip. Or turn clip so base of "L" is on top.

Fig. C

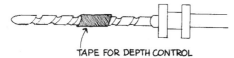

TAPE FOR DEPTH CONTROL

TIP: To avoid drilling all the way through end panel, wrap tape around the bit at the correct

depth (thickness of jig + 1/2" for clip post.) Or use a factory-made metal jig that clamps to the bit.

Fig. D

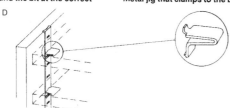

Shelf Supports with clips
    Another method of installing adjustable shelves uses purchased metal standards. The standards may be nailed or screwed into

position, or dadoed in.
    Use a level to align standard vertically. Make sure holes line up horizontally before attaching second standard.

Paints and Thinners

Flammable liquids, like paints, thinners, solvents, reducers, degreasers and the like, should be stored separately in a well-ventilated flammable storage liquid cabinet. If you have small children, seriously consider keeping these hazardous materials in a locked cabinet. These cabinets should be located on an outside wall of your shop, preferably next to one of the big bay door openings. It is absolutely paramount that these units be stored away from any sources of ignition, like hot water heaters, furnaces, wood burning stoves, and so on. Many flammable liquids, like gasoline, produce vapors that are heavier than air. These highly flammable vapors will creep along floors until they find an ignition source or dissipate in the atmosphere. This is why hot water heaters in home garages are positioned on top of stands or supports about 18-inches high. If gasoline leaks out of an automobile tank or fuel system, the theory is that the vapors would hug the ground and escape through the gap at the bottom of the garage door before they could reach a hot water tank pilot light more than 18 inches off of the floor.

Bona fide metal flammable liquid storage cabinets are available through autobody paint and supply stores. You might also find used models at swap meets, commercial salvage yards and possibly some major industrial plants that sell off salvage or excess supplies. Instead of a professional flammable liquid storage cabinet, you could build a similar unit out of wood. Although this unit will not be fireproof, it will at least serve as a place where such materials can be kept out of the way and under lock and key. Plan to locate this cabinet on an exterior wall. Then, install a fresh air vent through the wall so air can circulate through the cabinet and in and out of the vent. The type of vent needed is just a common one most generally found at most home improvement centers and lumber yards. Louvers prevent rain water and snow from getting into the cabinet and a screen will prevent bugs from getting in there, too.

Dismantled Part Storage

This is an area of automotive workshop storage that requires careful consideration and planning. A gorgeous workshop with plenty of counters, cabinets and workbenches may not be ideally set up for frame-off restorations. Why? Because there is no place to store all the hundreds of parts that will be coming off the project vehicle. Remember that many of these parts will be stored in dirty condition until the restorer finds time to clean, repair and restore them.

Large Parts

One way to simplify this problem is to erect a small shed outdoors for the storage of dismantled auto parts. This would make a great place to protect large items, such as bumpers, hoods, trunk lids, fenders, seats and the like. A shed will protect parts from vandals and the weather. Instead of a shed, you may have to design a shelving system in your garage or workshop to handle the increased storage load.

If possible, consider building a large floor to ceiling storage unit in a corner of your work area. Use 2x4's and 3/4-inch plywood to build a 3 foot wide by 8 foot long floor to ceiling rack consisting of four shelves. Each shelf could be set about 2 feet above the other, or you could stagger shelf heights to best accommodate the things that will be stored there. Start by measuring some of the things that will need to be stored. Take an inventory of those items to give you a good idea of how much of what will go on the unit. The lowest shelf should be saved for the heaviest items, with the lighter stuff going above. Also take into account the number of relatively flat items that will be stored, like upholstery panels, glass, doors and so on. This way, you might be able to situate a couple of shelves just a foot, or so, above the ones below them and have enough overall room for a fifth shelf.

For a 3 foot by 8 foot storage unit, make the frames for your shelves out of 2x4's with the outside dimensions at 3 feet by 8 feet. Install 2x4 supports in the middle of the frames at the 3 foot and 6 foot points. Then, cover the frames with 3/4-inch plywood. Plan to use at least six 2x4 upright supports that will run from the floor to the ceiling. Mark these upright 2x4's at the points where you want the shelves to be located. Then, stand the bottom shelf on its end and nail one of the uprights to it at the corner with the end of the 2x4 flush with the bottom of the shelf frame; have a helper assist you. Next, position the top shelf in line with its mark on that 2x4 upright and nail the two together. Follow up by nailing on the rest of the shelves to that single upright. With all the shelves nailed to the first 2x4 upright, position the second corner 2x4 upright on the other side of the shelves and nail it in place according to your shelf marks. With two of the uprights nailed onto one end of the shelves, you should be able to turn the unit over and nail on the other four uprights; two on each end of the shelves and one on each side of the middle of the shelves. After the rack has been placed in position, secure it to wall studs with lag bolts. If your work area does not offer an open space for such a storage rack, you might have to set up brackets along open wall spaces for the storage of bumpers, trim and longer parts. You may even be able to store door panels, fenders and the like, on nails that are partially driven into wall studs.

Small Parts

Although small auto parts are much easier to store, they can become a problem when it comes time to find them, especially if they are stored haphazardly. Therefore, organization must be a priority. Cupboard and cabinet space may be designated for just the storage of dismantled auto parts. If possible, store related parts in cardboard boxes that are clearly labeled with their contents. Then, to make it easiest on yourself, keep a log of the parts stored in cabinets on a piece of paper taped to the inside or outside the cabinet door. It is not always easy to store clean parts. In many cases, auto restorers have such a good time taking parts off project vehicles, they find it hard to stop in the middle to start cleaning parts for storage. If you find yourself frantically dismantling parts, stop. Realize that the problem of storage will only get worse. If you have the patience, take time to clean and dry each part as it comes off the vehicle. Then place the part in a clean box with all the other related parts that have also been cleaned and dried. If you don't quite have the temperament to clean each part in that manner, at least realize the importance of parts storage and develop another plan. One idea is to schedule a block of time for dismantling to be followed by another specific block of time for cleaning and storing. This way, you can know that you'll face each new restoration day with a clean shop and all the dismantled parts neatly put away. This is an especially important point for those enthusiasts who may only have the time to work on project vehicles during weekends and a few other times during the week.

Restored Parts

The preservation of restored parts must be taken very seriously. In some cases, parts may sit on a shelf or in a cabinet for months before they are needed. Parts that have been taken down to bare metal must be coated with a primer before being put into storage. If not, rust will quickly attack the metal and require additional work to bring the part back to satisfactory condition. Those parts that have been primed and painted must be protected from other workshop activities. This not only includes their physical protection against being knocked over or bumped into, but also protection against airborne pollutants like sanding dust and paint overspray. If parts must be stored on open shelves, plan to wrap them in soft cotton cloths and place them in labeled boxes to protect them from workshop dust and dirt. Ideally, though, try to find empty cabinet space for them. You should wrap cloths around painted parts even when they are stored in cabinets to guarantee shop dust and dirt will not accumulate on them. Consider using old clothing lockers to store small auto parts. These units are equipped with 12-inch by 12-inch doors that are great for all types of small storage, from power tools and headlights, to gauges and handles. Call around to the various salvage yards in your area to see if they have any of these units available. If not, check local newspaper classified ad sections under the "Building Materials" heading. You might even check with the head office for your local school district. Their maintenance division may have a number of old lockers in storage and would be delighted to get rid of them for a very economical price.

These Western Wood Products Association plans are for a system of storage under stairs. Such a system might be perfect for those with basement workshops. A variety of parts may be stored under stairs.

LOOK UNDER THE STAIRS FOR CONVENIENT, VERSATILE, STORAGE

The storage units shown here are designed to fit inside a two-foot space between the vertical dividers. (Other dimensions may be used; simply adjust the size of the units and the spacing between walls.)

Dividers are framed with 2x2s and finished on one side with 1x6 or 1x8 boards.

If you prefer to panel both sides of the dividers, allow 3 inches for wall thickness.

FRAMEWORK/DIVIDERS

Fig. 1

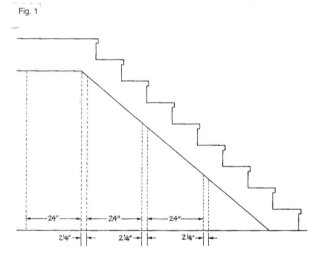

Lay out divider wall spacing on floor, allowing a 24-inch *inside measurement* between dividers plus 2¼ inches for thickness of finished wall. Then, using a plumb line, mark the underside of stairs directly above floor spacing.

Fig. 2

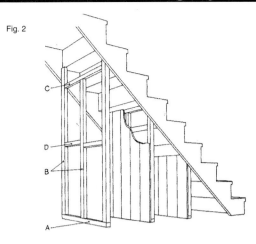

If stair stringers are exposed, attach 2x2 bottom frame (A) to wood floor with glue and nails; if floor is concrete, use tile mastic and/or concrete nails. Glue/nail vertical 2x2 supports (B) to stair stringers and floor frame.

Glue/nail horizontal 2x2s (C) between supports at top. Where span is more than 36 inches, add horizontal center support (D).

Apply paneling boards to one or both sides of frame.

If stair stringers are enclosed with drywall, plaster or paneling, locate position of stringer just as you would find studs in an existing wall: use magnetic stud finder; look for drywall nailing pattern, or "sound" them out by gently tapping with a hammer.

Fig. 3

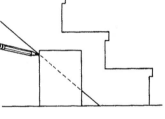

Determine stair angle by placing a piece of cardboard vertically where stair angle meets the floor. Make sure one side of cardboard is square to floor, then reach inside with a pencil and mark floor/stringer angle on cardboard.

Fig. 4

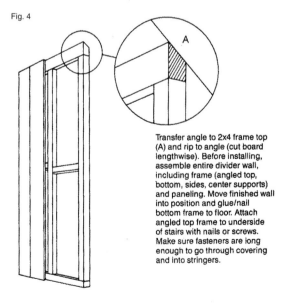

Transfer angle to 2x4 frame top (A) and rip to angle (cut board lengthwise). Before installing, assemble entire divider wall, including frame (angled top, bottom, sides, center supports) and paneling. Move finished wall into position and glue/nail bottom frame to floor. Attach angled top frame to underside of stairs with nails or screws. Make sure fasteners are long enough to go through covering and into stringers.

PULL-OUT STORAGE BIN

19" x 21" x 15" high, plus casters

MATERIALS LIST

BIN, Figs. 5, 6, & 7
Bottom frame: (2) 2x2s, 16½"
(2) 2x2s, 17½"
Corner posts: (4) 2x4s, 12¾"
Bottom boards: (5) 1x4s, 19½"
Top frame: (2) 2x2s, 16½"
(2) 2x2s, 14½"
Sides: (22) 1x4s, 15"
Casters:
(4) 2" casters and screws
Nails:
1 lb. 4d (1½"), ½lb. 8d (2½")
Yellow glue

Fig. 5

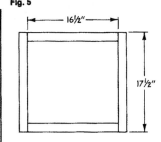

16½"

17½"

FIVE EASY STEPS

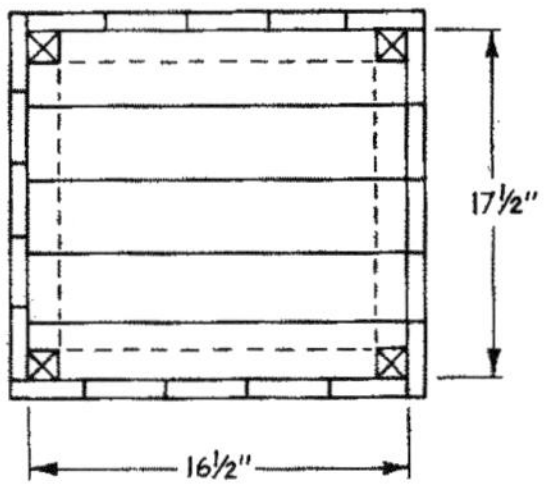

Fig. 5

1. Assemble bottom frame (A) with 8d nails and glue.

Fig. 6

2. Glue/nail the four 2x2 corner posts (B) to outside corners of two 1x4 bottom boards (C). Glue/nail the five bottom boards to frame with 4d nails, positioning boards with posts along outside edges.

Fig. 7

3. Glue/nail top frame (D) to corner posts 1-½" below top of post, using 8d nails.

4. Apply 1x4 sides (E) with glue and 4d nails.

5. Attach casters to bottom corners making sure widest part of caster doesn't extend beyond outer edge of box.

Fig. 6

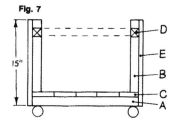

17½"

16½"

Fig. 7

D
E
B
C
A

15"

DRAWERS

23-½"wide x 30" long x 4-¼" deep

MATERIALS LIST

DRAWER, Figs. 10 & 11
Drawer front and back:
(2) 1x6, 22"
Drawer sides: (2) 1x6, 30"
Bottom supports:
1x1 (molding stock)
(2) 22" (front and back);
(2) 27" (sides)
Drawer bottom: ¼" plywood,
waferboard or hardboard;
22"x28½"
Drawer glides: (2) 2x2, 30"
Nails: ½lb. 3d (1¼");
½lb. 6d (2"); ½lb. 8d (2½")
Yellow glue

FOUR SIMPLE STEPS

Fig.10

1. Using a saber saw with fine tooth blade, cut 6-inch wide by 2-inch deep hand hole in center of drawer front(A).

2. Glue/nail sides (B) to front and back with 6d nails.

3. Glue/nail 1x1 drawer bottom supports (C) to inside of back, front and sides with 3d nails. Position supports ¼ inch from bottom edges. Check to be certain it's square, then glue/nail drawer bottom (D) in place.

Fig. 11

4. Position 2x2 drawer glides (E) 1 inch inside front edge of dividers. Glue/nail in place using 8d (2½") nails.

To install additional drawers, apply drawer glides 7-½ inches apart on center. A light coating of paste wax or candle wax on bottom of drawer sides will help unit side easily on glides.

Fig.10

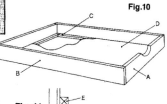

C
D
B
A

Fig. 11

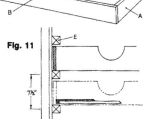

E

7½"

TABLE TOP

24"x 28-½"

Fig. 8

A

MATERIALS LIST

TABLE TOP, Figs. 8 & 9
Table Top:(2) 1x12s, 27"
Cross brace:(2) 1x2s, 22½"
Edge trim: (4)1x2s, 30"
Nails: ½lb. 3d (1¼")
Yellow glue

Fig. 9

1. Assemble 1x12s (A) for table top by spacing 1x2 cross braces (B) 21-¼ inches apart and equidistant from each end. Glue/nail in place, using 3d nails.

2. Cut to size and glue/nail 1x2 trim (C) vertically to table edges.

Fig. 9

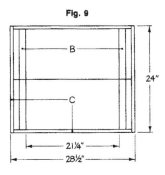

B

C

24"

21¼"

28½"

PULL-OUT SHELVES/CLOTHES STORAGE

36"wide x 22-½" deep x 61-½" high, plus casters

MATERIALS LIST

PULL-OUT UNIT, Figs. 12 & 13
Sides: (4) 1x12s, 60"
Shelf Supports: (8) 2x2s, 22"
Top and bottom: (4) 1x12s, 36"
Shelves: (8) 1x12s, 34½"
Back: (17) 1x4s, 36" or
¼" plywood, waferwood or
hardboard, 36"x61½"
Casters: (4) 2½" or 3" casters
and screws
Nails: ½lb. 4d (1½");
½lb. 6d (2")
Yellow glue

For clothes storage option:
Clothes rod and brackets
Nailing cleats: (6) 2x2s, 22"

CONSTRUCTION STEPS

1. For Shelf Unit: To assemble sides (A), glue/nail shelf supports (B) across 2x12s at desired spacing.

Fig. 12

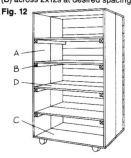

A
B
D

C

1a. For Clothes Storage Option: Glue/nail 2x2 nailing cleats (E) across 2x12s at top, bottom, and center of sides (Fig. 13). A shelf may also be added across top.

2. Glue/nail top and bottom boards (C) to sides.

3. Install 1x12 shelf boards (D) with nails.

4. Place unit face down on floor. To make sure it's square, measure opposite diagonal corners or use a large framing square. Apply 1x4s to back horizontally. Or use solid backing.

For clothes storage, install brackets and clothes rod at desired height.

5. Apply casters at bottom corners of unit.

Fig. 13

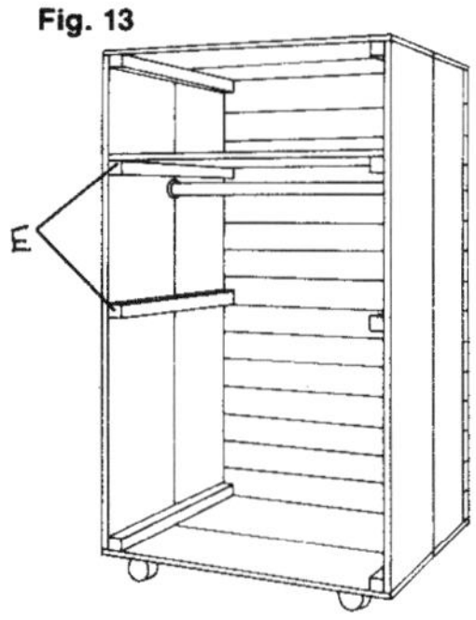

E

This is a 26-Drawer Combo tool chest from Stack-On Products. A large mobile tool chest like this may be perfect for those with limited work and storage space, especially if pegboard tool storage may be a security problem. Worktops on the wings of this unit are very handy when working on autos away from workbenches.

Like Ron Hoffer, Chuck Saydan installed a built-in set of racks for trays that hold all kinds of small automotive parts and fasteners. An open shelf below houses spray cans and other containers. Above the rack is a built-in slot for a radio. This wall separates the workshop area from the shop bathroom.

Tool and Equipment Storage

One of the best ways to keep track of your tools is by use of a roll-around tool chest. If you have a large assortment of hand tools and other specialty tools, you may think that bigger is better. Those huge tool chests that rise almost 6-feet off the ground are not always the most convenient. It may be difficult to spot tools in the top of these units which may be tucked away in back corners. For those who have quite a few tools, it might be smarter to invest in a couple of medium tool chests. Easier to organize and retrieve things from, each of these can be outfitted with tools that are related—mechanics wrenches, sockets and the like in one, autobody tools in the other, and so on.

A wide variety of tool chests with all sorts of different drawer and compartment combinations are available through Stack-On Products, Harbor Freight Tools, The Eastwood Company and other outlets. Prices vary according to quality and construction.

When buying a new tool chest, always look for the biggest wheels available. Small wheels are a pain in the neck. They can get blocked by almost any piece of debris on the floor and are difficult to maneuver, especially when heavily loaded.

Hand Tools

If your automotive workshop is set up in a secure area, where you have few worries about thieves or vandals, you may prefer to keep most of your hand tools out in the open. One of the easiest ways to accomplish this is with pegboard. If pegboard has been a problem for you in the past because hooks seemed to fall off each time you grabbed a tool, then invest in Sta-Put Color Pegs. These plastic pegboard hooks are available in different colors and designs. One model features three size rings, perfect for screwdrivers and other long skinny tools. (Check the sources section under Sta-Put) Paint pegboard white or another light color to increase its ability to reflect light. Then, once you have all the hand tools arranged the way you want them, trace their outline onto the pegboard with a black felt marker. This will help you to remember where each tool belongs. Should you choose to keep hand tools in a tool chest drawer, check out any of a number of different drawer organizers available through tool outlets and mail order companies. These handy devices go a long way toward keeping tools organized. Individual units are available for wrenches and sockets, and divider packages are available for other drawers.

Power Tools

Power tools may be stored in tool chest compartments, on lower workbench shelves, open wall shelves or in cabinets. The choice is up to you. However, to ensure the safety of these items, you should consider covered storage, like cabinets with doors. Storing power tools in protected cabinets or lockers keeps them out of sight and away from the normal workshop activities that create dusty atmospheres. Plan to store heavy power tools on lower shelves of a free standing shelf unit, like a book case. This will keep the unit from becoming top heavy. Better yet, secure the unit to the wall with lag screws or wall anchors. Set up the power tool storage area in such a way that all attachments and accessories are right next to the tool. Use a drill press to bore uniform sets of holes in a block of wood; one hole for each drill bit. The wood block will support the bits upright to make them convenient to recognize and easy to retrieve. A small section of pegboard secured to a couple of 1/4-inch runners on the inside of cabinet doors makes a great place for storing packages of hacksaw blades, sandpaper, wrenches and other items. Pegboard must stick out from the door surface by at least 1/4-inch to make room for the insertion of pegboard hooks.

Pneumatic Tools

Most all tools that operate on compressed air should be stored in the same general vicinity. This makes it easiest to locate certain tools when you need them. Organize cupboard space so tools have their own spot. Use 1/4-inch plywood or hardwood to make dividers. If you are good at woodworking, you might even consider routing 1/4-inch grooves or slots inside cabinet or cupboard spaces so that dividers can easy slip in. Consider using pegboard as dividers for small parts and maintenance items. You must also provide for the storage of tool accessories. These items may include sanding disks, burrs, drill bits and so on.

Some auto enthusiasts prefer to maintain power and pneumatic tools in their own distinctive metal tool cases. This is a good idea because cases are outfitted with bumpers and supports that keep tools from banging around while they are carried in the case. Print the name of the tool on the outside of the case with a felt marker. This will help you to quickly identify the tool when needed. To help keep your workplace tidy and safe, consider mounting retractable reel compressed air lines in your shop. You will have to run regular air line piping up to the ceiling so that the reels can be supplied with air. Once this extra work is done, you will have the convenience of compressed air without having hoses running all over the floor.

Autobody and Paint

Autobody and paint work requires the use of special tools and materials. Since autobody work must be done at a vehicle, it may make sense to have autobody tools maintained in a roll-around cart. Another option is the lower half of a two-piece tool chest. This way, all the tools and materials you would commonly need for autobody repair can be stored together and easily wheeled to the locations where you need them. On the other hand, painting tools and materials need to be protected from shop dust and other debris. They must remain clean so that they perform as expected. Therefore, plan to store paint guns, spare parts and tips, filters and other materials in an enclosed space.

Large Equipment Units

Stationary pieces of large equipment will require good amounts of floor space. If your work area is limited, seriously consider using bench top equipment units instead of the larger models. Should benchtop tools be something you want to pursue, plan to build workbenches with bottom shelves big enough to store benchtop units when not in use. Some large pieces of equipment must be bolted to the floor to ensure adequate support. Therefore, before you commit to boring holes in concrete floors, be absolutely certain that the locations chosen for tools are perfect. If not, place tools in those spots while you conduct normal work around the shop. It should not take much time to determine if those locations pose obstacle problems.

Ventilation

Ventilation is one of the more critical elements that you must consider during the planning of your auto workshop. Breathing polluted air can have serious long term effects on your health. Filter masks and respirators are essential, of course, but do you really expect to wear one all the time?

A good way to ensure adequate workshop ventilation is to have a window or small door open on one end of the shop and a big bay door open on the other. Cross ventilation will flush pollutants to blow out of the shop as clean air rushes in. This may be an excellent method of ventilation during warm dry weather, but what about winter? A number of magazines, especially those about woodworking, carry ads for various air filtration systems. These units rely upon a fan to draw in dirty air through filters at one end. This air is then forced out of the opposite end through another system of filters. Although not intended to serve as air purification systems, these economical units do a good job of filtering out a large amount of workshop air pollution.

Mike Holiman set up a large furnace-type squirrel cage fan in his shop. It is mounted on the wall about 18-inches down from the ceiling. It does an outstanding job of clearing out the air in his shop, especially during spray painting exercises while a bay door is open. The only drawback to this set up is the fan draws everything up first before it is exhausted. A better system would be to have the fan mounted about a foot off the floor. That way, all the dust and overspray would be pulled down before being exhausted.

Vehicle Exhaust

Automobile exhaust is loaded with carbon monoxide and other deadly gases. It is recommended that engines never be operated inside garages or auto workshops for any longer than it takes to get vehicles in or out. This poses a problem during engine tune-ups. In most cases, mechanics pull vehicles outdoors to test engine operations. However, what about during inclement weather?

About the only way to safely operate engines inside garages and workshops is with use of tubing specifically designed to channel vehicle exhaust outdoors. Crush-Proof Tubing manufactures and sells kits with tubing that fits over exhaust pipes and a vent that is installed on garage doors. As long as there are no exhaust system leaks, this system works well to keep home garage and small auto workshop atmospheres safe from exhaust poisons.

Professional auto garages use a similar system that includes a special fan that helps draw out vehicle exhaust, especially when the distance from vehicles to the outdoors is extensive. If you have plans to dial-in engines in your garage or workshop, a ventilating automotive exhaust system should be one of the first priorities on your planning list. Even while using such a system, it is a very good idea to keep a window or door open to ensure fresh air is circulating throughout your workplace.

Welding

Welding operations should be conducted next to an open bay door. Smoke from welding is harmful. Large welding jobs will most likely be done in an open space close to an open door. A fan may be used to help blow out the smoke. For small welding jobs, though, you might think about setting up a small benchtop welding center. An easy way to set up a benchtop welding center is to start with 16-gauge sheet metal. Build a box-like unit about 3-feet wide and as deep as your workbench—about 28- to 30-inches. Make the back and both sides about 18 to 24 inches high and the front about 6 inches high. Fill the bottom of the box with fire brick set in furnace cement (fireplace mortar). Some welders prefer dry sand as a base because it can be used to support small pieces being welded.

If you choose to use fire brick, plan the floor of your welding center for a size that will accommodate bricks exactly. This way, you will not have to cut any bricks to fit. At the top, build a support system for a range hood, similar to the one over your kitchen stove. Mount the hood a few inches higher than your head. Use range hood ducting to route exhaust to a vent cap installed at a desired location through the

Internal combustion engines cannot be operated inside enclosed spaces. During cold winter months when you prefer to have shop doors closed, consider using an ExhaustAway System from Crush-Proof Tubing. These specially made hoses are designed to funnel auto exhaust from exhaust pipes out through an adapter installed through a garage door. Units are available for single and dual exhaust vehicles.

wall to the outdoors. Store your welder under the welding center on a heavy-duty shelf built into the workbench. Store welding tools, clamps, face shields, gloves and other materials around the center for quick and easy access. Maintain a fire extinguisher nearby, too.

Should you decide to install a benchtop welding center, you must plan for this in advance. You will need 110-volt electrical power to the range hood and a 220-volt supply to the welder. In addition, you must be certain that all flammable and combustible storage is maintained away from the welding center. Even though the center's metal walls extend up a good distance, sparks could escape the enclosure to pose a fire hazard.

Sanding

Those with autobody repair experience realize the tremendous amount of sanding dust that is created while working to smooth car bodies. Sanding dust is very fine. It will go everywhere and get all over everything. Therefore, you should plan to minimize the effects of this problem before tackling autobody repair projects in your new workshop and especially in your home garage. One method entails the use of plastic sheets. Staple the end of a sheet of plastic to a 1x2 board. Wrap plastic around the board

Respirator

Save Your Breath
Used for dust and paint mists (lacquer, enamel, and organic vapors). Features of both professional and disposable respirators include: soft seal flanges for unmatched comfort, low breathing resistance, low nosepiece for use with eyewear, perspiration port to reduce facepiece slippage, and adjustable crownstrap.
Not For Use With Paints Containing Isocyanates.

8216	**Professional Respirator**
8216A	**Organic Vapor Cartridges, 10 pack**
8216B	**Prefilters, 20 pack**
8224	**Disposable Respirator, not shown**

Respiratory protection is critically important during dust producing auto endeavors. Although paper filter masks do a good job under specific conditions, a full blown filtered respirator should be used under heavy sanding conditions and when painting with almost any non-isocyanate paint product. This respirator from The Eastwood Company features disposable filters, adjustable straps, a low nosepiece for use with glasses or safety goggles and soft seal flanges for comfort.

a couple of times and then mount it on the ceiling between two garage bays or where you want to install a curtain. Staple the bottom of the sheet to another 1x2 board. Make three of these curtains to essentially design a three-sided enclosure with the fourth being the garage door opening. You can place a couple of bricks on the bottom boards to help them stay in place. Leave a little extra plastic at the corners of each sheet. Fold these corners together and secure them with clothespins. Use tape to hold plastic sheet flaps securely to the door opening. Now, run a small fan to the inside of the enclosure to help circulate air throughout it. When you have completed your sanding chores and have cleaned up the area, remove the tape from the doorway and release the clothespins at the corners. Roll up the sheets starting with the bottom. With a few hooks placed in the ceiling on each side of the sheets, use bungee cords or tie rope to secure the rolled up bundles of plastic sheets to the ceiling.

Basement Workshops

Since basements are not normally outfitted with large bay doors, you must set up some kind of a viable air filtration and ventilation system. In addition, you must be keenly aware that vapors, fumes and dust can easily penetrate your household. Because your household furnace is located in your basement, as is the hot water heater, you must understand that some auto repair, alteration and restoration activities cannot be performed in basements.

First, you will need to design and plan for a fan that ventilates directly outside. You may have to cut into the space between ceiling and floor joists to access the rim joist. The rim joist should be located above ground. This is where to install the ventilation cap. If not the rim joist, you may have to hire a concrete cutting company to cut a hole near the top of the concrete or block basement wall to access outside air. If your

basement has windows, install a fan in a window opening and close off the rest of the window with plywood, Plexiglas or another suitable material. Now, if you have a fan in the basement that will force out dirty air, just where will the new air come from to replace it? Consider installing a vent on an opposite wall that can be opened while the fan is operating and closed during other times. To keep sanding dust and other airborne debris from getting into your house, install weather-stripping along the door jambs on all doors that lead from the basement into the house. Materials for this purpose are readily available at hardware stores and home improvement centers. Be certain to include notes regarding basement ventilation on your planning notes. Ventilation should be a primary focal point and one of the first actions taken to remodel your basement into a suitable auto work area.

Workshop Security

Many auto workshops are built with no windows and no skylights. Owners of these shops would rather sacrifice the benefits of natural light than make it easier for thieves to break into their shops. This is no small consideration. Auto workshops are generally filled with expensive tools. Some are also loaded with expensive and hard to find auto parts. Therefore, you must seriously evaluate the security needs for your own workshop. If you live in the country with few neighbors and crime is not a major problem, you might prefer the warmth and sunshine offered through windows and skylights. If you live in an urban area and are concerned about break-ins and theft, perhaps you should eliminate all window and skylight plans and consider the installation of a security system.

General Security

The yellow pages can provide you with a large number of security companies. With many of these systems, sensors are set up at all doors and windows. When an owner unlocks and opens doors, he or she will have a preset amount of time to get to the alarm panel and disarm the system. Instead of an official alarm system, some auto enthusiasts have installed motion detector lights in their shops. Hooked up to a light switch, these lights can be turned off while owners are working in the shop. Switched on, the lights will switch on when they sense motion inside the area. Those with electronics experience could also wire in a siren to these lights. You will have to check with an experienced electronics person to learn how to set up such a motion detector light and siren system. Another good way to keep thieves at bay is to install steel doors and heavy-duty deadbolts to regular entrance doors. Install locking systems that extend from the center of the door through the door jamb on the interior sides of bay doors. Outside lighting is also a deterrent to theft. Consider installing regular floodlights or halogen lights all around your workshop or garage. If this setup will be a nuisance by shining into bedroom windows, perhaps motion detector lights will be preferable.

Fire Alarms

Smoke detectors are not generally a good idea for auto workshops. The smoke and dust produced in these spaces will cause smoke detectors to go off regularly. Instead, invest in heat detectors. Heat detectors are activated by either a sudden rise in temperature or when room temperature reaches a preset level. Plan to position heat detectors on the ceiling of your workshop. Place them above likely sources of fire. Some may be near flammable liquid storage cabinets, welding centers, dirty rag storage and electrical service panels. If possible, wire the heat detectors into your home's alarm system, especially if you have a detached workshop. If a fire does break out in your workshop while you are asleep, alarms in the house will sound off. Consult an engineer at a fire or security alarm system company for specifics.

While on the subject of security and safety, do not forget the importance of fire extinguishers! Your workshop should be outfitted with at least two extinguishers in case one does not operate properly. Fire extinguishers should be rated at 2A:10B:C minimally. This means that it is rated to extinguish twice as much fire in normal (Class A) combustibles, like paper and wood as a 1A; be sufficient to extinguish a 10-square foot area of a flammable liquid fire (Class B fire); and can be used on electrical fires (Class C fires).

Place fire extinguishers next to exits; like entrance doors and garage bay doors. You will not want to run deeper into a fire to reach fire extinguishers. Rather, you will want to reach them as you exit the building area. Along with heat detectors and fire extinguishers, you should have a telephone in

Below the television set in Chuck Saydan's shop are an intercom to the house, telephone, clipboard and fire extinguisher. A first aid kit is in the bathroom. Your shop must be equipped with at least one fire extinguisher rated at 2A:10B:C or better. In addition, you should wire in a telephone for both convenience and emergencies.

your workshop. This will allow you to quickly call for help in an emergency. Telephones are also convenient to have in your workshop. Cordless telephones can fill this need quite nicely and allow you to walk over to an engine or auto part and describe it to the person at the auto parts store.

Overview

There is a lot to consider when planning the fundamental layout of your new auto workspace. As was stated at the beginning of this chapter, it is easy to become overwhelmed with all the possible options. Focus on the basics first. The extras will fall into place eventually. Take advantage of the time you have to plan. Write down the projects you hope to undertake in your work area and the specific things you will have to do. This should help you determine which features to focus on. Be sure to write down or draw in all the ideas that come to mind. The more you study your overall plan, the more you'll get out of your home workshop.

Chapter 4
FLOOR PLANS

Drawing floor plan layouts for your auto workshop or garage is easy. Diagrams do not have to look anything like those from a professional architect. Remember that these plans are for you alone. No one has to decipher your work. However, once you arrive at a plausible set of plans, make the effort to draw a final set neatly with legibly written notes. As eager as you might be to get started putting your new workspace together, it may be months before you get the chance to complete some of the outfitting projects. This is the time when neatly drawn plans that are easy to read and decipher will be most appreciated.

Purchase a pad of graph paper, preferably the type that features lines spaced at 1/4-inch intervals. Scale your drawings so that one square on paper equals 1 foot in real dimensions. If you want larger plans, make two or more squares equal 1 foot in real dimensions. Purchase an inexpensive drafting ruler, too. These rulers are generally three-sided, with different measuring increments on each side, like, 1 inch, 1/4 inch, 3/8 inch, and so on. The 1/4 inch increment ruler makes it easier to quickly determine the lengths of drawn lines, as opposed to counting graph paper squares each time you want to know the length of a line.

Start out your floor plan with the dimensions of the walls and doors. Then draw in the actual size of your project vehicle, especially its length. This will show you how much room is available at the front of the garage with the car or truck parked inside. Remember that you will need at least 3 feet at the front of the garage or workshop for maneuvering. Continue to adjust that "bird's eye view" floor plan until you develop a satisfactory layout.

With the floor plan mostly complete, work on plans for each wall. These will be horizontal viewing plans; diagrams of the walls, workbenches and storage units as they look while you are standing in the center of your garage. Be certain the height measurements from the floor to ceiling are accurate. Try to design upper storage units so that their bottom assemblies are located at least 2 inches above your head as you stand directly under them. This way, you should be able to walk under upper shelves or cupboards while working on your car or truck without banging your head. This rule does not apply to shelves and cupboards that are located over workbenches or counters.

Draw horizontal views of all four walls, including the one that supports the garage door. These drawings do not have to be three-dimensional. However, you should note on the plans how deep each unit will be, to help you later when it comes time to determine how much plywood and other materials will be needed.

Plans for the wall that supports the garage door may include pegboard panels for the inside of the door and storage shelves above the garage door along the header that supports the opening. Note: Anything stored on pegboard panels attached to garage doors must be lashed top and bottom before the door may be safely raised. Plans for other walls should include pegboard and/or hinged pegboard panels; storage shelves or cupboards; and anything that may be suspended from rafters or ceiling joists.

Be sure to include measurements for everything. Write measurements down on the plans next to the

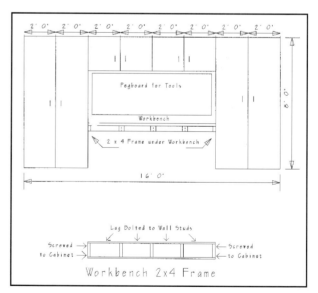

An 8-foot workbench is designed between two large cabinets. With a 2x4 frame secured to the wall in back and cabinets on both sides, there is little need for legs, unless you plan to put engines and other heavy parts on top of it. Notice that the plan calls for a series of 2-foot wide cabinet and cupboard doors. This was done to maximize the use of plywood that comes in 4-foot by 8-foot sheets.

This is a set of plans from the Western Wood Products Association that shows how to build an office work center in the open space beneath basement stairs. Many concours competitors would find this area convenient for researching material about their cars. Along with automotive text material, storage units can hold clean auto materials, parts and supplies.

UNDERSTAIR WORK CENTER

The drawers and filing cabinet are designed to fit between paneled dividers, spaced 24" apart. The 2x2 framework is finished on both sides with vertical 1x4 or 1x6 boards.

The design of the work center is totally flexible and depends upon your requirements and the size and shape of your stairwell.

Here are some options you'll want to consider:

Fig. A

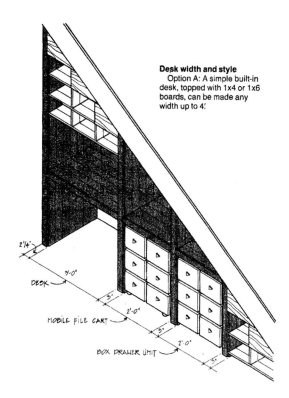

Desk width and style
Option A: A simple built-in desk, topped with 1x4 or 1x6 boards, can be made any width up to 4.'

Fig. B

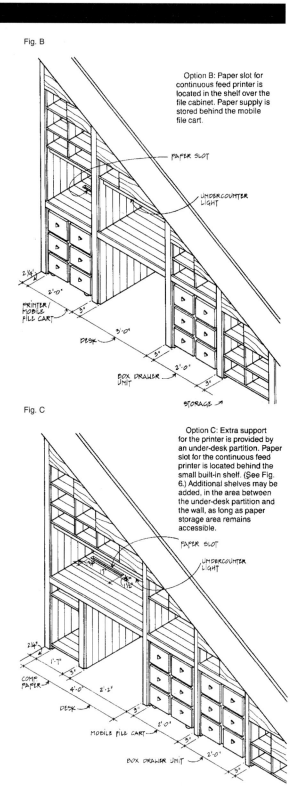

Option B: Paper slot for continuous feed printer is located in the shelf over the file cabinet. Paper supply is stored behind the mobile file cart.

Fig. C

Option C: Extra support for the printer is provided by an under-desk partition. Paper slot for the continuous feed printer is located behind the small built-in shelf. (See Fig. 6.) Additional shelves may be added, in the area between the under-desk partition and the wall, as long as paper storage area remains accessible.

Depth

The work center may be built to the total depth of the stairwell. However, it is difficult to reach the back of a desk top deeper than the standard 28" to 39". If stairs are wider than 39", you may want to install a false wall—at least behind the desk area.

For false wall, follow the same framing and finishing methods used in building the dividers: Nail or screw 2x2 frame to floor, ceiling and dividers; add center support and horizontal braces as needed; finish with 1x4 or 1x6 boards.

Electrical wiring

Before you start construction, make a list of all the office equipment you will use, such as a typewriter, computer, printer, calculator, desk lamp, clock, answering machine and pencil sharpener. Then decide how many outlets you will need and where they should be located. Be sure to include wiring for any indirect lighting you want to add. Your electrician will be able to install the wiring so most of it will be concealed when the project is finished.

Cubbyholes

If you plan to build cubbyhole dividers as pictured (instead of simple shelves), lay out partition locations on a modular grid so cubbyhole sizes will be similar in each section. We recommend a 1' grid for the cubbyholes, a 2' opening for box drawers and file cabinet and a 3' space for the desk.

You may want to consider installing a false back to prevent small items from getting lost. For easy access, depth of cubbyholes shouldn't exceed 24". Or, instead of cubbyholes, simple shelves may be installed above the work areas.

Allow at least 2' between top of desk and bottom of cubbyholes or over-desk shelving—more if desk is deeper than 3'.

CAUTION: Be certain that you review and understand all steps of construction and verify all dimensions before cutting your material. While every effort has been made to ensure accuracy in the design and drawing of WWPA plans, the possibility of error always exists and WWPA cannot accept responsibility for lumber improperly used or designs not first verified.

MATERIALS LIST FOR SHADED AREAS IN FIG. A

Materials vary depending on how you decide to build your understair work center and on the size of your space. Our calculations are based on a depth of 39", adjust accordingly.

We recommend you measure your space and decide where you want the dividers (See Fig. 1); chalk in lines on your floor (the file cabinet and box drawer units each require a 24" wide bay); measure the height of the dividers in your space (write in your measurements on Fig. 1); and decide on the depth of your work center.

DIVIDERS AND PANELING

1. Based on your depth and divider heights, calculate the amount of 2x2 framing. See Fig. 2 and steps 2 & 3.
2. To calculate the amount of 1x4 or 1x6 paneling you will need, keep in mind that the end wall and both sides of each divider are paneled. It will take 11, 1x4s or 7, 1x6s to panel each of the seven surfaces. In addition, you will need 4, 1x3s to trim the front-facing edge of the paneled end wall and the three dividers. (See Figs. 7, 7A, &8.) The lengths of all boards are determined by the height of your dividers and end wall.

DESK AND SHELVES

For desk and desk-height shelves (shaded in Fig. A), the following applies if your desk is 36" wide, bays are 24" wide and the understair area is 39" deep:

DESK

Top: (11) 1x4, 36" or (7) 1x6, 36"
Back ledger: (1) 2x2, 36"
Side nailers: (2) 2x2, 35½"
Front spreader: (1) 2x2, 36"
Center support: (1) 2x2, 35½"
Front trim: (1) 1x3, 37"

SHELVES AT DESK-TOP HEIGHT

Black ledgers: (2) 2x2, 24"
Side nailers: (4) 2x2, 35½"
Front spreaders: (2) 2x2, 24"
Shelves: (22) 1x4, 24" or (14) 1x6, 24"
Front Trim: (2) 1x3, 25"

individual accessories. This will help you to determine and calculate how much material will be needed to construct and install the items noted.

All floor plans for one-car garage workshops must focus primarily upon usable floor space. Maneuvering room and vehicle access is severely limited in one-car garages. Therefore, focus upon workshop accessories that will not obstruct what little open space is available.

Plans for shelves and storage cabinets should be directed toward upper garage walls, rafter areas and spaces above existing doors. Maintaining storage 6 feet and more above the floor is not necessarily convenient, but it will provide open areas below while you work around your project vehicle. For tools and equipment you plan to use most often, install plenty of pegboard around the garage. Arranged neatly, you might be surprised by the amount of tool and small item storage pegboard can accommodate.

If security is a problem and you prefer to keep hand tools and other items out of sight, consider hanging pegboard from rafters with heavy-duty hinges. Frame pegboard with 1x4 boards, hinge units to rafters just above walls and install a locking system along center rafter areas where free pegboard ends can be hooked or secured. This way, the pegboard and tools on it will rest suspended above the garage floor and out of sight while not in use.

Folding tables, fold out workbenches and other hinged accessories may prove most useful in one-car garages. Although you may have to roll project vehicles into the driveway to use fold out units, when the work is done, you will be able to park vehicles completely inside.

Two-car Garages

Drawing plans for two-car garages is the same as for one-car garages. The only difference is size. If the paper is not quite big enough, tape a couple of pieces of paper together. Unless your home features a separate laundry room or full basement, your two-car garage is likely to contain plenty of non-automotive items. Factor these extra items into your plans. Maybe some storage above the garage doors will suffice for camping gear, summer things, etc. Consider designating one wall exclusively for household storage. Try to keep your automotive inventory separate.

Typical two-car garages should offer room for workbenches or storage units along side walls. However, they generally leave little in the way of extra room at the front. In these cases, you might want to reserve the front of the garage for maneuvering room and fill the side wall spaces with accessories. This way, your project vehicle could remain parked completely in the garage while work is done under the hood or on the front end. Since two-car garages are wide, there should be plenty of room on the sides for access, especially when the car or truck is parked in the middle of the garage.

DIVIDERS

Fig. 1

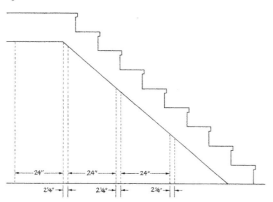

— 24" — — 24" — — 24" —
2¼" — 2¼" — 2¼" —

1—Lay out divider wall spacing on floor, allowing 24" **inside measurement** between dividers. (Desk will require 36" to 48".) Allow 3" for the thickness of finished walls. If you frame and panel the end wall, as illustrated, allow 2¼" for end wall.

Using a plumb line, mark the underside of stairs directly above floor spacing.

Fig. 3

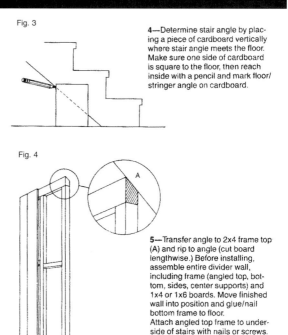

4—Determine stair angle by placing a piece of cardboard vertically where stair angle meets the floor. Make sure one side of cardboard is square to the floor, then reach inside with a pencil and mark floor/stringer angle on cardboard.

Fig. 4

5—Transfer angle to 2x4 frame top (A) and rip to angle (cut board lengthwise.) Before installing, assemble entire divider wall, including frame (angled top, bottom, sides, center supports) and 1x4 or 1x6 boards. Move finished wall into position and glue/nail bottom frame to floor.

Attach angled top frame to underside of stairs with nails or screws. Make sure fasteners are long enough to go through covering and into stringers.

Fig. 2

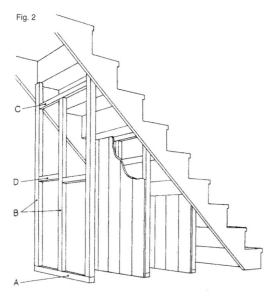

2—If stair stringers are exposed, attach 2x2 bottom frame (A) to wood floor with glue and nails; if floor is concrete, use tile mastic and/or concrete nails. Glue/nail vertical 2x2 supports (B) to stair stringers and floor frame.

Glue/nail horizontal 2x2 (C) between supports at top. Where vertical span is more than 36", add horizontal center supports (D).

Glue/nail 1x4 or 1x6 boards to both sides of frame with 6d (2") nails.

3—If stair stringers are enclosed with drywall or paneling, locate position of stringers just as you would find studs in an existing wall: use a magnetic stud finder; look for the drywall nailing pattern, or "sound" them out by gently tapping with a hammer.

DESK, SHELF FRAMING

Fig. 5

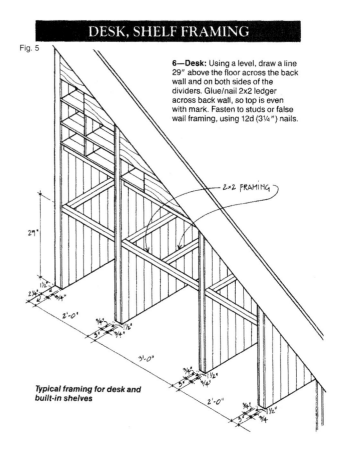

6—**Desk:** Using a level, draw a line 29" above the floor across the back wall and on both sides of the dividers. Glue/nail 2x2 ledger across back wall, so top is even with mark. Fasten to studs or false wall framing, using 12d (3¼") nails.

Typical framing for desk and built-in shelves

2x2 FRAMING

29"

2'-0"
3'-0"
2'-0"

7—Measure distance from front of divider to face of ledger; subtract 1½" and cut 2x2 nailers to that length. Butt 2x2s to ledger on back wall and attach to paneling, using glue and 2¼" screws.

8—Measure width between each divider and cut 2x2s to that length; glue/nail front 2x2 to ends of 2x2 nailers, using 10d (3") nails.
9—For Option A and B, glue/nail a 2x2 support in the center of the desk area.

Fig. 6

Option C

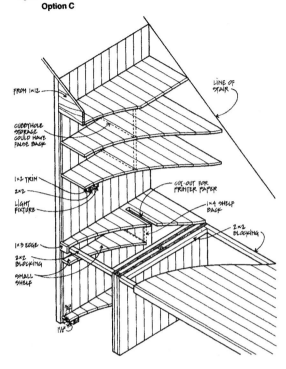

FROM 1x12
CUBBYHOLE STORAGE COULD HAVE FALSE BACK
1x2 TRIM
2x2
LIGHT FIXTURE
1x3 EDGE
2x2 BLOCKING
SMALL SHELF
LINE OF STAIR
CUT-OUT FOR PRINTER PAPER
1x4 SHELF BACK
2x2 BLOCKING

Fig. 7

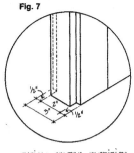

TYPICAL CENTER PARTITION AT BASE

Fig. 7A

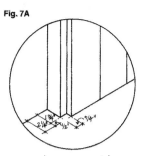

TYPICAL END PARTITION AT BASE

Fig. 8

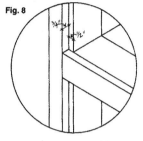

TYPICAL END PARTITION AT DESK

Vertical trim: Rip 1x3 to 2" wide; center trim on front face of divider walls, allowing 1/2" reveal on either side, Fig. 7. Glue/nail in place. For end wall, rip 1x3 to 1¾" wide and install flush with wall, Fig. 7A.
12—To trim face of desk and shelves, measure distance between vertical trim and cut 1x3s to that length. Glue/nail to front edge of desk and shelves, flush with top of decking. Trim will overlap dividers by 1/2", Fig. 8.

To permanently install box drawers, wait until unit is in place before attaching 1x3 trim.
13—Install tube light fixture under cubbyholes or stair stringers, (See Fig. 6.) Inset fixture approximately 6" from front edge. Glue/nail 2x2 in front of fixture and trim with 1x2.

10—**Option C:** Note: Position of support wall and paper slot may have to be adjusted to accommodate your printer. (See Fig. C.)

Frame the support wall as you did for the divider walls and finish both sides with 1x4 or 1x6 boards.

Bottom shelf: For front and back shelf supports, cut two 2x2 nailers to 1'7". (Adjust length if you have changed support wall location.) Glue/nail one nailer to back of compartment, flush with floor and back wall. Position second nailer across front of compartment, flush with floor and 2¼" inside front edge of divider and support wall; glue/nail in place. (See Fig. 6 and Fig. C.) Glue/nail 1x2 trim to front face of nailer.

For side supports, measure distance between front and back nailers and cut two 2x2 nailers to that length. Position 2x2s on each side of compartment between front and back nailers, flush with floor and side walls. Glue/nail in place.

Starting at the front edge, flush with front edge of dividers, glue/nail 1x4 or 1x6 decking to 2x2 nailers. (Decking extends beyond front 2x2 to form toe-kick.)

Small shelf: Cut 1x4s to length and edge glue to form shelf surface. (Notice that shelf stops 1½" to 2" short of paper slot.) For light loads, shelf may be toenailed into position; for heavier loads, use 1x1 shelf cleats.
11—**Desk top, Options A, B & C:** Starting at the front and flush with framing, glue/nail 1x4 or 1x6 decking to framework.

For continuous-feed printer, determine location of paper slot and cut 1½"x17" slot in one decking board. Check your paper and make certain this slot is the correct size for your equipment.

Draw plans as described earlier. Make notes of where you want compressed air outlets, electrical outlets, switches, and other conveniences. Designate spots for rag storage, used motor oil storage and all the accessories that require space. The more realistic your floor plan and horizontal view plans are, the better off you will be. To ensure accuracy, measure everything first before drawing up your plans.

Three-car Garages

Three-car garages offer the most in auto workshop versatility. With two bays saved for daily drivers, you should have an open space for a project vehicle. You may also be able to dedicate one bay to workbenches, an open work table or an "L" shaped work center. In addition, you should have the flexibility to park a project vehicle in the center bay and have plenty of working room around it. Although you will have a large amount of room to work with, do not get carried away. Remember that you will need room for a shop vacuum, work carts and other mobile items. Plan their parking spaces, too.

FILING CABINET

Fig. 1

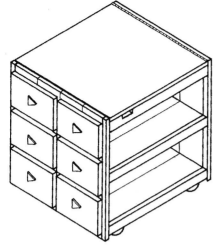

Fig. 3

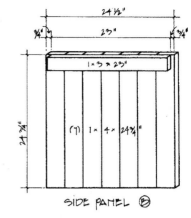

SIDE PANEL Ⓑ

2—Edge glue and clamp (7) 1x4s for side panel (B). Glue/nail 1x3 to top of panel, flush with top edge and 3/4″ from each end.

Fig. 2

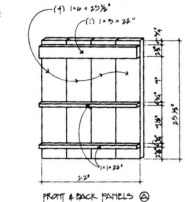

FRONT & BACK PANELS Ⓐ

1—Edge glue and clamp front and back panels (A), using (4) 1x6s per panel. When glue sets, glue/nail (2) 1x1 shelf supports to each panel, using 1¼″ nails. (See Fig. 2 for position.) Glue/nail 1x3 to top of panel, 3/4″ from top edge. (See *Woodworking Tips* on making solid wood panels.)

Fig. 5

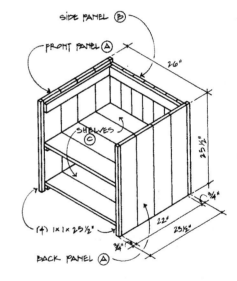

SIDE PANEL Ⓑ
FRONT PANEL Ⓐ
SHELVES Ⓒ
BACK PANEL Ⓐ

4—Glue/nail shelves in place. Glue/nail 1x1 vertical trim to outside edges of front and back panels.

5—Glue/nail side panel (B) in place, flush with bottom. Glue/nail along long edges to front and back panels, using 4d (1½″) nails; glue/nail to shelves and to ends of 1x3s on front and back panels, using 6d (2″) nails. (Note that side panel is 3/4″ shorter than front and back panels.)

Fig. 4

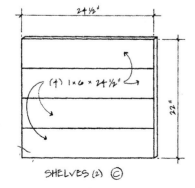

SHELVES (2) Ⓒ

3—Edge glue and clamp (4) 1x6s for each of two shelves (C).

Fig. 6

Fig. 7

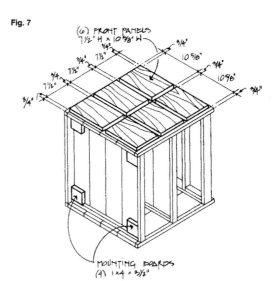

6—Attach 1x3 spreader (E) to open side of cabinet. Glue/nail to ends of 1x3s on front and back panels.

7—Glue/nail 1x2 edge trim to front edge of shelves and flush with top of shelves.

11—Cut (6) panels from 1x10 lumber, each 10⅝" wide by 7½" high. (Grain runs horizontally.) Position on front of cabinet, allowing 3/4" between panels and around outside edges. Glue in place and secure with 1¼" nails.

12—From 1x4 lumber, cut (4) mounting boards, each 3½" long. Glue/nail to corners of base, as shown, using 1¼" nails. Install casters on mounting boards. (See Fig. 8 and note following.)

Detail 6A

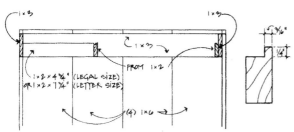

8—Hanging file rails: Cut 1/4" x 13/16" rabbet (notch) along one edge of 1x2s, as shown in Detail 6A. Finished lip is 3/16" wide by 1/4" high. If the file cabinet will receive heavy usage, the top edge of the rail can be protected by a vinyl guard, available at most office supply stores. Many office supply outlets also carry metal file rails or inserts which may be used in place of wood rails.

9—For standard file folders:
Install 1x2 x 7¾" nailer to front and back panels, flush with bottom of horizontal 1x4s. Glue/nail in place, using 6d (2") nails.
For legal-size file folders:
Install 4¾" nailers, as above.
10—Glue/nail or screw rail to enclosed side of cabinet, flush with base of 1x3. Lip is in, with notched side flush with 1x3. Use 6d nails or 1½" screws.
Glue/nail or screw second rail to ends of nailer, lip in.

Fig. 8

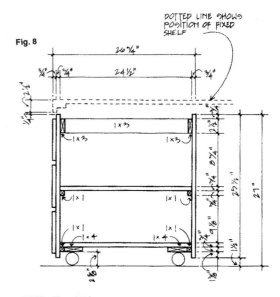

NOTE:—To maintain same height as drawer unit and still allow clearance below built-in shelf, caster wheels must extend 1½" below sides of filing cabinet. See *Materials List* for specifications. If another caster is selected, adjust bottom shelf to accommodate height. Mount casters far enough inside the corners to allow wheels to swivel freely.

Fig. 9

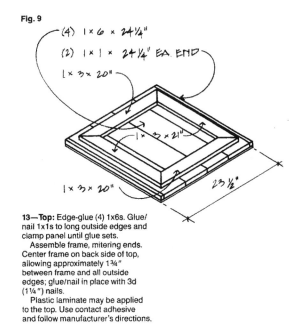

(4) 1 x 6 x 24¼"

(2) 1 x 1 x 24¼" EA. END

1 x 3 x 20"

1 x 2 x 21"

1 x 3 x 20"

23½"

13—Top: Edge-glue (4) 1x6s. Glue/nail 1x1s to long outside edges and clamp panel until glue sets.

Assemble frame, mitering ends. Center frame on back side of top, allowing approximately 1¾" between frame and all outside edges; glue/nail in place with 3d (1¼") nails.

Plastic laminate may be applied to the top. Use contact adhesive and follow manufacturer's directions.

Fig. 10

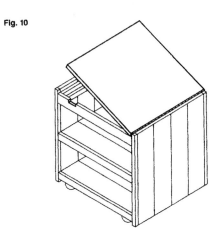

14—Attach top with piano hinge along back inside edge of cart. Cut 3/4"x3" handhold on side of cart.

15—Install lid stays according to manufacturer's directions. Attach decorative drawer pulls on front panels.

MATERIALS LIST FOR MOBILE FILE CART	
Front and Back (A):	(8) 1x6, 25½"
	(4) 1x1, 22"
	(2) 1x3, 22"
Side Panel (B):	(7) 1x4, 24¾ "
	(1) 1x3, 23"
Shelves:	(8) 1x6, 24½"
Trim:	(4) 1x1, 25"
Spreader:	(1) 1x3, 24½"
Rails:	(2) 1x2, 23"
Nailers:	(2) 1x2, 7¾" or 4¾"
Edge Trim:	(2) 1x2, 24 1/2"
Front panels:	(6) 10⅝" wide x 7½" high (grain runs horizontally) (Cut from 7' of 1x10)
Caster boards:	(4) 1x4, 3½"
Casters:	(4) 2½" swivel Hafele 660.15.361
Top:	(4) 1x6, 24¼"
	(2) 1x1, 24¼"
	(2) 1x3, 20"
	(2) 1x3, 21"
Plastic laminate:	(optional) 23½" x 24¼"
Lid stays:	1 pair
Decorative drawer pulls*:	(6)
Nails:	3d, 4d, 6d finishing nails
Screws:	1½" flathead
Carpenter's glue	

*The triangular drawer pulls shown here and in illustration are #625 Isosceles Right Triangles.

Available from:
Greenstreet Details
821 SW Green, No. 4
Portland, OR 97205

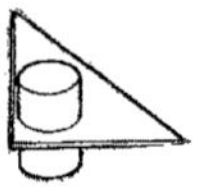

If possible, attempt to locate your auto work area on the outside wall of a three-car garage. This will help to reduce the amount of workshop noise that reverberates into the house. In addition, since family things will be located closer to the house than your auto workshop stuff, chances are better that children will stay away from the auto area. This may be a safety factor, as well as a way to help protect freshly painted things you may have just restored.

To make sure your plans are complete and big enough for you to decipher, you may want to tape two pieces of graph paper together. You might even choose to designate separate pieces of paper for each bay.

Separate Workshops

You might think that a detached auto workshop will provide huge amounts of room. This may be true, but be careful. With seemingly unlimited space, it may appear that you can fit everything you could ever want into the shop. This may not be true.

One of the most frequent statements about auto workshops is, "I wish I had more room." This is a big clue for those planning to outfit a new auto workshop. You must do one of two things during the planning stage: Make plans for expansion, which is highly recommended; or, leave open room for the addition of new pieces of equipment or project endeavors in the future.

If you have the room, you will feel free to buy more equipment, parts and other things to fill your shop. Why would you plan to fill your new shop right

off the bat with workbenches, cabinets, counters and other built-ins? Plan and organize it with what you have, what you contemplate getting soon and what may be a pipe dream today. In other words, leave some open room for future options.

If possible, set up your shop for two separate areas: one for dismantling and other dirty work; and another for assembly and clean work. This can be

BOX DRAWER UNIT

Fig. 1

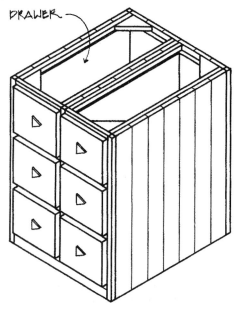

DRAWER

Two drawer plans are provided for the box drawer unit. The simpler version uses a dado joint to support a plywood bottom. The other, recommended for experienced woodworkers, uses a solid wood bottom with both rabbeted and dado joints.

Fig. 2

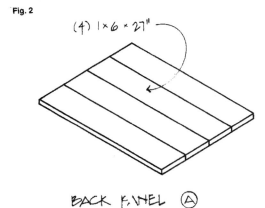

(4) 1×6×27"

BACK PANEL Ⓐ

1—Edge glue and clamp (4) 1x6s for back panel (A). (See *Woodworking Tips* on making solid wood panels.)

done with plastic curtains suspended from the ceiling, regular walls and partitions made from 1x4 boards and pegboard. Lay out a frame of 1x4 boards and cover them with pegboard on both sides. Hang the partition in the center of two bays and either secure them to the floor with turnbuckles or weight them down with chain.

A pegboard partition serves a couple of different purposes. First, it separates two work areas. Second, it serves as a handy tool storage point for the items you'll need while working on a certain side of a project vehicle - be it dirty work or clean work.

Make sure your plans look realistically at your budget, auto aspirations and other workshop interests. Many auto enthusiasts also enjoy woodworking. A dedicated workshop will have to serve as both an auto work center and woodworking haven. This facility will also have to accommodate your home improvement needs. Keep in mind that the sawdust, sanding dust and other airborne debris created by woodworking can interfere with automotive projects. This is a very important factor when planning the layout of a home based detached workshop. Again, consider partition walls. Also, seriously consider paneling this partition wall with pegboard. It can hold woodworking tools on one side and automotive tools on the other.

Basement Workshops

Automotive workshops in basements require close scrutiny. This is due to the likelihood of there being hot water heaters and furnaces already installed. Both of these heating units pose significant points of fire ignition. Therefore, you must make certain your plans for an auto workshop in a basement do not include any sort of painting activity and that all cleaning tasks are achieved with non-flammable (bio-degradable) cleaners. In addition, understand that many petroleum products produce vapors that are heavier than air, such as gasoline, kerosene and others. In a basement, vapors from these flammable liquids could easily accumulate and cause a reduction in the room's oxygen content.

Basement auto workshops are also severely space limited. You will not be able to fit an entire vehicle in this space but just how much of it can you fit in? That depends upon the basement and the means of access to it. Basements are equipped with stairways that go up to the main floor of a house. The space under stairways can provide a large amount of storage space if used properly. Plan to take advantage of this space for either condensed storage or a combination storage and desk area. Another major concern with basements is access. Be certain that your floor plans and horizontal view plans take this into account.

Another major concern with basements is access and egress. Be certain that your floor plans and horizontal view plans keep those in mind. Spend adequate time designing an air ventilation plan. Air circulation is important no matter what type of automotive activity you carry on in your basement. Be sure you have a way to bring in fresh air and exhaust polluted air, before starting any aerosol can painting task or cleaning with potent chemicals.

Fig. 3

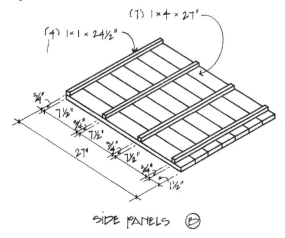

(7) 1×4×27"

(4) 1×1×24½"

¾"
7½"
¾"
7½"
¾"
7½"
¾"
27"
1½"

SIDE PANELS Ⓑ

2—Edge glue and clamp two panels for sides (B), using (7) 1x4s per panel. Glue/nail 1x1 drawer runners to one side of panels, using 1¼" nails. Space runners as shown in Fig. 3. Glue/nail 1x1 vertical trim to front and back edges of panels, using 4d (1½") nails. (See Fig. 5.)

Fig. 4

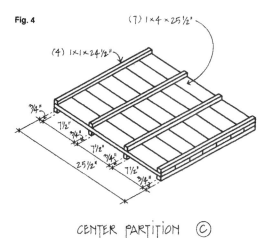

(7) 1×4×25½"

(4) 1×1×24½"

¾"
7½"
¾"
7½"
¾"
25½"
7½"
¾"

CENTER PARTITION Ⓒ

3—Edge glue and clamp (7) 1x4s for center partition (C). Apply 1x1 drawer runners to **both** sides of center panel. Glue/nail 1x1 vertical trim to front edge of partition (See Fig. 5).

Fig. 5

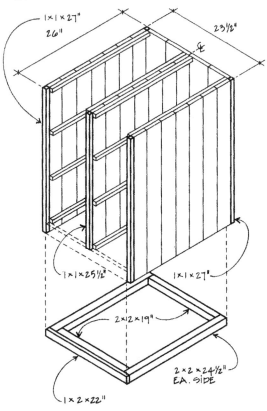

1×1×27"
26"
23½"

1×1×25½"
1×1×27"
2×2×19"
1×2×22"
2×2×24½"
EA. SIDE

BASE

4—Attach back to sides. (Back fits inside 1x1 trim on side panels and flush with drawer runners.) Glue/ nail to 1x1 vertical trim and to drawer runners, using 4d (1½") nails.

5—Glue/nail partition to center of back, flush with top of back and sides, using 6d (2") nails.

6—Assemble and glue/nail 2x2 base, as shown in Fig. 5; trim front of base with 1x2. Position cabinet so base is flush with front of cabi- net; sides and back of base fit inside cabinet. Glue/nail in posi- tion, using 8d nails.

Fig. 6

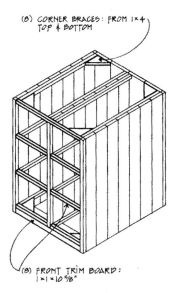

(8) CORNER BRACES: FROM 1×4
TOP & BOTTOM

(8) FRONT TRIM BOARD:
1×1×10⅝"

Fig. 8

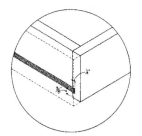

10—Sides: Cut 1/4″ groove for drawer bottom, using dimensions shown in Fig. 8.
11—Assembly: Apply glue to notch in drawer sides and slide plywood drawer bottom into position. Make sure sides are square and glue/nail drawer front and back in place, between sides, using 4d nails. (Fig. 7) Apply glue to drawer front and fascia. From inside of drawer, nail front to fascia with 3d nails, keeping edges even. Install drawer pulls to match filing cabinet. **NOTE:**—Fascia is slightly larger (⅛″) than drawer face to allow for any variations in size.

7—Corner braces: Cut (4) 3½″ lengths of 1x4 on the diagonal to produce (8) triangular braces. Make sure cabinet is square and glue/nail braces to each corner, top and bottom.

8—Horizontal trim: Glue/nail (8) 1x1 trim boards to vertical and horizontal 1x1s, as shown in Fig. 6.

MATERIALS LIST FOR BOX DRAWER UNIT

Back panel: (4) 1x6, 27"
Side panels: (14) 1x4, 27"
(8) 1x1, 24½"
Partition: (7) 1x4, 25½"
(8) 1x1, 24½"
Trim: (4) 1x1, 27"
(1) 1x1, 25½"
Corner braces: (4) 1x4, 3½"
Front trim: (8) 1x1, 10⅝"
Drawer parts (cut from 1x10):
Sides: (12) 7⅜" x 25¼"
Bottom: (6) 1/4" plywood,
9½" x 25¼"
Front & Back: (12) 9" x 6⅝"
Fascia: (6) 10⅝" x 7½"
(fascia grain runs horizontally)

For solid wood drawers:
Sides: (12) 7⅜"x 25¼
Bottom: (6) 9½ x 25"
Front & Back: (12) 10½ x 7⅜"
(grain runs horizontally)

Base:
Sides: (2) 2x2, 24½"
Front/Back: (2) 2x2, 19"
Trim: (1) 1x2, 22"
(6) Decorative drawer pulls
(See file cabinet Materials List)
Nails: 4d,6d,10d finishing nails
Carpenter's glue

Fig. 7

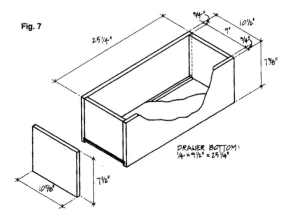

25¼"
¾"
10½"
9"
½"
¼"
7⅞"
7½"
10⅝"

DRAWER BOTTOM:
¼ × 9½" × 25¼"

9—Drawer: Cut components for six drawers as follows: (Cut from 1x10)
Sides: (12) 7⅜"x25¼"
Front/Back: (12) 6⅝"x9"
Bottom: (6) 1/4"-plywood,
9½"x25¼"
Fascia: (6) 7½"x10⅝" (grain runs
horizontally)

ALTERNATE DRAWER DESIGN

Fig. 9

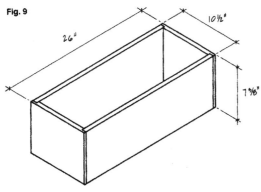

26" 10 1/2" 7 3/8"

12—For solid wood drawers: Cut components according to dimensions given in Figs. 9 and 10 (or *Materials List*).

Fig. 10

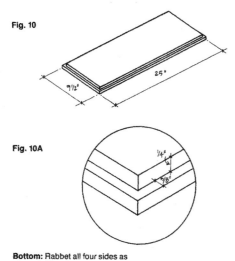

9 1/2" 25"

Fig. 10A

1/4" 3/8"

Bottom: Rabbet all four sides as shown in Fig. 10.

Fig. 11

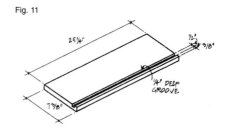

25 1/4" 1/2" 3/8" 1/4" DEEP GROOVE 7 3/8"

Sides: Cut dado in sides as shown in Fig. 11.

Fig. 12

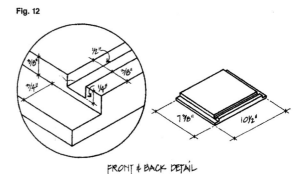

1/2" 3/8" 3/8" 3/4" 1/4" 7 3/8" 10 1/2"

FRONT & BACK DETAIL

Front and Back: Rabbet sides and cut dado as shown in Fig. 12.

To assemble, glue/nail front and two sides; apply glue to grooves and slide bottom into position. Glue/nail back in place. Install drawer pulls.

14—Slide drawer unit into position below built-in shelf, with front of cabinet even with divider. Attach 1x3 face trim to shelf.

15—Slide drawers into cabinet. Drawer fronts will extend 3/4" beyond cabinet. For smoother operation, apply paraffin wax to drawer bottoms above runners.

WOODWORKING TIPS

Fig. A

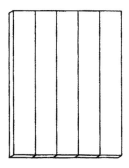

How to make solid wood panels
 Glued or edge-laminated panels are fairly simple to assemble and, when properly glued and clamped, are strong and aesthetically appealing.

Fig. B

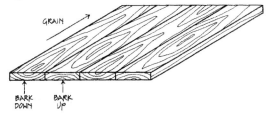

1—Cut boards to length. (You may want to allow an extra inch or two and trim panel to length after glue sets.) Lay out boards side by side with grain running the same direction.

2—Next, look at the end grain and arrange boards so end grain alternates from bark-side up to bark-side down. This will help reduce risk of warping. Mark and number one end of boards to keep them in proper sequence for laminating.

Fig. C

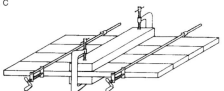

3—Apply carpenter's glue liberally to board edges. Line up boards and attach bar or pipe clamps, using scraps of wood to protect board edges. After boards are clamped into position, wipe off excess glue with a damp rag.

If boards tend to cup or warp, clamp a 2x4 or 2x6 across the face of the panel on both sides. Secure with a C-clamp at each end. (See Fig. C.)
4—Allow at least 24 hours for glue to set, then sand or plane surface to a smooth finish.

USING COMPUTER SOFTWARE FOR WORKSHOP DESIGNS

The workshop layouts and floor plans in this book were first drawn on 1/4-inch graph paper with a pencil. A scaled ruler and heavy duty eraser served as useful accessories. Once the rough drawn plans were made legible, my wife, Janna, entered them into a personal computer using a software program designed for making house plans.

The software program we used sold for about $40 in 1993. It was advertised as 'user friendly' for those who want to draw up simple two-dimensional renditions of floor plans for houses. Janna found that this program requires a great deal of computer memory, is somewhat cumbersome with numerous commands to follow, and a few of the mouse commands mandate an exceptionally sensitive touch.

Computer Aided Design (CAD) software programs have greatly improved over the years. They are available in computer software stores, many office supply stores and in some computer hardware outlets.

The intended use for and cost of these programs vary widely. A few CD-ROM "Draw Your House Plans" type programs can be found for $9.99, while other architect/engineer dedicated software program packages have price tags of $279.99, $499.99, and even higher. However, for the non-architect/engineer and automotive do-it-yourselfer wanting to use a computer to draw up clean copies of workshop floor plans, there are very good programs on the market ranging in price from $40 to $100.

Knowledgeable computer software representatives have suggested that most programs selling for under $100 are not as useful, user friendly or sophisticated as those priced at $100 and more. They recommend the $100 units.

For under $100, you can expect to get a simple program designed to draw lines and insert symbols in just two-dimensions, with the possibility that some may have three-dimensional ability. For $275 and higher, programs may be more complicated, but capable of pumping out intricate plans of such items as electronic circuit boards, diagrams of internal machinery assemblies and a lot more.

But, for about $99.99 (plus tax where applicable), you should be able to pick up a decent CAD program with the ability to draw up floor plan layouts, plumbing and electrical lines and workshop wall layouts with cabinets and cupboards. These programs also have the ability to provide outside elevation views, in both two- and three-dimensions. The programs are easy to use, and have useful features for other tasks, like drawing plans for cabinets, cupboards and other storage units. About the only thing these programs will not have are pre-programmed symbols for engine hoists, engine stands, above ground lifts and other automotive related equipment pieces. Use boxes, rectangles and other shapes to depict such items on your plans.

The decision to use a computer program or graph paper and pencil to draw automotive workshop floor plans and layouts is simply a matter of choice. If you have a lot of experience with computers and relish the thought of learning and using a new program, go for it. On the other hand, if the thought of a computer makes your head hurt, reach for a pad of 1/4-inch graph paper, a scaled ruler and a sharp pencil with a new eraser.

For those in the middle who may be leaning toward use of their home PC but are confused over the hardware requirements and general capabilities of the different CAD programs, plan to visit a local computer software store. If possible, make your visit during the week, as Saturdays are generally quite busy. Ask to speak with a sales representative, and present him or her with the project you have in mind.

Software package literature will list the types of computer hardware required to run the program. It will also indicate the kinds of designs and symbols the software is capable of producing.

Once you have narrowed your selection down to one or two programs, ask if you can try the programs out on an in-store computer. This hands-on test drive will give you the best idea of which program is most likely to produce the types of plans you require, with the ease of operation you prefer, and at a price you can afford.

Expect to draw up a dozen or more different workshop floor plans before you finally arrive at the one you like the best. So, if a CAD program can help you draw and re-draw plans more quickly and accurately, it may be worth its weight in gold. It will save you time and the frustration of drawing plans over and over again by hand with paper and pencil. After all, the changes between floor plans and layouts may only be subtle. A single CAD designed plan may be easily altered to produce numerous plans, each with particular characteristics, differing from previous plans by only a feature or two.

Making slight alterations on an original floor plan is very fast and easy on a CAD program; making similar changes on paper may require completely new drawings or erasing features to make way for new changes.

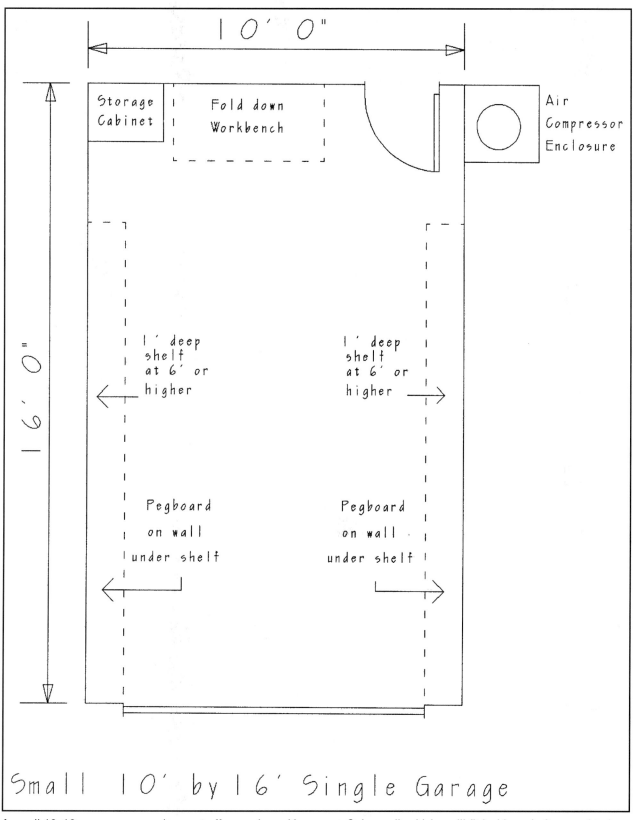

10' 0"

16' 0"

Storage Cabinet

Fold down Workbench

Air Compressor Enclosure

1' deep shelf at 6' or higher

1' deep shelf at 6' or higher

Pegboard on wall under shelf

Pegboard on wall under shelf

Small 10' by 16' Single Garage

A small 10x16 one-car garage does not offer much working room. Only small vehicles will fit inside and often need to be moved out into the driveway to access the front end. Cramped workspaces like this call for fold-down work tables, cupboards built high enough so you won't bump your head and plenty of pegboard storage. Setting up an air compressor outdoors in a small enclosure will not only provide extra working room but will reduce noise inside the garage.

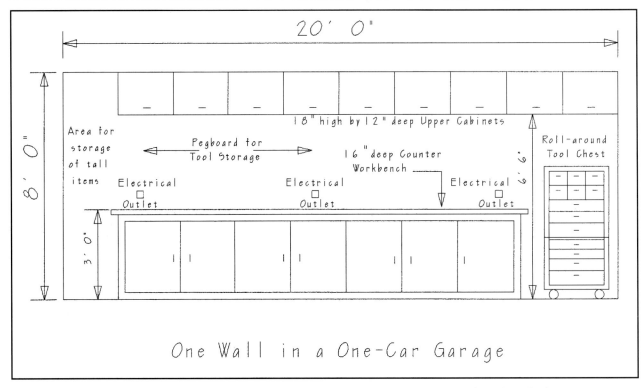

20' 0"

8' 0"

Area for storage of tall items

Pegboard for Tool Storage

18" high by 12" deep Upper Cabinets

16" deep Counter Workbench

Roll-around Tool Chest

Electrical ☐ Outlet

Electrical ☐ Outlet

Electrical ☐ Outlet

6' 9"

3' 0"

One Wall in a One-Car Garage

Horizontal diagrams will help you determine the best dimensions for various counters, cupboards and other storage accessories. This counter is designed for a 16-inch depth. It is a bit narrow but will accommodate the limited space in this one-car garage. Note the area to the left for the storage of tall items, like brooms, mops and the like. Upper cupboard doors are designed to lift up and are planned high on the wall to prevent them from becoming head bumping obstacles.

A 12x20 one-car garage is not uncommon. As with typical southwest home garages, the clothes washer and dryer are located in this space. If desired, the shop vacuum could be stored under the workbench and the air compressor housed outdoors to make room for more storage or another small workbench. Note the 30-inch deep fold-down workbench at the front right corner of the garage.

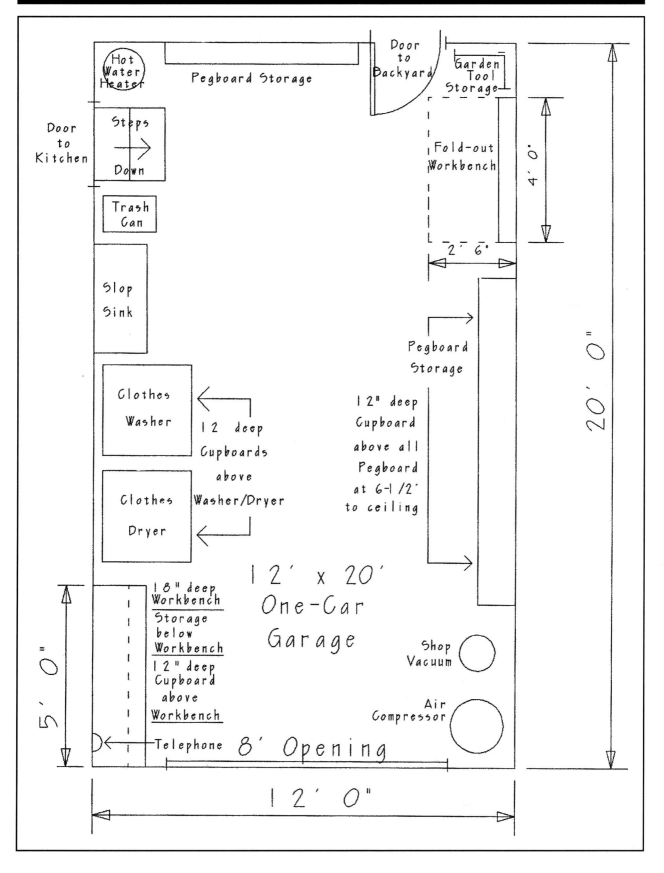

Hot Water Heater

Pegboard Storage

Door to Backyard

Garden Tool Storage

Door to Kitchen

Steps Down

Fold-out Workbench

4' 0'

2' 6'

Trash Can

Slop Sink

Pegboard Storage

Clothes Washer

12 deep Cupboards above Washer/Dryer

12" deep Cupboard above all Pegboard at 6-1/2' to ceiling

Clothes Dryer

20' 0"

18" deep Workbench
Storage below Workbench
12" deep Cupboard above Workbench

12' x 20'
One-Car
Garage

Shop Vacuum

5' 0"

Air Compressor

Telephone   8' Opening

12' 0"

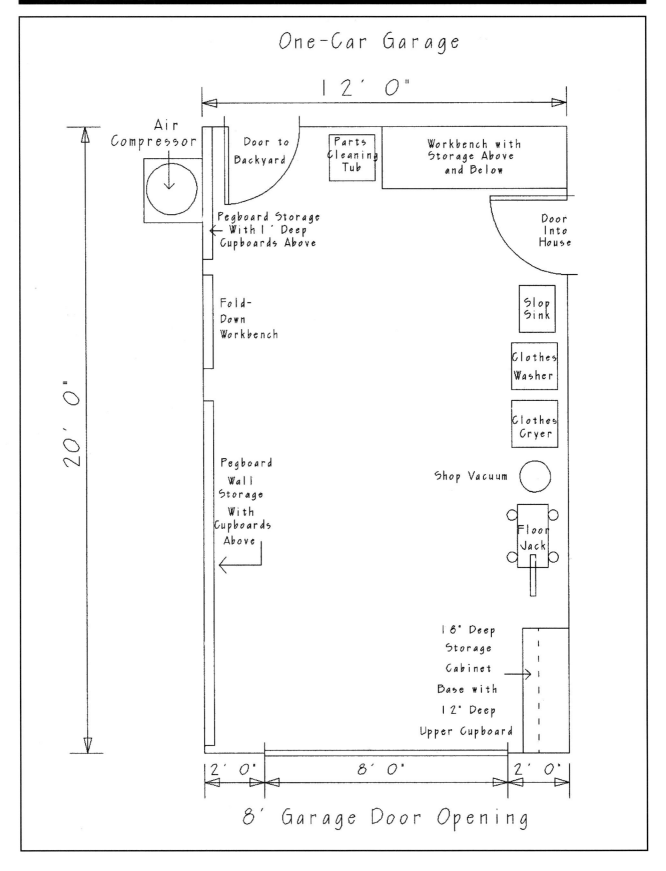

One-Car Garage

12' 0"

20' 0"

Air Compressor

Door to Backyard

Parts Cleaning Tub

Workbench with Storage Above and Below

Door Into House

← Pegboard Storage With 1' Deep Cupboards Above

Fold-Down Workbench

Slop Sink

Clothes Washer

Clothes Dryer

Shop Vacuum

Pegboard Wall Storage With Cupboards Above

Floor Jack

18" Deep Storage Cabinet Base with 12" Deep Upper Cupboard →

2' 0"

8' 0"

2' 0"

8' Garage Door Opening

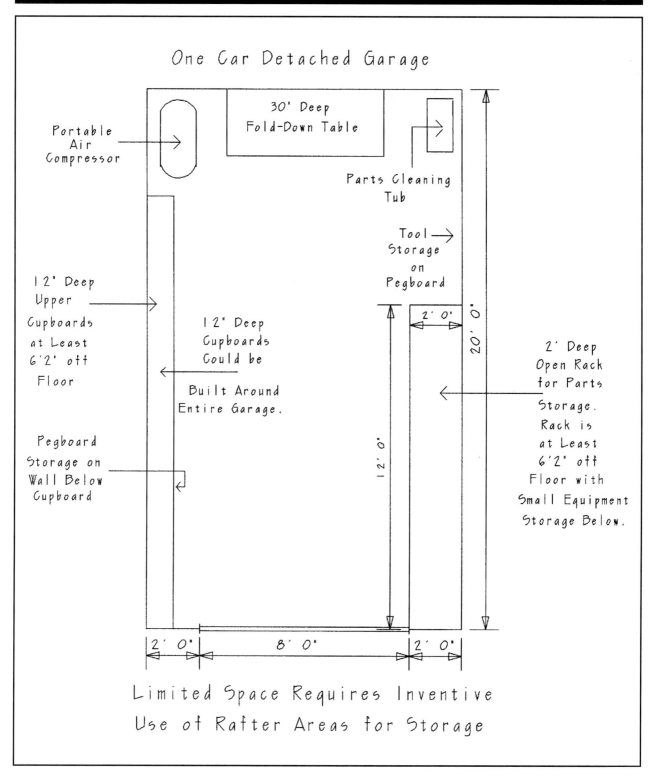

One Car Detached Garage

Portable Air Compressor

30' Deep Fold-Down Table

Parts Cleaning Tub

Tool Storage on Pegboard

12" Deep Upper Cupboards at Least 6'2" off Floor

12" Deep Cupboards Could be Built Around Entire Garage.

Pegboard Storage on Wall Below Cupboard

2' 0'

20' 0'

2' Deep Open Rack for Parts Storage. Rack is at Least 6'2" off Floor with Small Equipment Storage Below.

12' 0'

2' 0'   8' 0'   2' 0'

Limited Space Requires Inventive Use of Rafter Areas for Storage

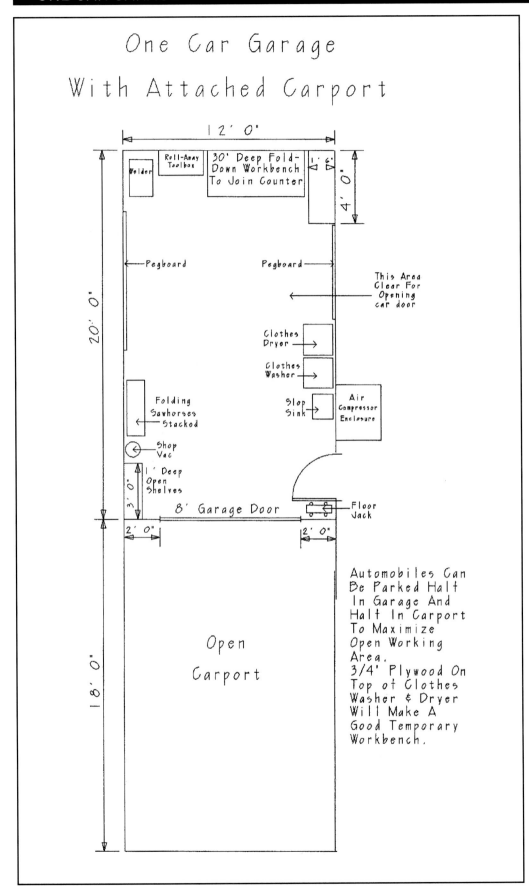

One Car Garage
With Attached Carport

12' 0"

Welder

Roll-Away Toolbox

30' Deep Fold-Down Workbench To Join Counter

1' 6"

4' 0"

20' 0"

←Pegboard

Pegboard→

This Area Clear For Opening car door

Clothes Dryer →

Clothes Washer →

Folding Sawhorses Stacked ←

Slop Sink →

Air Compressor Enclosure

Shop Vac ←

1' Deep Open Shelves

3' 0"

8' Garage Door

Floor Jack

2' 0"

2' 0"

18' 0"

Open

Carport

Automobiles Can Be Parked Half In Garage And Half In Carport To Maximize Open Working Area.
3/4' Plywood On Top of Clothes Washer & Dryer Will Make A Good Temporary Workbench.

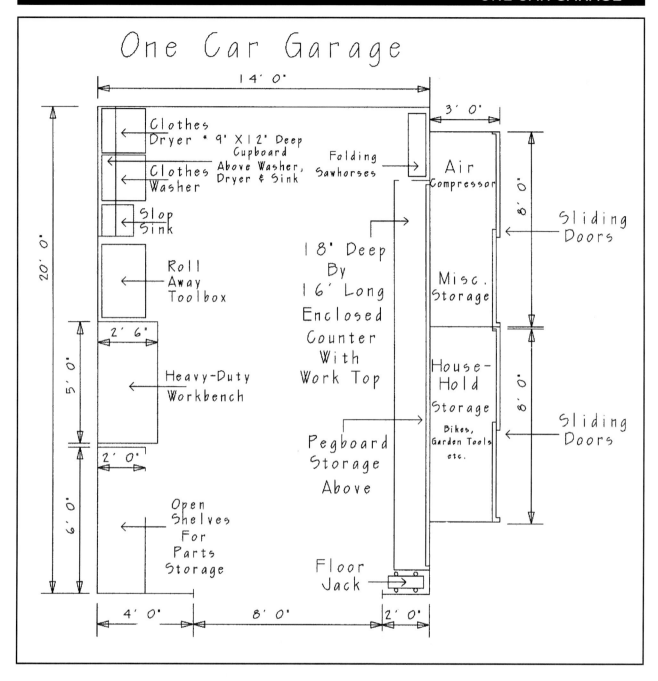

One Car Garage

14' 0"

Clothes Dryer * 9' X 12' Deep Cupboard Above Washer, Dryer & Sink

Clothes Washer

Slop Sink

Roll Away Toolbox

2' 6"

Heavy-Duty Workbench

2' 0"

Open Shelves For Parts Storage

20' 0"

5' 0"

6' 0"

4' 0"   8' 0"   2' 0"

18' Deep By 16' Long Enclosed Counter With Work Top

Pegboard Storage Above

Floor Jack

Folding Sawhorses

3' 0"

Air Compressor

Misc. Storage

House-Hold Storage

Bikes, Garden Tools etc.

8' 0"

8' 0"

Sliding Doors

Sliding Doors

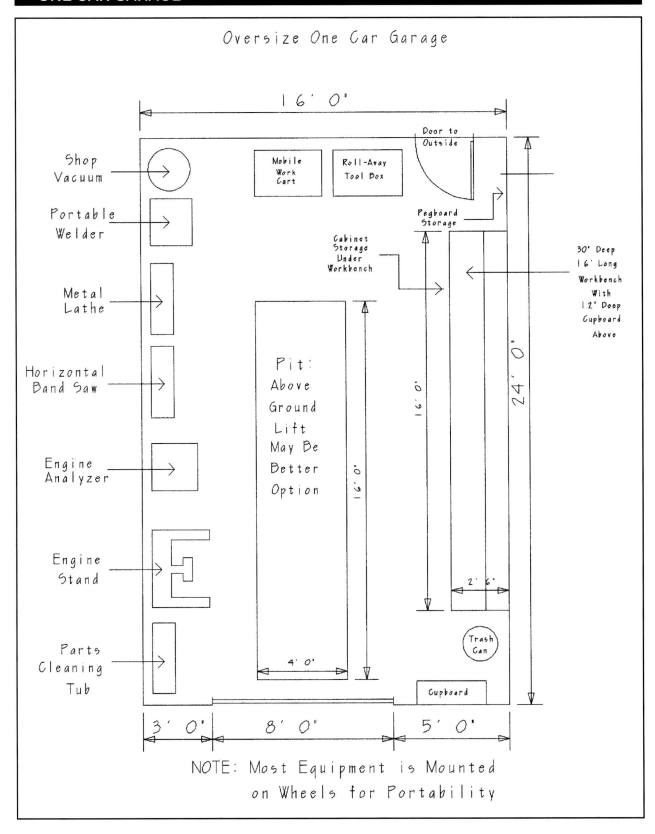

Oversize One Car Garage

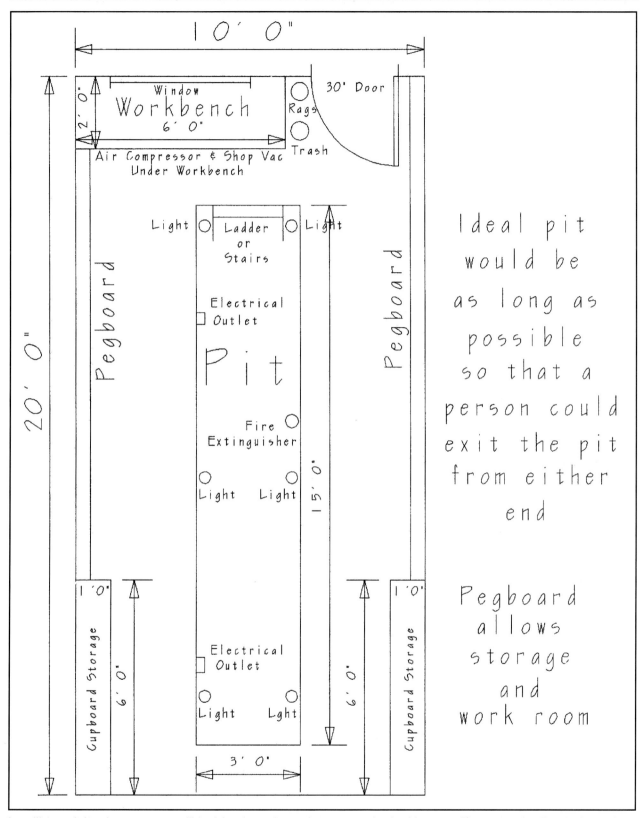

10' 0"

20' 0"

2' 0"

Window
Workbench
6' 0"

Rags

30' Door

Air Compressor & Shop Vac
Under Workbench

Trash

Light

Ladder
or
Stairs

Light

Electrical
Outlet

Pit

Fire
Extinguisher

Light   Light

15' 0"

Pegboard

Pegboard

1' 0"

Cupboard Storage

6' 0"

Electrical
Outlet

Light   Lght

6' 0"

Cupboard Storage

1' 0"

3' 0"

Ideal pit
would be
as long as
possible
so that a
person could
exit the pit
from either
end

Pegboard
allows
storage
and
work room

Installing a pit in a home garage will be labor intensive and you must check with your utility companies first to determine if any electrical, natural gas or water lines run underground through the space. Pegboard storage is designed along the side walls to maximize maneuvering room along the sides of vehicles. Plan to outfit pits with lights, electricity, air lines and a fire extinguisher.

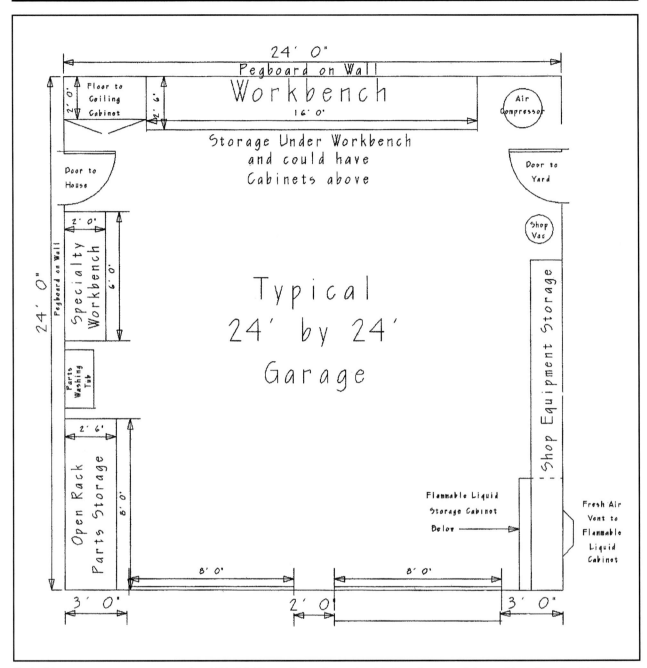

Typical two-car garages measure about 24x24. These dimensions should allow for complete workbench and cabinet storage at the front and along the sides. For garages with two separate garage doors, consider using wheel dollies to move project vehicles to the center for maximum working room.

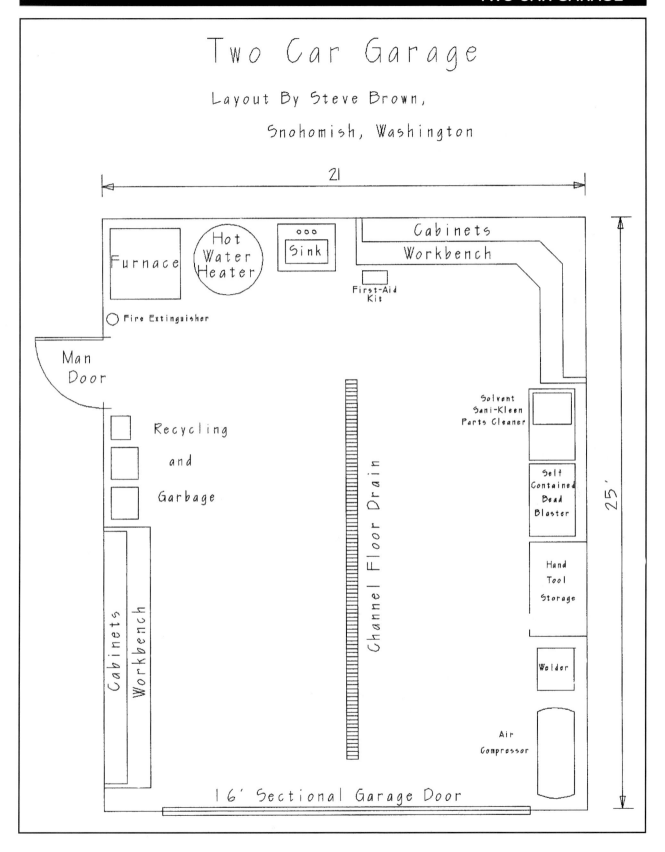

Two Car Garage

Layout By Steve Brown,

Snohomish, Washington

21

25'

Furnace

Hot Water Heater

Sink

Cabinets
Workbench

First-Aid Kit

Fire Extinguisher

Man Door

Recycling

and

Garbage

Solvent
Sani-Kleen
Parts Cleaner

Self
Contained
Bead
Blaster

Hand
Tool
Storage

Channel Floor Drain

Cabinets Workbench

Welder

Air
Compressor

16' Sectional Garage Door

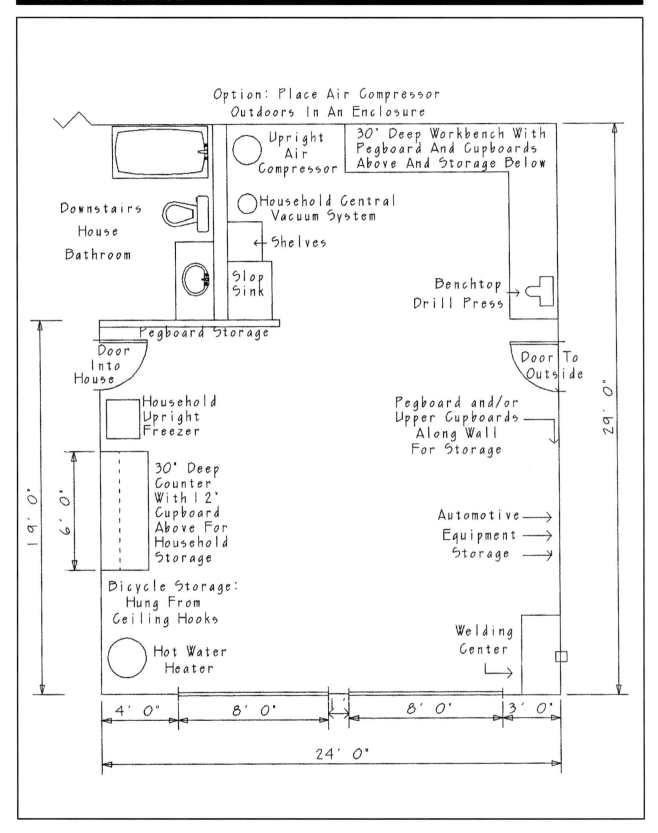

Option: Place Air Compressor
Outdoors In An Enclosure

Upright Air Compressor

30" Deep Workbench With Pegboard And Cupboards Above And Storage Below

Downstairs House Bathroom

Household Central Vacuum System

← Shelves

Slop Sink

Benchtop Drill Press

Pegboard Storage

Door Into House

Door To Outside

Household Upright Freezer

Pegboard and/or Upper Cupboards Along Wall For Storage

30" Deep Counter With 12" Cupboard Above For Household Storage

Automotive →
Equipment →
Storage →

Bicycle Storage: Hung From Ceiling Hooks

Hot Water Heater

Welding Center

19' 0"

6' 0"

29' 0"

4' 0"   8' 0"   8' 0"   3' 0"

24' 0"

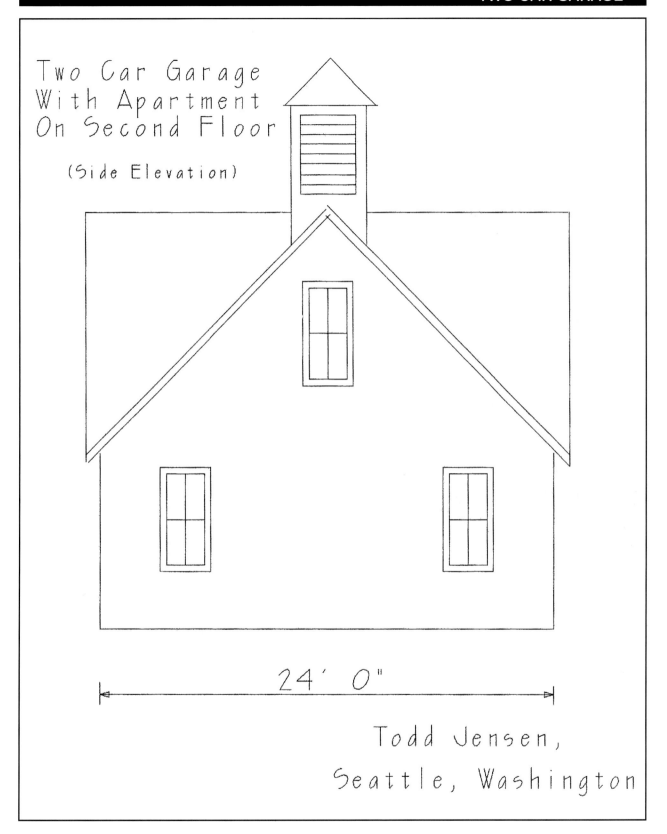

Two Car Garage
With Apartment
On Second Floor

(Side Elevation)

24' 0"

Todd Jensen,
Seattle, Washington

Two Car Garage
With Apartment
On Second Floor

13'

9'

32'

Todd Jensen,
Seattle, Washington

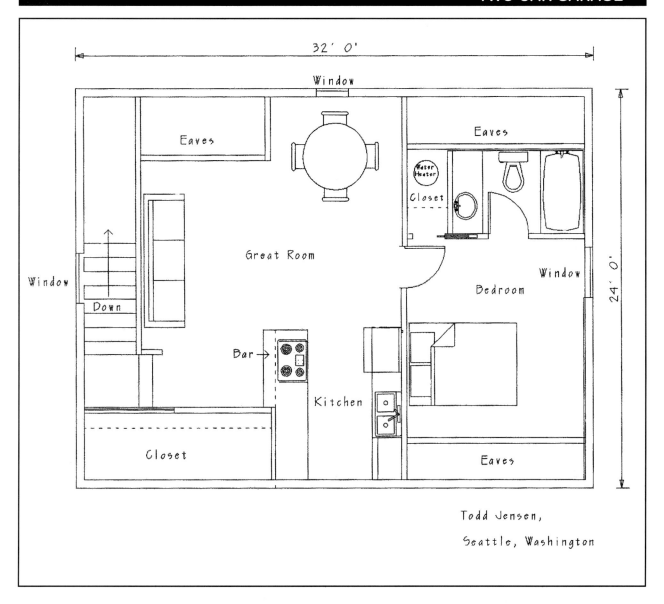

Todd Jensen,
Seattle, Washington

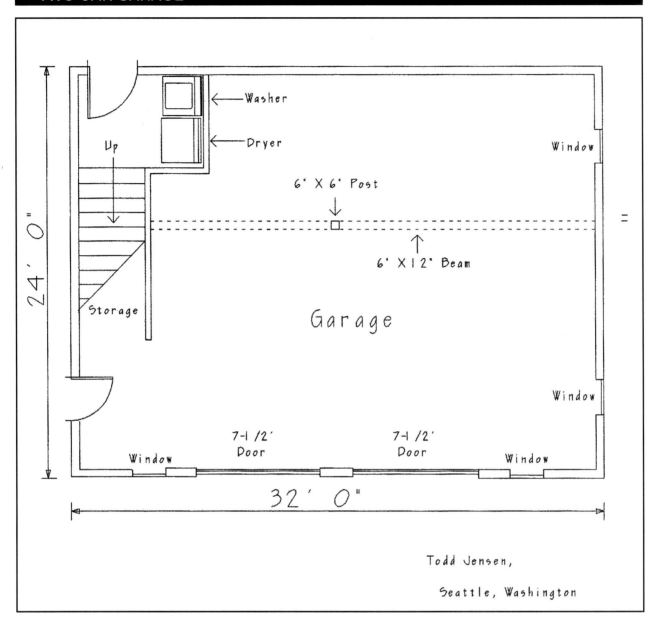

Washer

Dryer

Up

6" X 6" Post

6" X 12" Beam

Window

Storage

Garage

Window

Window

7-1/2' Door

7-1/2' Door

Window

24' 0"

32' 0"

Todd Jensen,

Seattle, Washington

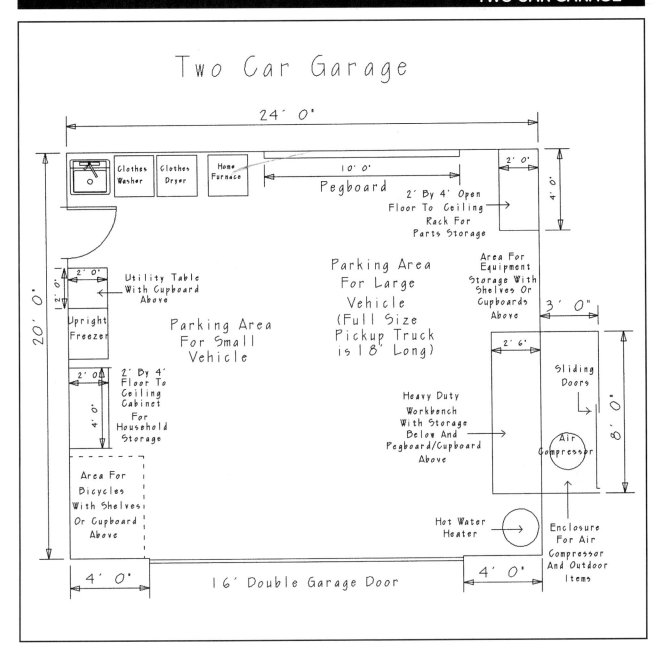

Two Car Garage

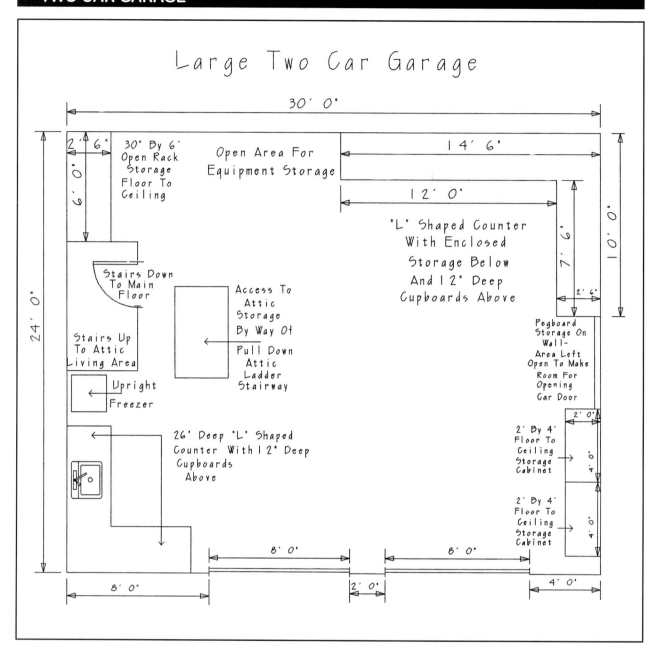

Large Two Car Garage

Two Car Garage

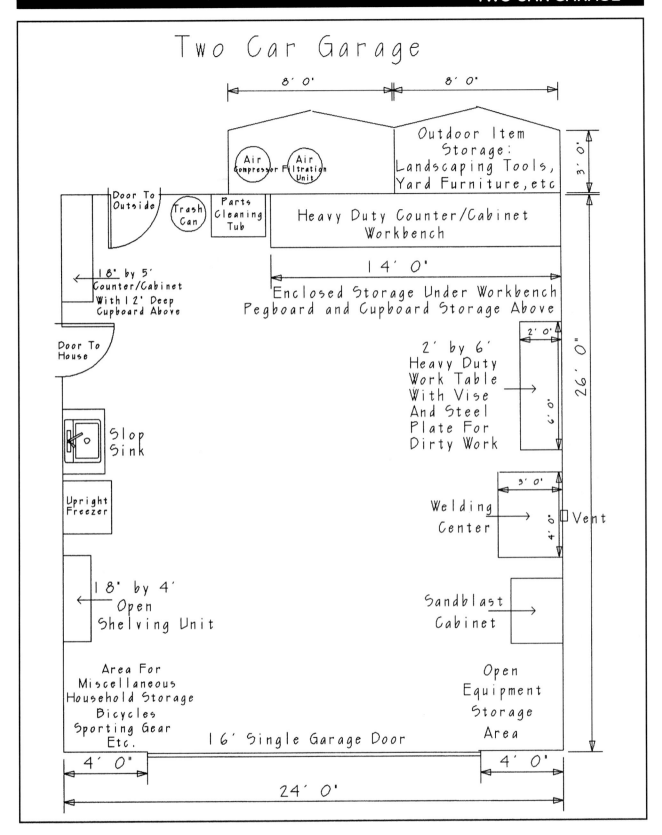

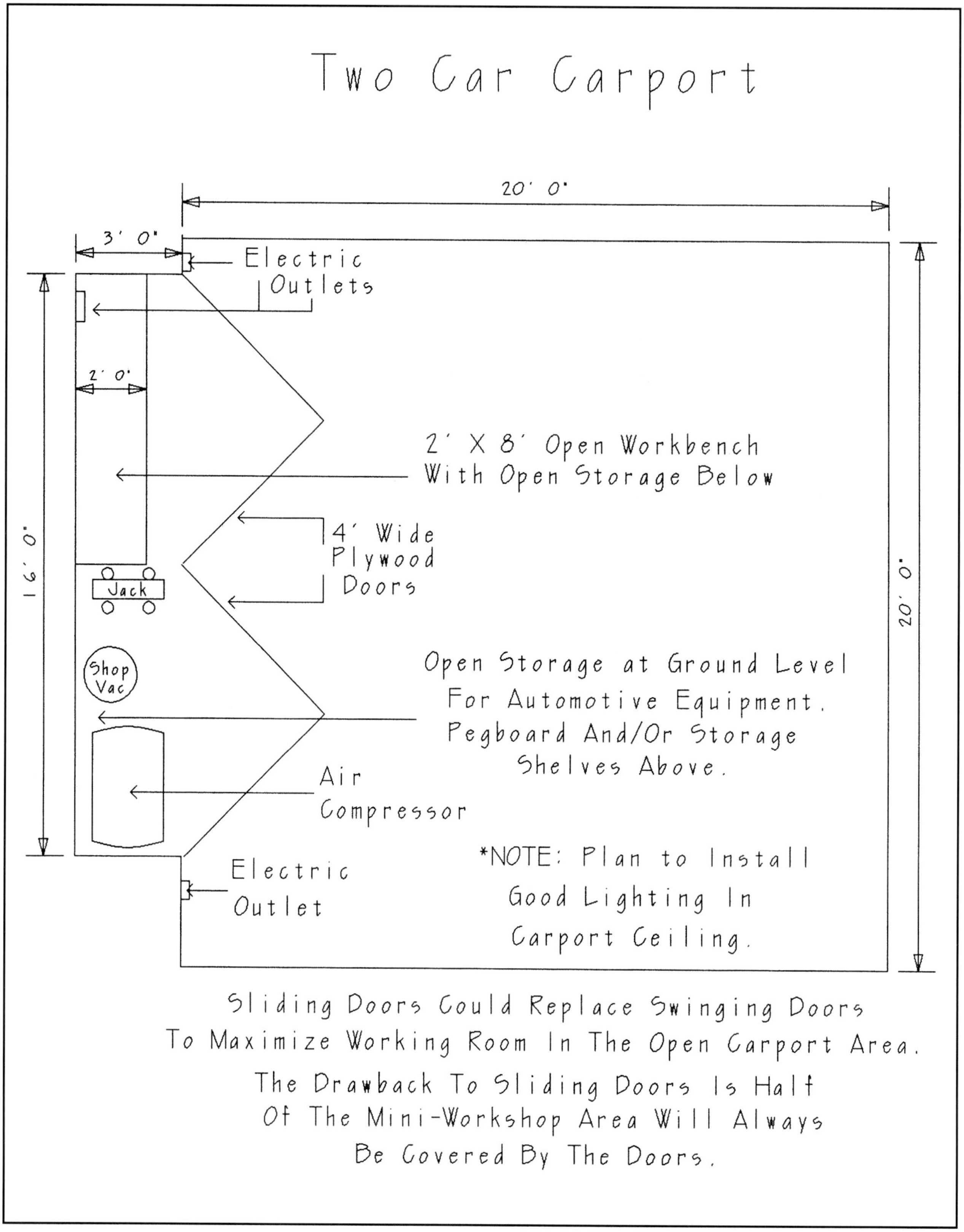

Two Car Carport

20' 0"

3' 0"

Electric
Outlets

2' 0"

16' 0"

2' X 8' Open Workbench
With Open Storage Below

4' Wide
Plywood
Doors

Jack

20' 0"

Shop
Vac

Open Storage at Ground Level
For Automotive Equipment.
Pegboard And/Or Storage
Shelves Above.

Air
Compressor

Electric
Outlet

*NOTE: Plan to Install
Good Lighting In
Carport Ceiling.

Sliding Doors Could Replace Swinging Doors
To Maximize Working Room In The Open Carport Area.
The Drawback To Sliding Doors Is Half
Of The Mini-Workshop Area Will Always
Be Covered By The Doors.

Two Car Carport with 5´ X 20´ Secured Enclosure

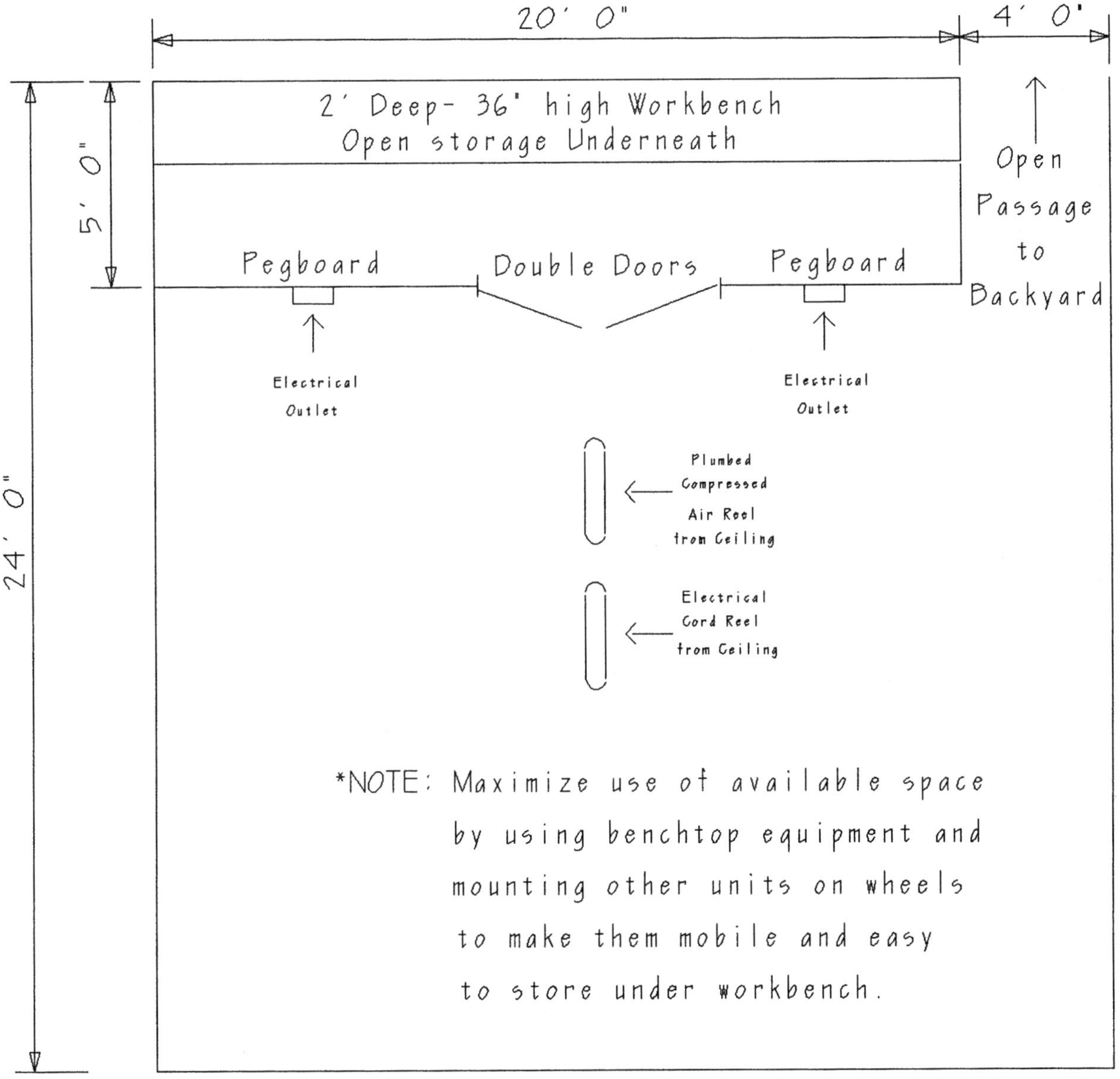

20´ 0"

4´ 0´

5´ 0"

24´ 0"

2´ Deep- 36´ high Workbench
Open storage Underneath

Pegboard

Double Doors

Pegboard

Open

Passage

to

Backyard

↑
Electrical
Outlet

↑
Electrical
Outlet

← Plumbed
Compressed
Air Reel
from Ceiling

← Electrical
Cord Reel
from Ceiling

*NOTE: Maximize use of available space
by using benchtop equipment and
mounting other units on wheels
to make them mobile and easy
to store under workbench.

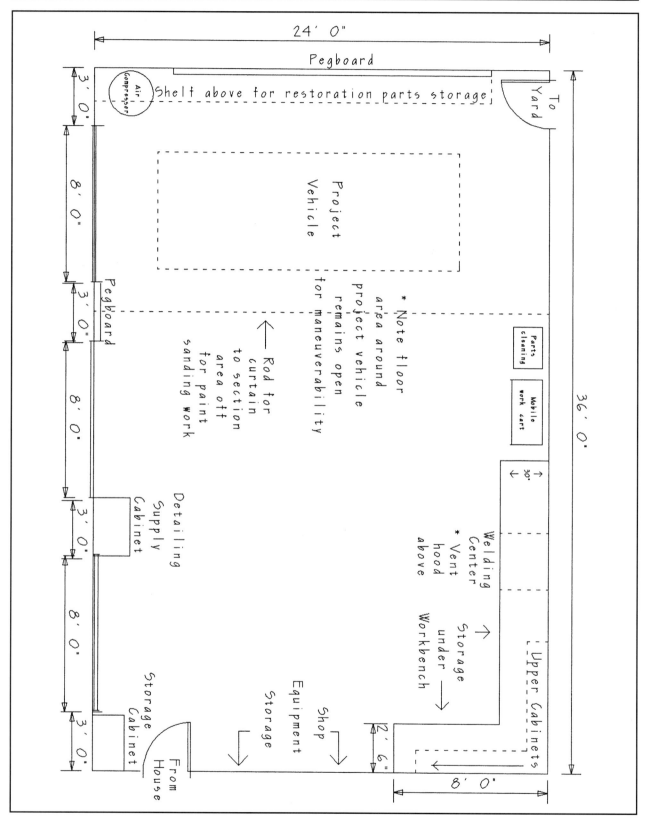

Three-car garages offer plenty of working and storage space. In this plan, a viable work center is designed for one corner with the opposite side left clear. This large amount of storage would be ideal for restoring an old vehicle.

Three Car Garage

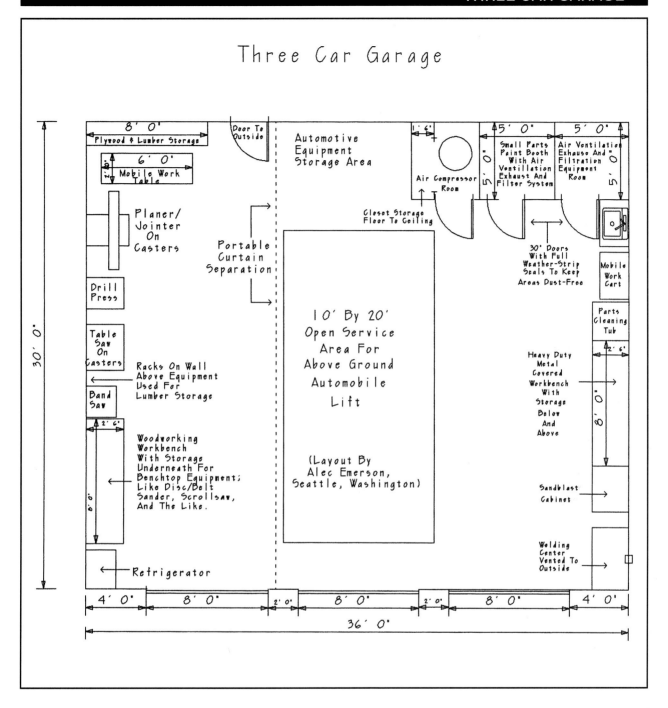

(Layout By Alec Emerson, Seattle, Washington)

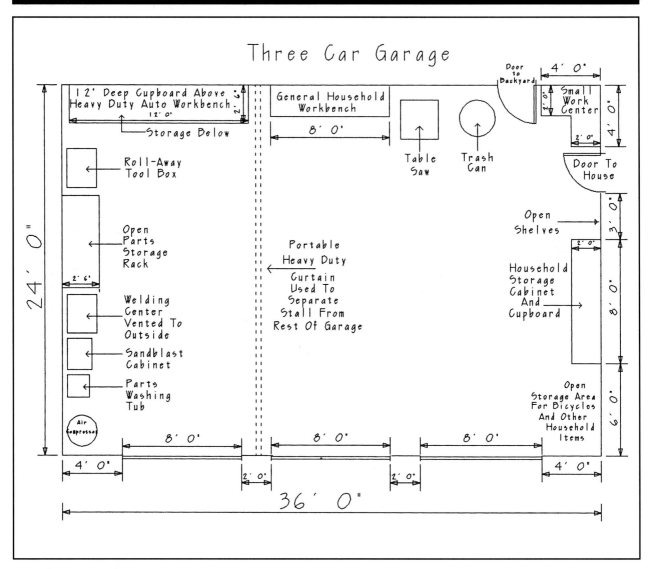

Three Car Garage

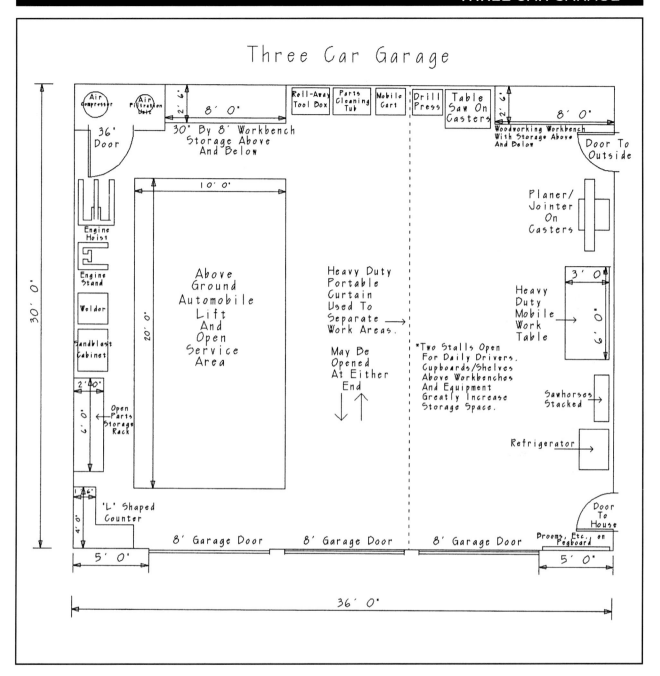

Three Car Garage

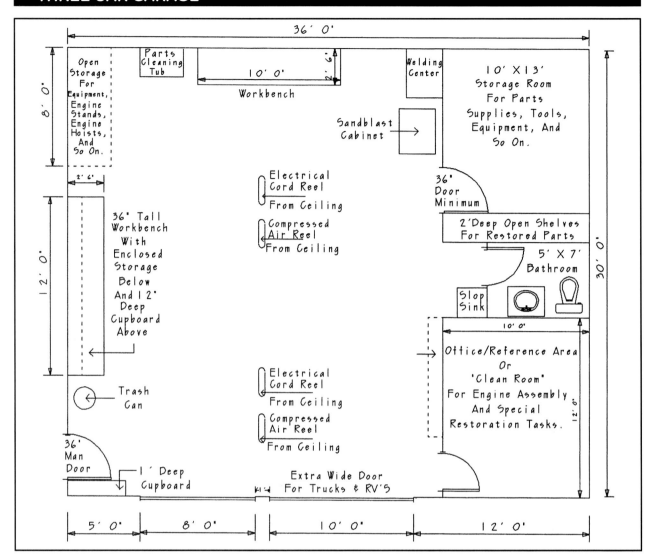

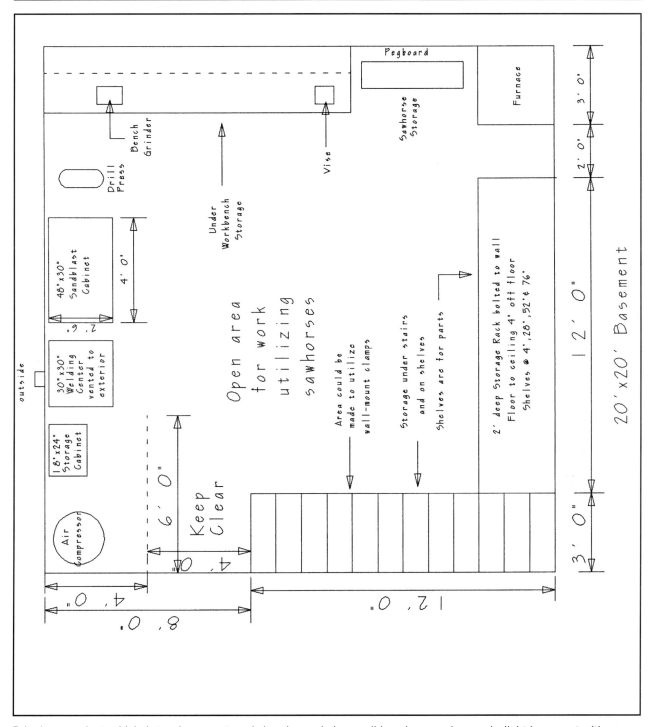

Bringing a project vehicle into a basement workshop is nearly impossible unless you have a daylight basement with a large door. However, you can still set up a quality basement automotive workshop. Keep the area at the base of stairs clear and use plywood and sawhorse workbenches to take advantage of open center areas. A wall mounted clamp unit from the Adjustable Clamp company outfitted with a piece of plywood could also be used as a temporary workbench.

Daylight Basement Workshop

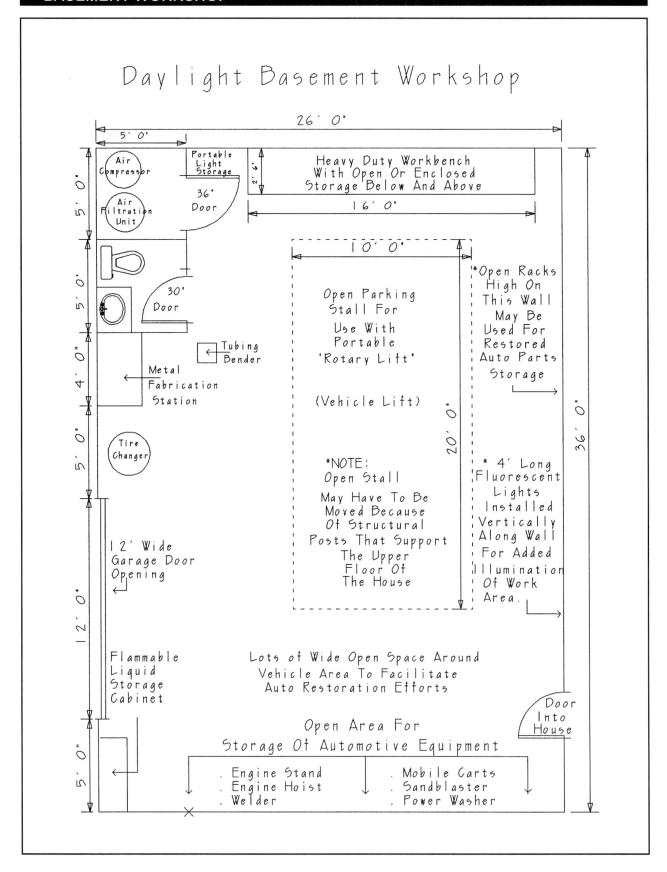

26' 0"

5' 0"

Air Compressor

Air Filtration Unit

Portable Light Storage

36' Door

Heavy Duty Workbench
With Open Or Enclosed
Storage Below And Above

2' 6"

16' 0"

5' 0"

5' 0"

30' Door

10' 0"

Open Parking
Stall For
Use With
Portable
'Rotary Lift'

(Vehicle Lift)

*Open Racks
High On
This Wall
May Be
Used For
Restored
Auto Parts
Storage

Tubing Bender

Metal Fabrication Station

4' 0"

5' 0"

Tire Changer

*NOTE:
Open Stall
May Have To Be
Moved Because
Of Structural
Posts That Support
The Upper
Floor Of
The House

20' 0"

* 4' Long
Fluorescent
Lights
Installed
Vertically
Along Wall
For Added
Illumination
Of Work
Area.

36' 0"

12' 0"

12' Wide
Garage Door
Opening

Flammable
Liquid
Storage
Cabinet

Lots of Wide Open Space Around
Vehicle Area To Facilitate
Auto Restoration Efforts

Door
Into
House

Open Area For
Storage Of Automotive Equipment

5' 0"

. Engine Stand
. Engine Hoist
. Welder

. Mobile Carts
. Sandblaster
. Power Washer

Daylight Basement Workshop

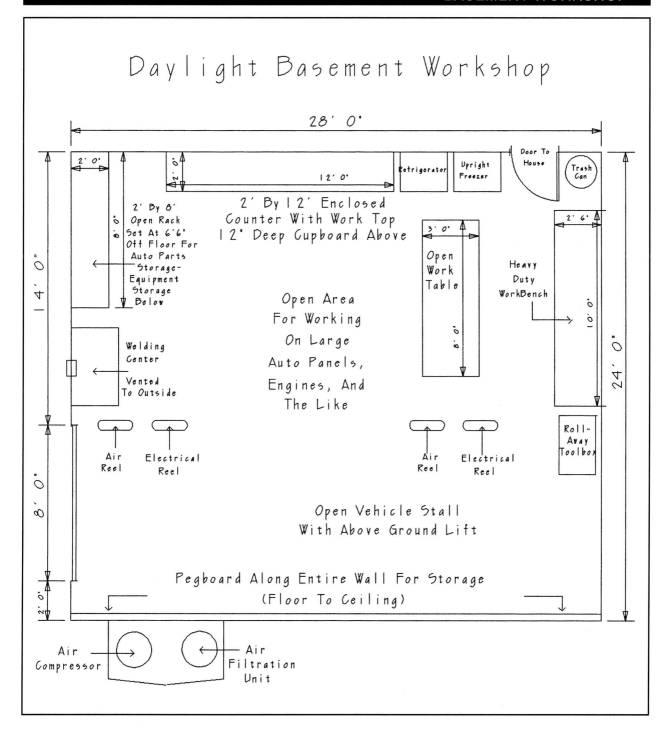

28' 0"

2' 0"

2' 0"

12' 0"

Retrigerator

Upright Freezer

Door To House

Trash Can

2' By 8' Open Rack Set At 6'6" Off Floor For Auto Parts Storage- Equipment Storage Below

2' By 12' Enclosed Counter With Work Top 12" Deep Cupboard Above

3' 0"

Open Work Table

8' 0"

Heavy Duty WorkBench

2' 6"

10' 0"

14' 0"

Open Area For Working On Large Auto Panels, Engines, And The Like

24' 0"

Welding Center

Vented To Outside

Air Reel

Electrical Reel

Air Reel

Electrical Reel

Roll- Away Toolbox

8' 0"

Open Vehicle Stall With Above Ground Lift

Pegboard Along Entire Wall For Storage (Floor To Ceiling)

2' 0"

Air Compressor

Air Filtration Unit

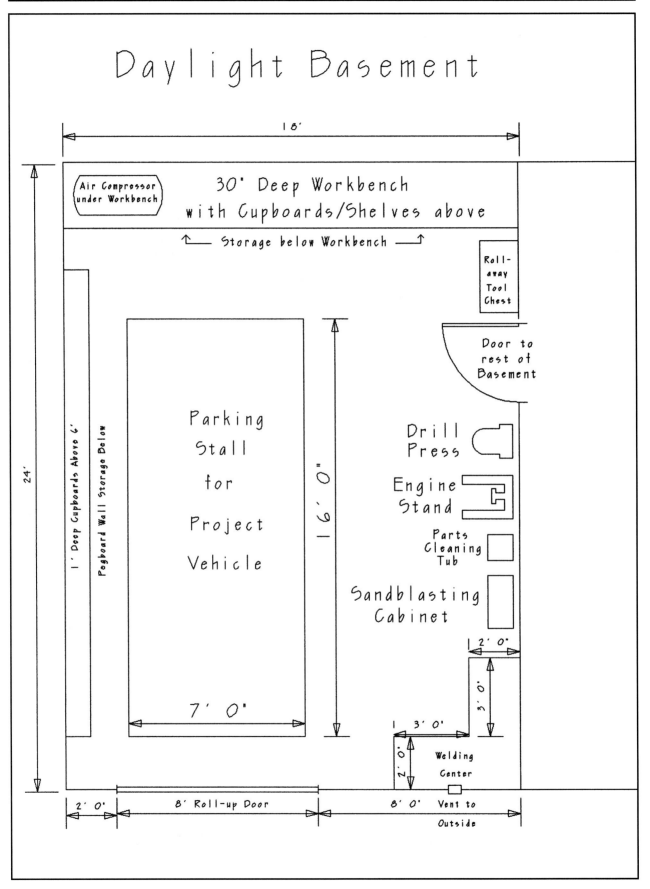

Daylight Basement

18'

Air Compressor under Workbench

30" Deep Workbench with Cupboards/Shelves above

← Storage below Workbench →

Roll-away Tool Chest

Door to rest of Basement

24'

1' Deep Cupboards Above 6'

Pegboard Wall Storage Below

Parking Stall for Project Vehicle

16' 0"

Drill Press

Engine Stand

Parts Cleaning Tub

Sandblasting Cabinet

2' 0"

3' 0"

7' 0"

3' 0"

2' 0"

Welding Center

2' 0"

8' Roll-up Door

8' 0"

Vent to Outside

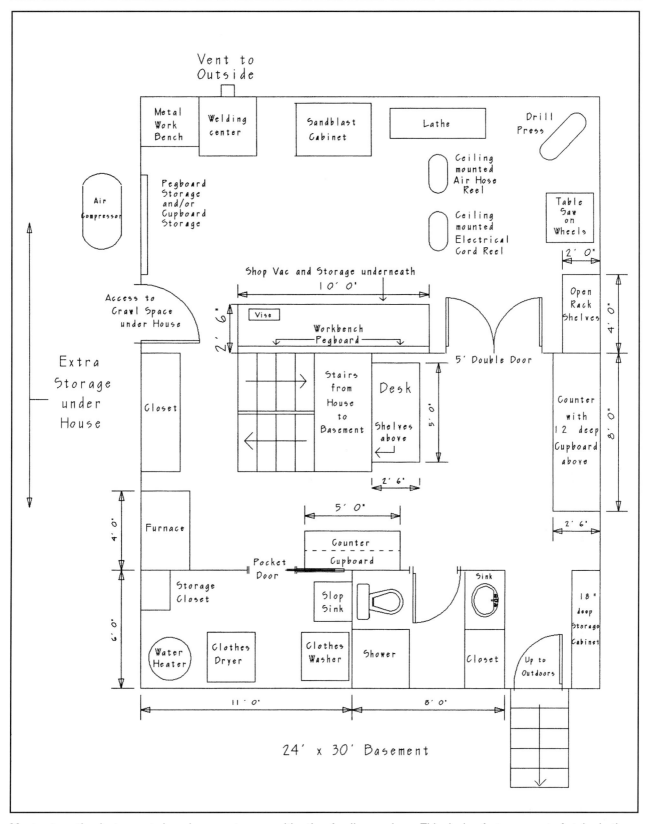

Vent to Outside

Metal Work Bench

Welding center

Sandblast Cabinet

Lathe

Drill Press

Air Compressor

Pegboard Storage and/or Cupboard Storage

Ceiling mounted Air Hose Reel

Ceiling mounted Electrical Cord Reel

Table Saw on Wheels

2' 0"

Access to Crawl Space under House

Shop Vac and Storage underneath
10' 0"

2' 6"

Vise

Workbench Pegboard

5' Double Door

Open Rack Shelves

4' 0"

Extra Storage under House

Closet

Stairs from House to Basement

Desk

Shelves above

5' 0"

Counter with 12" deep Cupboard above

8' 0"

2' 6"

2' 6"

Furnace

4' 0"

5' 0"

Counter
Cupboard

Pocket Door

Storage Closet

6' 0"

Slop Sink

Clothes Washer

Shower

Sink

Closet

18" deep Storage Cabinet

Water Heater

Clothes Dryer

Up to Outdoors

11' 0"

8' 0"

24' x 30' Basement

Most auto enthusiasts must share basement space with other family members. This design features a set of stairs in the center of the basement. On one side of the stairs is a laundry center, bathroom, and utility space complete with a desk and chair. The other side serves as a household workshop. A 5-foot double door on one side and a pocket door on the other help to keep dust and workshop debris away from the other half of the basement.

Chapter 5
WORKBENCHES

Every auto workshop needs at least one workbench. Many auto related repair, alteration and restoration tasks will be accomplished here. Should your workload be diverse and workspace large enough, additional workbenches with special accessories may prove convenient. In some situations, a workbench may consist of a sturdy cardboard box, a simple table or a piece of plywood set over sawhorses. Your workbench simply needs to be a place where you can work on car parts comfortably. Most people, however, would prefer a sturdy and stable workbench that is tough enough to withstand pounding.

Wood and metal workbenches are available through mail order tool and equipment outlets, like Harbor Freight Tools. Some auto enthusiasts, especially those with limited workspaces, prefer to employ roll-around tool chests equipped with wood tops that double as workbenches. These accessories offer convenience and mobility, while taking up very little workshop space. Combination roll-around tool chest/workbenches can be moved out of the way to make room for various auto repair activities.

Basic Workbench

Simple workbenches may be constructed from either wood or metal. This is true for the frame, as well as the top. In either case, framing members must be sturdy and fastened together securely. Wood workbench framing should be built with 2x4 or 4x4 dimension lumber. Tops may consist of 2x6 or larger dimension material, or 3/4-inch to 5/4-inch AC grade plywood. For metal workbenches, plan to use heavy gauge angle iron or square tubing for the frame and metal plate for the top. Members may be welded or bolted together.

Along with stability, workbenches must be built to dimensions that conveniently fit users. If you are over 6-feet tall, a 30-inch high workbench will be most uncomfortable for you to stand over for any length of time. A better workbench height would be 36- to 40-inches. In contrast, auto enthusiasts that stand less than 6-feet tall may be best served with workbench heights from 30- to 36-inches. An easy way to determine comfortable workbench height is to stand at a kitchen counter and tackle a small task.

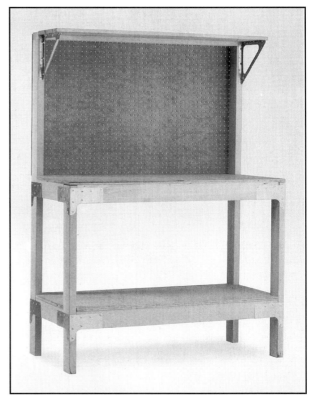

Simpson Strong-Tie Connectors were used to make this handy workbench with 2x4s, 3/4-inch plywood and 1/4-inch pegboard. It is a simple and sturdy design that can be built in just a few hours. For maximum strength and stability, plan to use Simpson Steel Screws instead of nails.

Spread out a newspaper or piece of cardboard to protect the countertop and spend some time cleaning small auto parts; like badges or light lenses that do not require solvents or other petroleum products. Use a toothbrush and other small cleaning implements that may require you to bend over the counter. It shouldn't take long to discover if the height is right for you. If the counter height is too low, place a couple of books on the counter and put a breadboard on top of them. Is the increased working height more comfortable? Use books of varying

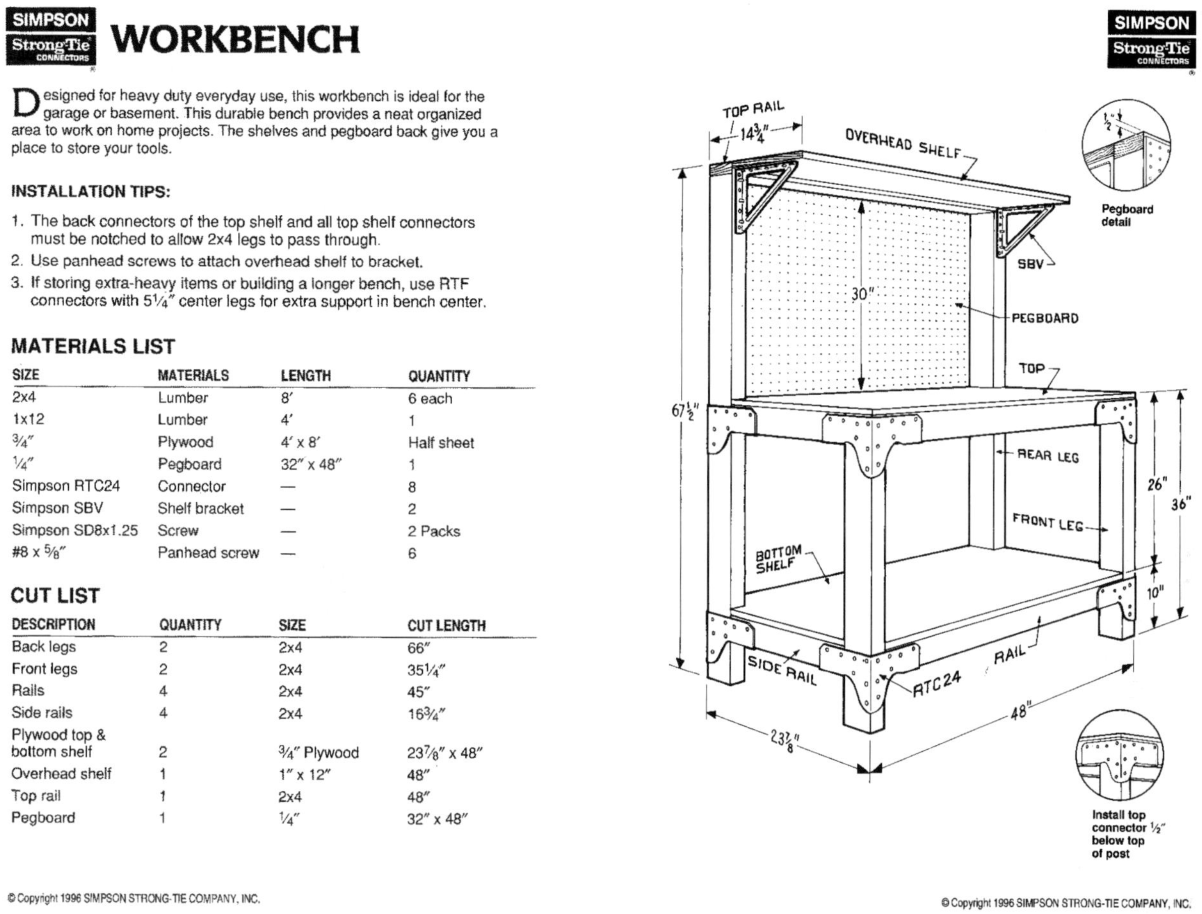

WORKBENCH

Designed for heavy duty everyday use, this workbench is ideal for the garage or basement. This durable bench provides a neat organized area to work on home projects. The shelves and pegboard back give you a place to store your tools.

INSTALLATION TIPS:

1. The back connectors of the top shelf and all top shelf connectors must be notched to allow 2x4 legs to pass through.
2. Use panhead screws to attach overhead shelf to bracket.
3. If storing extra-heavy items or building a longer bench, use RTF connectors with 5¼" center legs for extra support in bench center.

MATERIALS LIST

SIZE	MATERIALS	LENGTH	QUANTITY
2x4	Lumber	8'	6 each
1x12	Lumber	4'	1
¾"	Plywood	4' x 8'	Half sheet
¼"	Pegboard	32" x 48"	1
Simpson RTC24	Connector	—	8
Simpson SBV	Shelf bracket	—	2
Simpson SD8x1.25	Screw	—	2 Packs
#8 x ⅝"	Panhead screw	—	6

CUT LIST

DESCRIPTION	QUANTITY	SIZE	CUT LENGTH
Back legs	2	2x4	66"
Front legs	2	2x4	35¼"
Rails	4	2x4	45"
Side rails	4	2x4	16¾"
Plywood top & bottom shelf	2	¾" Plywood	23⅞" x 48"
Overhead shelf	1	1" x 12"	48"
Top rail	1	2x4	48"
Pegboard	1	¼"	32" x 48"

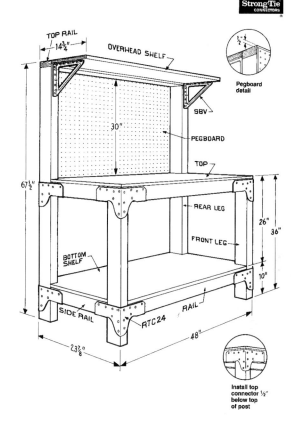

These are the plans and materials list for the Simpson Strong-Tie Workbench.

This workbench is 10 feet long and 30 inches deep. It was built 78 inches tall so it would fit under exposed household pipes. It rests about 10 inches off the floor to provide just enough room for some spare tires. These cabinets provide abundant storage along with the pegboard that sits above the work surface built at a height of 36 inches. The unit is made out of 2x4s and 3/4-inch AC plywood. A small section was cut out of the pegboard to provide access to an electrical outlet.

thickness to alter the working height until you arrive at a perfect level. Measure that height and build your workbench to it. If the counter is too high, simply place books on the floor and stand on them until you arrive at a comfortable working height.

Workbench Depth

The distance your workbench extends out into the workshop area may depend upon the amount of room you have to work with. One-car garages will most likely limit workbench depths to about 12 to 24 inches. Wider and deeper two-car and larger garages should allow workbenches to extend up to 30 inches out from walls. Workbenches deeper than 30 inches are not practical. This is because it is difficult to reach tools and other things located on pegboard or near the back of workbenches any deeper than 30 inches. You will also find that many things will inadvertently get shoved toward the back of deep workbenches, making them hard to retrieve and easy to misplace.

Workbench Length

As with depth, workbench length might also be limited by the amount of available workshop space. Although you can get by with a 4-foot long work-

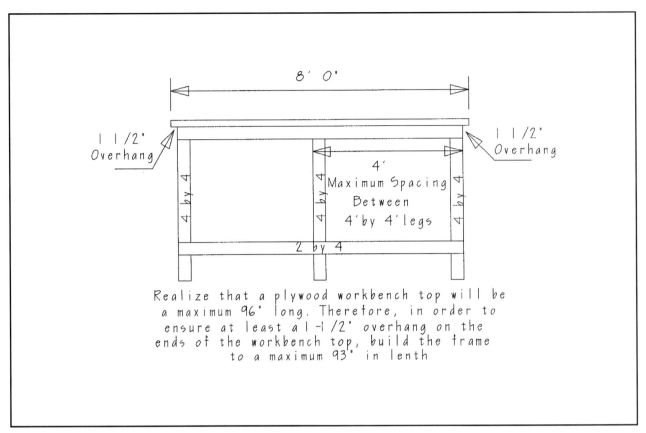

8' 0"

1 1/2" Overhang

1 1/2" Overhang

4 by 4

4 by 4

4 by 4

4'
Maximum Spacing
Between
4' by 4' legs

2 by 4

Realize that a plywood workbench top will be
a maximum 96" long. Therefore, in order to
ensure at least a 1 -1/2" overhang on the
ends of the workbench top, build the frame
to a maximum 93" in lenth

When working with wood, realize that dimension lumber comes in even lengths and sheets of plywood measure 4 feet by 8 feet. When designing workbenches, take these figures into account so you can maximize wood usage. For example, a 30-inch plywood workbench top will leave behind a 17 7/8-inch piece; deduct 1/8-inch for the saw blade kerf. That piece can be used as an upper shelf or cut in half lengthwise for two smaller shelves.

bench, a 5-foot long workbench will prove much more convenient. Ideally, try to set up your shop with a 6- to 8-foot workbench. You must also consider what kind of work you expect to tackle when planning workbench length. Longer workbenches are convenient for many auto related tasks, like straightening long trim pieces and upholstering bench seats. However, long workbenches may be unwarranted for tasks that involve just the repair of electronic parts or the restoration of small assemblies. While planning your workshop area, take into account the space available for workbenches and the space needed for storage. Should your shop area be filled with large workbenches, where will all the other things be kept?

Under workbench storage

One of the easiest ways to accommodate both workbench and storage concerns is to incorporate storage into your workbench unit design. If you have a number of equipment pieces mounted on wheels, like a welder, shop vacuum, and portable air compressor, build a workbench on top of a 2x4 frame that is mounted to wall studs. Instead of workbench legs that rest on the floor, framing could consist of

2x4s that run from the wall to the workbench top at a 45-degree angle. This design will allow open space under the workbench top for the storage of wheeled equipment units.

Where you simply need shelf storage, build a workbench with legs and then install shelves between the legs. If you need storage for large items, install just one shelf at the workbench floor level. Should you need a large amount of storage for smaller items, build a shelf at floor level and another one half way between the lower shelf and the workbench top. This arrangement can be altered, with one side of the workbench storage area left open for big things and the other side outfitted with an extra shelf for smaller objects.

Above workbench storage

Installing 1/4-inch thick pegboard on the wall just above workbenches will provide a handy storage spot for hand tools and other frequently used items. However, you must limit pegboard height to that which you can conveniently reach. It would be pointless to run pegboard from the level of the workbench top to the ceiling because you will not be able to retrieve items located high above your head. Retriev-

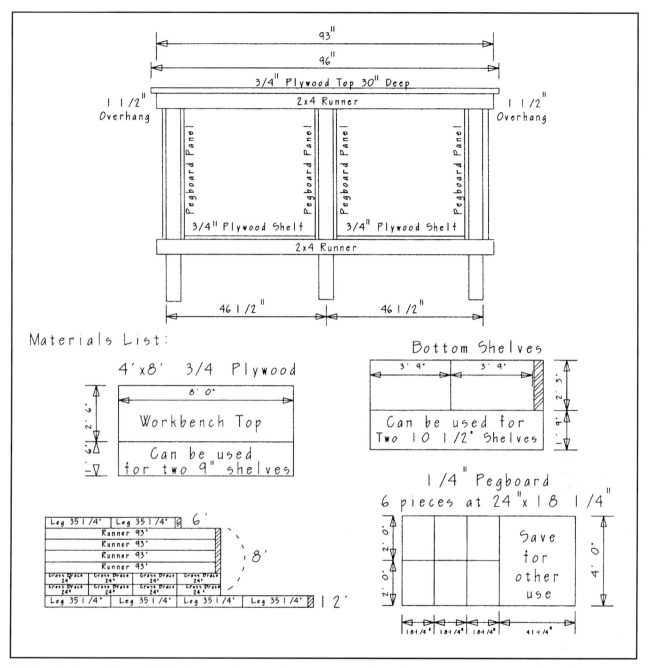

This is a design and materials list for an 8-foot long, 30-inch deep workbench/table. Notice that the frame measures 93 inches long. Using this design, an 8-foot plywood sheet will overhang the frame by 1 1/2 inches on both ends. Overhangs prove useful when using clamps. Plan to use straight 2x4s and 3/4-inch AC plywood.

ing high pegboard items will be even more difficult if your workbench extends out from the wall 30-inches. Therefore, plan to install 1/4-inch thick pegboard to a height that is comfortable for you to reach.

Above that, install a 9- to 12-inch deep shelf or cabinet. Save that storage space for things infrequently needed because you will most likely need a stool or ladder to safely reach things stored inside. Limit the depth of above workbench storage shelves or cabinets to a maximum of 12-inches. Made deeper, it may be dif-

ficult to see and retrieve things stored in the back.

If shop security or tool cleanliness is a factor and you prefer to minimize pegboard storage, you could install a 4 to 6-inch deep cabinet above the workbench for tool storage. Install pegboard on the inside of the cabinet and on the doors to maximize storage room and convenience. Be sure to use heavy duty hinges, maybe even piano hinges, for the doors to ensure they are secured strongly while supporting pegboard and the things hung from it.

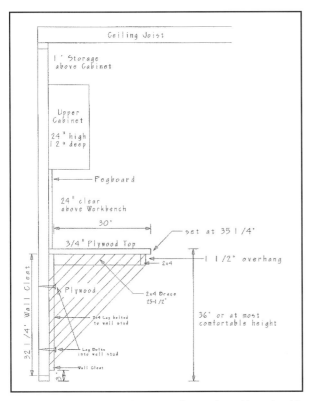

This is a simple design for a cantilevered workbench with pegboard and cupboard storage above. Room is left open under the workbench for a shop vacuum and mobile air compressor. Wall cleats are bolted to the wall so that the plywood has something to be nailed to. Plywood braces should be located every 32 inches for maximum support.

A Fold-Down Work Center would be ideal for small garages, basements and other workshop areas limited in open space. It may also be handy for specialty auto work, like electronics and small parts detailing. The WoodsmithShop catalog offers a complete set of plans and hardware for this unit. The plans contain everything except the wood and fluorescent light; you supply the tools, too. (Check the sources section for the address and telephone number for WoodsmithShop.)

Any number of above workbench storage designs may be implemented. It all depends upon your needs and preferences. You can use pegboard or install shallow cabinets. Reserve a space along the wall in the middle of the workbench and install 12 to 18-inch deep cabinets on each side. This way, you will have an open area in the center of the workbench for use when working on large auto parts, like bucket seats or panels. Instead of cabinets, install open shelves in any arrangement that suits your needs.

In all cases, take time to plan your workbench storage design. Look around your current auto workspace to see what will need to be stored. Envision scenarios with various storage options, i.e. pegboard versus cabinets and shelves versus room for wheeled equipment units. Where do you want things stored? Will they be needed close to the workbench or mainly used away from it? Remember the workshop convenience factor and plan to store related tools and supplies close to each other.

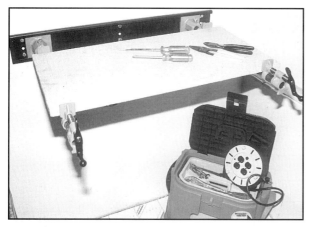

The Adjustable Clamp Company offers this very handy "Pony" Mounted Clamp Collars unit that can be used for a wide variety of projects. The base is bolted to wall studs with lag bolts provided in the package and the collars slip into the mounting bracket. 3/4-inch black pipe is inserted into the collars and secured with thumb screws. The unit will support up to 200 pounds with pipe measuring up to 3 feet. Below the temporary workbench is a nifty Power Toolbox from Lasko Metal Products. It features three trays, a wind-up extension cord and serves as a step stool.

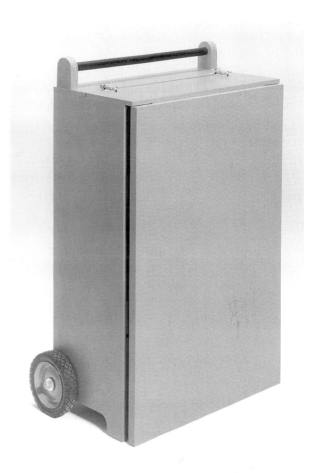

This is a Car Care Cart built from plans provided by the American Plywood Association. Designed to hold a variety of tools and equipment, this cart quickly folds out. The entire unit, including the top cabinet, retracts into an easy to store rectangle. The cart is made from 1 1/2 sheets of 1/2-inch AC plywood.

Fold-out Work Centers

Workbenches may be designed to fold out when needed and closed up when space is required for the parking of automobiles or other activities. These are most convenient in small workshops, like one-car garages. You can design 45-degree angled supports that are hinged to wall studs and simply place a piece of plywood on top for a simple workbench. Another option is to use a long piano hinge to support a worktop with legs hinged to the outer edge of the top for added support.

If the work area is wide enough, consider building a 6 or 9-inch deep tool cabinet and attach a hinged work table underneath. This way, you will have a small storage area along with a fold-out work table.

Another simple method uses sawhorses. If you have a space where two sawhorses can be stored, plan to use them with a sheet of plywood for a top. Plywood can be tilted up against a wall for storage or you can drill a couple of holes in the sheet at one end and hang it from sturdy hooks when not in use.

Old doors may prove useful as fold-out work tops. Hollow core wood doors are not strong enough to use as workbench tops. Plan to employ solid core wood or metal doors. These

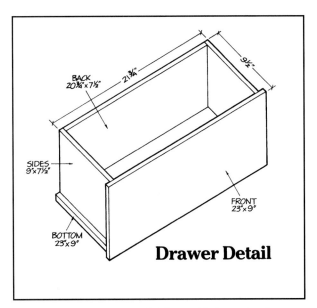

BACK 20¾″×7½″
2¾″
9½″
SIDES 9″×7½″
FRONT 23″×9″
BOTTOM 23″×9″

Drawer Detail

These are the plans, material list and information for building the Car Care Cart.

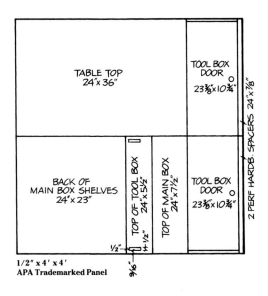

TABLE TOP 24″×36″

TOOL BOX DOOR 23⅜″×10¾″

BACK OF MAIN BOX SHELVES 24″×23″

TOP OF TOOL BOX 24″×5½″

TOP OF MAIN BOX 24″×7½″

TOOL BOX DOOR 23⅜″×10¾″

2 PERF. HARDB. SPACERS 24″×⅞″

1½″
½″
9/16″

1/2″ x 4′ x 4′
APA Trademarked Panel

Panel Layout

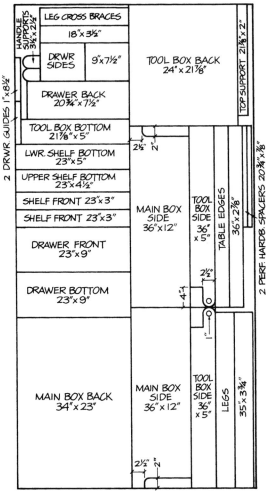

HANDLE SUPPORTS 3½″×2½″

LEG CROSS BRACES 18″×3½″

DRWR SIDES 9″×7½″

TOOL BOX BACK 24″×21⅞″

DRAWER BACK 20¾″×7½″

2 DRWR. GUIDES 1″×8½″

TOP SUPPORT 21⅞″×2″

TOOL BOX BOTTOM 21⅞″×5″

LWR. SHELF BOTTOM 23″×5″

UPPER SHELF BOTTOM 23″×4½″

SHELF FRONT 23″×3″

SHELF FRONT 23″×3″

DRAWER FRONT 23″×9″

MAIN BOX SIDE 36″×12″

TOOL BOX SIDE 36″×5″

TABLE EDGES 36″×2⅞″

2 PERF. HARDB. SPACERS 20¾″×⅞″

2½″
2″

DRAWER BOTTOM 23″×9″

2½″

4″

MAIN BOX BACK 34″×23″

MAIN BOX SIDE 36″×12″

TOOL BOX SIDE 36″×5″

LEGS 35″×3¾″

2½″
2″

1/2″ x 4′ x 8′ APA Trademarked Panel

units have solid edges to which hinges can be attached and will hold up under most normal workbench activities. You will need to support the outer edges with a sawhorse or legs hinged to the outer corners.

Mobile Workbenches

A small workbench on wheels may be perfect for any number of auto workshop activities. Outfitted with shelves and pegboard on the outside, you can bring your tools and supplies with you while working anywhere around vehicles. When jobs are complete, simply roll the mobile workbench back to an out of the way storage space.

Mobile workbenches must be outfitted with sturdy wheels. Plan to use 3- or 4-inch locking wheels. Bigger wheels are always better. Small wheels will jam against pebbles or other debris on workshop floors and driveways. In addition, they will make moving heavy workbenches difficult. Be sure the wheels are equipped with locking mechanisms. This way, you won't have to worry about units rolling away on slanted driveways and you can be assured that units will stay in place while you work on top of them.

As with any other workbench, be sure to allow space for a vise on top of your workbench. Vises are perhaps the single most useful workbench accessory around. Be selective when choosing a vise. Although bigger models may be capable of supporting great weight and withstanding significant impacts, the work surfaces they are on must also be able to handle the same. A small fold-out workbench cannot endure the same workload as a large heavy-

Materials List

Recommended panels: **APA trademarked Medium Density Overlay (MDO), overlaid both sides, if available, or**

APA trademarked A-B or A-C, or

For unique appearance, APA trademarked reconstituted wood panels

PANELS

Quantity	Description
1	1/2 in. x 4 ft. x 8 ft.
1	1/2 in. x 4 ft. x 4 ft.

OTHER MATERIALS

Quantity	Description
1	1 in. x 23 in. wood dowel
2	Approx. 1 in. wide x approx. 6-8 in. diameter wheels with axle, 4 nuts and 6 washers (drill axle holes in plywood sides according to wheel size)
2	1-1/16 in. x 18 in. continuous hinges w/screws (for attaching tabletop)
4	1 in. x 1-1/2 in. butt hinges w/screws (for attaching toolbox doors)
2	Barrel bolt latches w/screws (for securing toolbox)
2	Magnetic catches w/screws (for toolbox doors)
1	24 in. x 21-7/8 in. perforated hardboard with miscellaneous hanger hardware as desired
As required	Wood screws, finishing nails, white or urea resin glue, wood dough or synthetic filler, fine sandpaper, top quality finish (see finishing section)

This plan is one of the winners of the Panel Project Contest sponsored annually by the American Plywood Association and *Popular Science* magazine. Watch for contest rules and entry forms in upcoming issues of *Popular Science.*

Designed by **Mark McClanahan, Clio, Michigan**

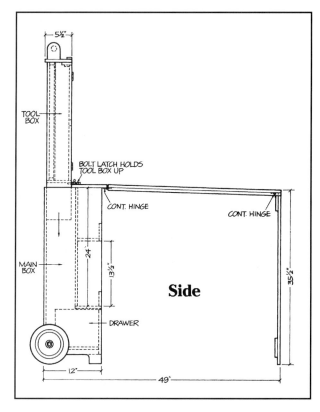

Side

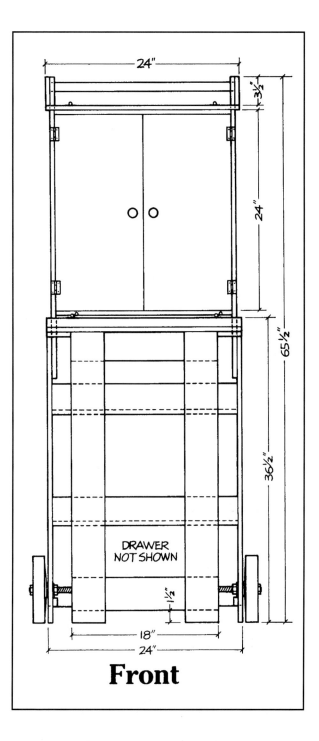

Front

duty vise. Therefore, match the vise size with the workbench. For fold-out workbenches that are unable to accommodate any storage, mount a small vise to a piece of 3/4-inch plywood. When the vise is needed, simply place the plywood mounted vise on the worktop and clamp the plywood to the fold-out top with two or more clamps. In fact, you can employ the same technique anywhere that workbench top space is limited. When not needed, remove the vise from the workbench and store it.

BUILDING HINTS

These general hints will help you achieve the best possible results in working with plywood and other APA panel products. They apply not only to this plan but to all projects you may undertake using APA trademarked panels. Since building methods and interpretation of suggestions may vary, the American Plywood Association cannot accept responsibility for results of an individual's project efforts.

PLANNING. Before starting, study the plan carefully to make sure you understand all details.

MAKING LAYOUT. Following the panel layout, draw all parts on the panel using straightedge and carpenter's square for accuracy. Use a compass to draw corner radii. Be sure to check the width of your saw cut and allow for saw kerfs when plotting dimensions.

CUTTING. When hand-sawing, support panel firmly with the best side facing up. Use a 10 to 15 pt. cross-cut saw. Use a fine-toothed coping saw for curves. For inside cuts, start hole with a drill and use a coping or keyhole saw. When power sawing on a radial or table saw, the best side of the panel should be face up. A plywood blade gives excellent results but a sharp combination blade may be used. When using a portable power saw, the best side of the panel should be down. For curved cuts, use a jigsaw, bandsaw or sabre saw. Be sure blade enters the face of the panel. Use the finest tooth possible for a smooth and even cut. For prolonged cutting of nonveneered panels and those containing layers of reconstituted wood, a carbide-tipped blade is suggested.

Reduce panel to pieces small enough for easy handling with first cuts. Plan to cut matching parts with the same saw setting. Scrap lumber clamped or tacked securely in place beneath the panel prevents splintering on the back side.

Overlaid panels can be worked in the same manner as regular grades with these exceptions: sawing and drilling should always be done with the cutting edge of the tool entering the panel face. To minimize chipping at the point of tool exit, use a piece of scrap wood as a backup or place tape along the line of the cut.

DRILLING. Support panel firmly. Use brace and bit for larger holes. When point appears through panel, reverse and complete hole from back. Finish slowly to avoid splintering.

PLANING. Remember, edge grain of the panel runs in alternate directions so plane from ends toward center. Use shallow set blade.

SANDING. Many APA panels are sanded smooth in manufacture — one of the big time-savers in their use — so only minimum surface sanding is necessary. Use 3-0 sandpaper after sealing and in direction of grain only. You may find it easier to sand cut edges smooth before assembling each unit. Use 1-0 or finer sandpaper before sealer or flat undercoat is applied.

ASSEMBLY. Construction by section makes final assembly easier. Drawers, cabinet shells and compartments, for example, should be handled as individual units. For strongest possible joints, use glue with screws or nails. Check for a good fit by holding pieces together. Contact should be made at all points for lasting strength. Mark nail location along edge of piece to be nailed. In careful work where nails must be very close to an edge, predrill using a drill bit slightly smaller than nail size. Always predrill for screws.

Apply glue to clean surfaces according to manufacturer's instructions. Press surfaces firmly together until bead appears. Check for square, then nail and apply clamps if possible to maintain pressure until glue sets. For exterior exposure, use resorcinol-type (waterproof) glue; for interior work use liquid resin (white) or urea resin type glues. Other glues are available for special gluing problems.

FINISHING FOR INTERIOR USE. Little, if any, surface preparation is usually required. Sanded panels require only light sanding to remove blemishes or to smooth fillers which might be used to patch any dents or openings in the surface. Sand in the direction of the grain only with fine sandpaper. If an opaque finish is to be used, cover any knots, pitch streaks, or sap spots with shellac or a stain-resistant sealer. Do not apply finishes over dust, glue, or spots of oil.

Three types of finishing systems may be used for interior applications: paints, stains and natural finishes.

When using paint systems, a solvent-thinned (oil-based) primer should be used to minimize grain raise and prevent staining. Gloss and semi-gloss enamel top coat provide a washable, durable surface. The top coat may be oil-based or alkyd-based (solvent-thinned) or latex (water-thinned), provided it is compatible with the primer.

Panels used for natural finishes should be carefully selected for pattern and appearance. For the most natural appearance, use two coats of a clear finish, such as a urethane, varnish, or clear sealer. To pleasantly subdue any grain irregularities or repairs, a light stain finish may be applied either by color toning, which uses companion stain and non-penetrating sealer, or light staining, which uses a pigmented sealer, tinting material (stain, thin enamel or undercoat), and finish coat (varnish or lacquer). Finish Medium Density Overlaid panels with solid-color acrylic latex stain or a two-coat paint system (primer plus companion top coat).

FINISHING FOR EXTERIOR USE. A top quality stain or paint will help maintain the panel's appearance and protect it from weathering. Since end grain absorbs and loses moisture rapidly, panels should be edge-sealed to help minimize possible damage. Use paint primer to seal panels to be painted, or use a paintable water-repellent preservative for panels which are to be stained.

For rough or textured panels, either high quality stain or acrylic house paint systems are recommended. Use a solvent-thinned semi-transparent stain for maximum grain show-through. Use only acrylic latex solid-color stain when it is desirable to hide the grain and color of the wood surface, but not its texture. Maximum protection of the wood is obtained by using a house paint system which consists of a stain-resistant primer and one or more acrylic latex top coats. Finish Medium Density Overlaid panels with solid-color acrylic latex stain or a two-coat paint system (primer plus companion top coat).

Best performance is achieved by applying the first coat of finish by brushing. If the first coat of finish is sprayed on, it should be back-brushed or back-rolled to work it well into the wood surface. Additional coats may be sprayed without back-brushing.

Whatever finishing method is used — paint or stain — always use top quality materials and follow the manufacturer's instructions.

HOW TO BUY APA PANELS

APA trademarked panel products are manufactured in two basic types: panels for permanent exposure to the weather or moisture, and panels for interior or protected applications when only temporary exposure to moisture or the weather is required. Within each type are numerous grades — sheathing grades, panels with smooth sanded surfaces on one or both sides, textured panels and panels with overlaid surfaces. The right grade to use for this project is given in the materials list.

American Plywood Association trademarks, such as those shown below, appear only on products manufactured by APA member mills. The marks signify that the manufacturer is committed to APA's rigorous program of quality supervision and testing and that panel quality is subject to verification through APA audit — a procedure designed to assure manufacture in conformance with APA performance standards or U.S. Product Standard PS 1-83 for Construction and Industrial Plywood.

Always insist on panels bearing the **mark of quality** — the APA trademark.

Although every effort is made to be accurate in the design and drawing of all APA plans, the possibility of error exists. Be sure that you review and understand all steps of construction and verify all dimensions before cutting your material. Quality of workmanship and the conditions under which panels are used vary widely. Because the Association has no control over these elements, it cannot accept responsibility for panel performance or designs as actually constructed.

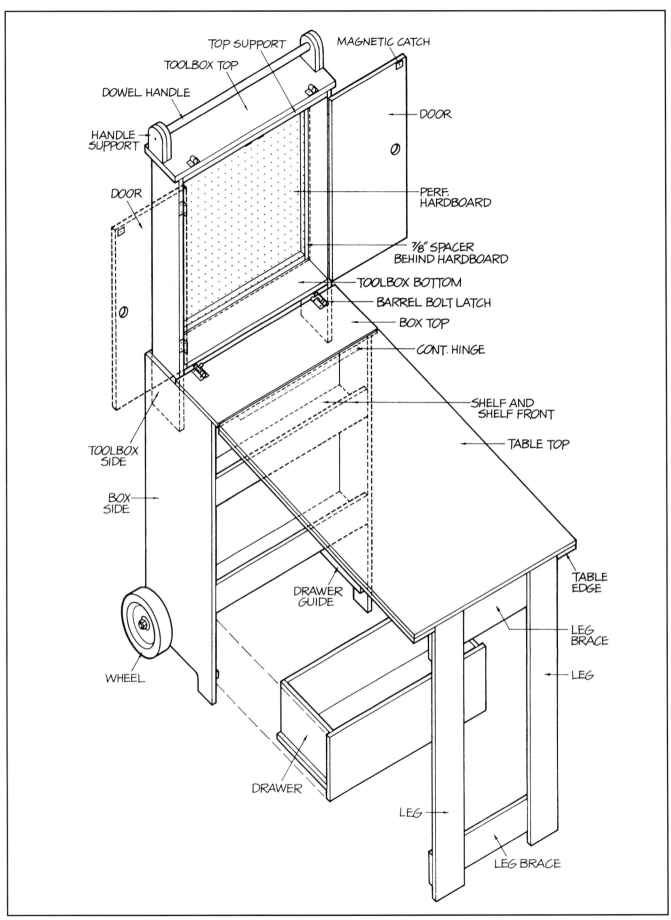

TOP SUPPORT

TOOLBOX TOP

MAGNETIC CATCH

DOWEL HANDLE

HANDLE SUPPORT

DOOR

DOOR

PERF. HARDBOARD

⅞" SPACER BEHIND HARDBOARD

TOOLBOX BOTTOM

BARREL BOLT LATCH

BOX TOP

CONT. HINGE

SHELF AND SHELF FRONT

TABLE TOP

TOOLBOX SIDE

BOX SIDE

TABLE EDGE

LEG BRACE

LEG

DRAWER GUIDE

WHEEL

DRAWER

LEG

LEG BRACE

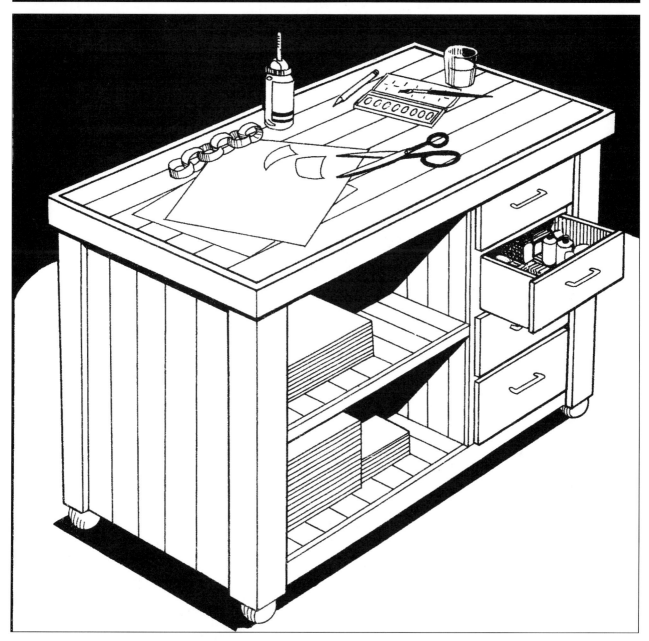

These are the plans for a Mobile Workbench provided by the Western Wood Products Association.

MATERIALS LIST

(lumber shown in linear feet)
1x1, 22'
1x2, 40'
1x4, 195'
1x6, 15'
1x8, 30'
2x2, 30'
2x4, 10'
4x4, 11'
Nails: 3d (1¼"); 4d (1½");
6d (2"); 10d (3")
(4) drawer pulls
1¾" or longer machine
screws (for drawer pulls)
See Note, Step 27
(4) locking swivel casters
Carpenter's glue

CAUTION: Be certain that you review and understand all steps of construction and verify all dimensions before cutting your material. While every effort has been made to insure accuracy in the design and drawing of all WWPA plans, the possibility of error always exists and WWPA cannot accept responsibility for lumber improperly used or designs not first verified.

TOOLS LIST

Hammer
Table saw
Framing square
Tape measure
Electric drill
Screwdriver
Chisel
Miter box
Optional: Router, radial arm
  saw or power miter saw

MOBILE WORKBENCH OFFERS STORAGE AND WORKSPACE

In addition to a generous-size work area. the workbench incorporates two open shelves and four large drawers for tools and supplies.

Two drawer plans are included. The one featuring the solid wood bottom uses both dadoed and rabbeted joints and is recommended for durability. However, for ease of construction, we've also included plans for an alternate drawer with a plywood bottom which requires only a quarter-inch groove in drawer sides.

Note: In the following illustrations, dimensions shown without inch marks (1x2, for example) are nominal sizes; those shown with inch marks ($1\frac{1}{2}"$x$2\frac{1}{2}"$) are actual sizes.

Mobile Workbench

Overall Dimensions: Height $35\frac{1}{2}"$ (including casters)
Length 54"
Width 26"

Fig. 1

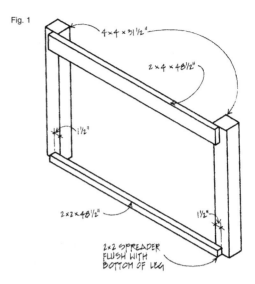

1—Frame: Assemble two side sections, using 2x2 spreader at the base and a 2x4 at the top. Spreaders overlap 4x4 posts $1\frac{1}{2}$." Fasten with glue and 10d nails or $2\frac{1}{2}"$ screws.

Fig. 2

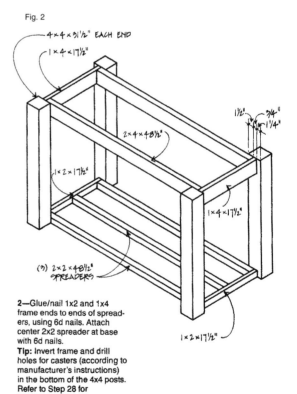

2—Glue/nail 1x2 and 1x4 frame ends to ends of spreaders, using 6d nails. Attach center 2x2 spreader at base with 6d nails.
Tip: Invert frame and drill holes for casters (according to manufacturer's instructions) in the bottom of the 4x4 posts. Refer to Step 28 for installation.

Fig. 3

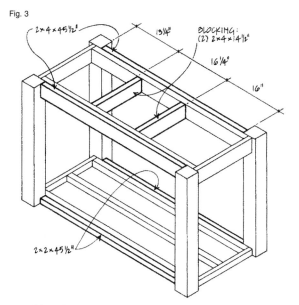

Fig. 5

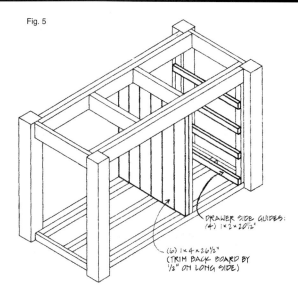

3—Glue/nail two 2x4s to outside of top frame; toenail to posts. Glue/nail two 2x2s to outside of base frame, flush with base.
4—Install two 2x4 blocks between top frame. Position

one 2x4 16″ in from inside of right leg and the other 13¼″ in from inside of left leg. Secure with glue and 10d nails.

9—Starting at the front of the unit, glue/nail six 1x4s to back side of divider, as shown in Fig. 5. Trim last 1x4 to 3″ wide and use at the back of the divider.
10—**Drawer side guides:** (Right side.) Cut four 1x2s to length; install one across the bottom flush with outside

edges of vertical 1x2s, front and back. Use 3d nails.
Tip: To ensure accurate spacing of side guides, cut two temporary vertical spacing blocks 5⅛″ long. Set blocks on bottom 1x2 and position next 1x2; glue/nail in place. Repeat for remaining side guides.

Fig. 4

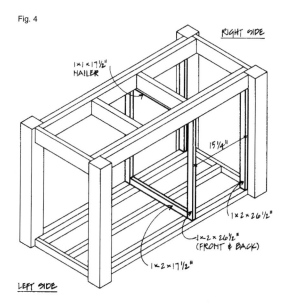

Fig. 6

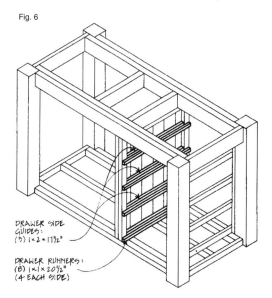

5—**Drawer frame:** On right side of workbench, glue/nail 1x2s to 4x4 legs, front and back, flush with inside edges of legs. (Also see Figs. 8 and 10 for plan view.)
6—Toenail vertical 1x2s between top and bottom frame, front and back, flush with inside face of 2x4 blocking at top. 1x2s are flush with

outside edge of top and bottom frames. There is 15¼″ (inside measurement) between vertical 1x2s.
7—At the base of the divider, glue/nail 1x2 between verticals. Toenail in place.
8—At the top, glue/nail 1x1 nailer below 2x4 blocking and between 1x2 verticals. (Also see Fig. 8.) Attach with 4d nails.

11—**Drawer side guides:** (Left side.) Cut three 1x2s, each 17½″ long, and glue/nail in place between vertical 1x2s; use 3d nails. Spacing is same as for right side. (Also see Fig. 8.)

12—Cut eight 1x1 drawer runners, each 20½″. Glue/nail flush to bottom of all side guides, using 3d nails.

109

Fig. 7

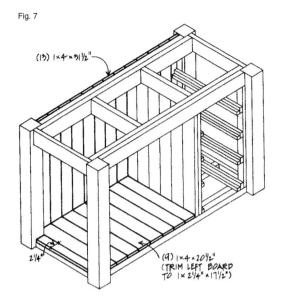

(13) 1×4×31½"

(9) 1×4×20½"
(TRIM LEFT BOARD
TO 1×2¼"×17½")

2¼"

13—Glue/nail thirteen 1x4s to back of workbench, using 6d nails.
Tip: Start at each end and adjust width of center board, if necessary.

Starting next to the partition on the left side of the drawer unit, apply nine 1x4s to the base. Rip last board to width and trim to fit between legs.

Fig. 8 Detail A

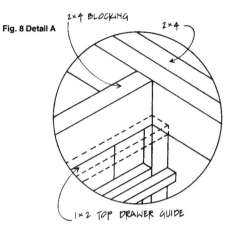

2×4 BLOCKING

2×4

1×2 TOP DRAWER GUIDE

Fig. 8 Detail B

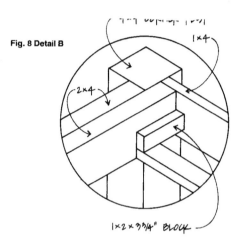

1×4

2×4

1×2×3¾" BLOCK

Fig. 8

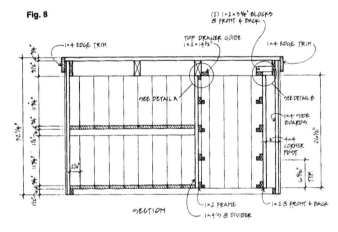

1×4 EDGE TRIM

TOP DRAWER GUIDE
1×2×14½"

(2) 1×2×3¾" BLOCKS
@ FRONT & BACK

1×4 EDGE TRIM

SEE DETAIL A

SEE DETAIL B

1×4 SIDE BOARDS

4×4 CORNER POST

52¼"

2¼"

SECTION

1×2 FRAME

1×4's @ DIVIDER

1×2 @ FRONT & BACK

26½"

6⅝" TOP

14—**Top drawer guide:** Cut two 1x2 drawer guides to length.
On the left side, position guide so bottom of guide is flush with bottom of 2x4 frame and blocking (Detail A.) Glue and toenail in place.
On right side, cut two 1x2 blocks, each 3¾". Glue/nail

blocks to each end of drawer guide, as illustrated in Detail B. Glue/nail block to frame, front and back, so bottom of guide is flush with bottom of 2x4 side frame and back of block butts 1x4 end frame. (See Fig. 9.) Blocking puts guide in line with drawer runners.

Fig. 9

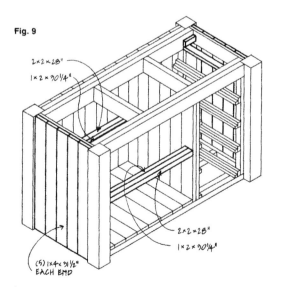

2×2×28"

1×2×30¼"

2×2×28"

1×2×30¼"

(5) 1×4×31½"
EACH END

15—Glue/nail five 1x4s to both ends of workbench, using 3d nails.

Fig. 10

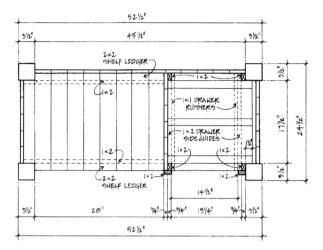

PLAN

16—Shelf ledgers: Cut two 2x2s, each 28". Glue/nail one to back of workbench, between 4x4 leg and partition, 11¾" above bottom shelf. Use 6d nails. (See Figs. 9 and 10.)
Tip: For ease of installation, cut two vertical spacing blocks, each 11¾" long.
17—Cut two 1x2s, each 30¼". Glue/nail one to front face of first ledger, overlapping 4x4 leg. Use 6d nails.

18—Using 11¾" spacing blocks, toenail second 28" ledger across front of opening, between leg and partition. Front of 2x2 is flush with front of partition; back is flush with back of 4x4 leg. Glue/nail second 30¼" ledger to back side of front ledger, overlapping 4x4 leg.

Fig. 11

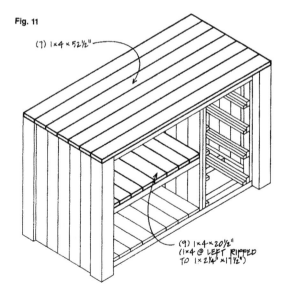

(7) 1x4 × 52½"

(9) 1x4 × 20½"
(1x4 @ LEFT RIPPED TO 1 2¼" × 17½")

19—Starting next to partition, glue/nail 1x4s to shelf ledgers. Notch last board for legs. (Last board may also require ripping.)

20—Top: Glue/nail seven 1x4s in place, using 6d nails.

Fig. 12

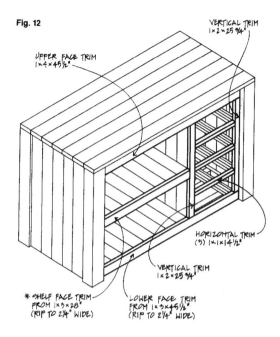

Fig. 12A

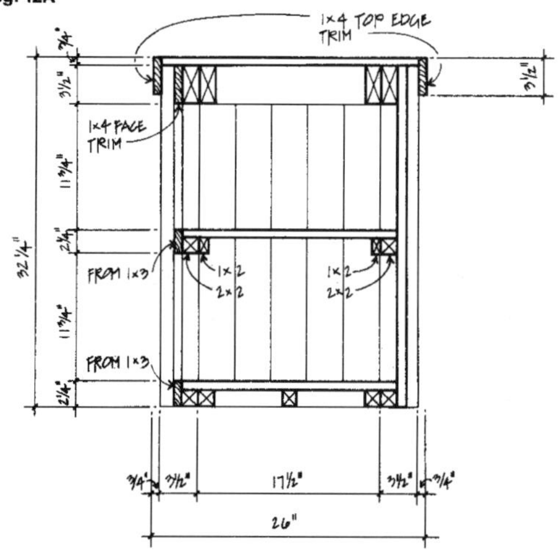

21—Top face trim: Attach 1x4 trim to face of 2x4 frame, between legs.
Lower face trim: Rip 1x3 to 2¼" wide; glue/nail flush with top of shelf.

Vertical trim: Glue/nail 1x2 to front edge of partition, flush left. Glue/nail second 1x2 to right side of drawer frame, flush with 4x4 leg on right.
Drawer trim: Glue/nail horizontal 1x1 trim to front edge of drawer runners.

Fig. 13

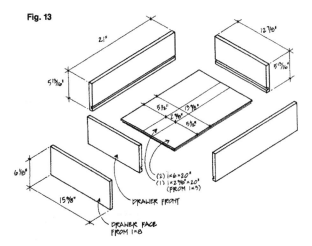

Solid Wood Drawer

The drawer described here, with the sturdy, solid wood bottom, is designed to handle heavy tools and years of hard use. However, if you prefer to build a simpler drawer, with a plywood bottom, see *Alternate Drawer Construction* section at the end of this Plan Sheet.

22—Cut drawer parts as follows:
Sides (from 1x8):
(8) 5¹³/₁₆″ x 21″
Fronts & Backs (from 1x8):
(8) 5¹³/₁₆″ x 12⅞″
Drawer bottom:
(8) 1x6, 20″
(4) 1x3, 20″
(Rip 1x3s to 2³/₈″)

Fig. 14

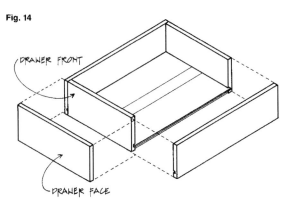

25—Apply glue to grooves in drawer front and back and insert drawer bottom. Glue side grooves and install drawer bottom, with sides overlapping front and back. Square sides and bottom and nail in place.

Fig. 13A   **Fig. 13B**

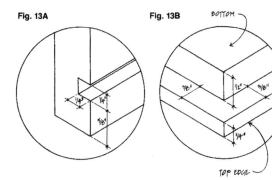

Cut 1/4″ x 1/4″ grooves in fronts, backs and sides, 5/8″ from bottom edge, as shown in Fig. 13A.
23—Drawer bottom: With 1x6s on outside and ripped board in center, edge glue and clamp bottom.

24—Rabbet bottom edge all around, producing a 1/4″ lip. (See Fig. 13B.)

Fig. 15

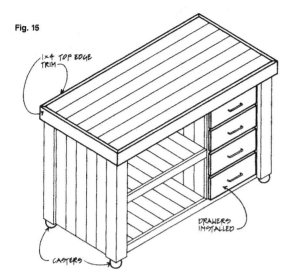

26—Cut four drawer faces from 1x8s, each 6⅛″ x15⅜.″ Drill for drawer pulls. Fasten to drawer fronts with glue and 3d nails, allowing ½″ overhang each side and 5/16″ at top.
27—Finish drilling holes, using pre-drilled face as a guide. Attach pulls.
Note: Some styles of drawer pulls may require a 1¾″ or longer machine screw in order to achieve a secure fastening.

28—**Edge trim:** Miter ends of 1x4s and nail flush to top at front, sides and back.

Attach locking swivel casters to the base of 4x4 legs according to manufacturer's instructions.

Fig. B

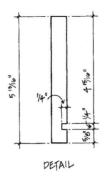

DETAIL

2—**Sides:** Cut ¼″ groove for drawer bottom, using dimensions shown in Fig. B.
NOTE: Two ¼″-deep cuts with a circular saw will produce the ¼″ groove. Mark cut lines as illustrated and set saw guide so blade is on the inside of the first cut line. Set saw depth to ¼″ and make the first cut. (Once guide is set, make the initial saw cuts in all drawer sides.)
Reset the guide so the blade is on the inside of the second cut line and make the second cut. Remove any remaining wood with a chisel.
If the joint is too tight, sand the edges of the plywood bottom to fit.

Fig. C

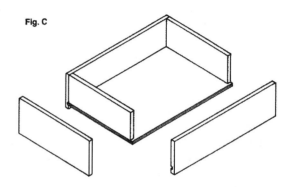

3—Apply glue to grooves and slide drawer bottom into position. Make sure sides are square and glue/nail drawer front and back in place, between sides. Use 4d nails.

4—Drill holes for drawer pulls in fascia. Apply glue to drawer front and fascia; from inside, nail front to fascia with 3d nails, allowing ½″ overhang each side and 5/16″ at top.
5—Finish drilling holes for drawer pulls, using fascia holes for guide.

ALTERNATE DRAWER CONSTRUCTION

While drawers with solid wood bottoms are extremely sturdy, they may prove difficult to construct unless you've mastered the technique of making dadoed and rabbeted joints. There is a simpler method,

described here, which uses a plywood bottom. By changing the dimensions, this version may be adapted to any drawer plan calling for an overlapping front fascia.

Fig. A Plywood-bottom drawer

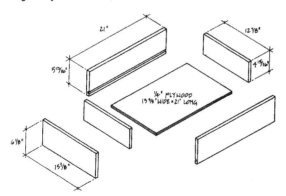

1—Cut drawer parts as follows:
Sides: (8) 5¹³/₁₆″ x21″
Front and back:
(8) 4¹⁵/₁₆″ x12⅞″

Bottom: (4) ¼″ plywood, 13⅜″ Wx21″ L
Drawer fascia: (4) 6⅛″ x15⅜″

Chapter 6
BASIC STORAGE

Simple basic storage generally starts with a nail driven part way into a wall stud upon which an extension cord is hung. In no time, it seems, garages and workshop areas soon become filled with things hanging from nails. Although quick and economical, this is not the best, safest nor most convenient method of providing auto workshop storage.

Fundamental workshop storage must be big enough to accommodate the things being stored and sufficiently sturdy to support those loads. Storage systems are available in many different models and materials. You will find a variety of storage systems at home improvement centers, hardware stores, some lumber yards and through mail order companies like The Eastwood Company and Harbor Freight Tools. Choose storage systems in plastic, metal or wood, depending upon the size needed and strength required.

Instead of purchasing ready to assemble storage units or systems, you may prefer to build your own out of wood. Custom made shelves or cabinets can be made to fit your workspace and the things you need to store. Should this be the option of choice, plan to use 3/4-inch material for shelves and cabinet structures. The most common materials are AC plywood, particle board or Melamine; each comes in 3/4-inch thick sheets that measure 4-feet by 8-feet. If you prefer to work with materials smaller than 4x8 sheets, consider solid pine or other boards that are available in 3/4-inch thick by 4 to 12-inch widths and in lengths from 4- to 12-feet. Lumber yards may carry some longer boards.

Plywood is graded by letters, with "A" being the most smooth and "D" having the most knots and defects. A plywood sheet graded AC means that one side (A) is very smooth and free of defects, while the other side (C) is less smooth and may have a few shallow knot holes. When working with AC plywood, plan to have the "A" side face up on shelves so things are easy to slide across them. For cabinet side panels, plan to have the "A" side face out to make the cabinet look its best. Particle board is heavy and requires a carbide tip saw blade for cutting. This material will

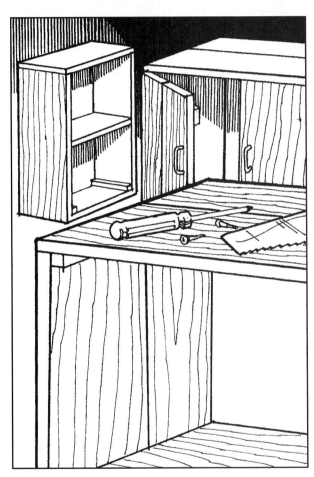

Basic workshop storage starts with simple boxes that are secured to or hung from walls to create cabinets and cupboards. This is a set of plans from the Western Wood Products Association for a system of Flexible Stackable Storage.

hold up well for lightweight storage as long as it never gets wet. Once a section of particle board gets wet, it will swell and when it dries it will most likely start to crumble apart. Plan to use plywood for shelves and cabinets unless you plan to cover a medium to high density particle board counter-

FLEXIBLE STACKABLE STORAGE

Storage units may be made any height or width. However, for ease of illustration, the units shown are all 30-7/8 inches wide and use "nominal" 1x8 lumber for the major components. (See actual sizes below.)

If you prefer a different size, it's best to base the module design on standard size lumber. It will save you time and money because you won't have to rip the boards (saw them lengthwise.)

Standard-size lumber: 1x4 (actual size, 3/4"x 3-1/2"); 1x6 (3/4"x 5-1/2"); 1x8 (3/4"x 7-1/4"); 1x10 (3/4"x 9-1/4").

DEEP MODULE

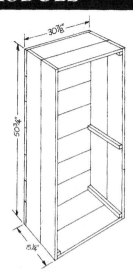

Size of units may be adapted to fit space.

Modules two or more boards deep may be constructed by tying boards together at the corners with 1x1 or 1x2 nailing cleats.

If unit is more than 48-inches high, add cleats at midpoint, as illustrated above, right.

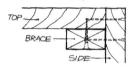

Assemble top and bottom of unit by installing nailing cleats at each end of boards. Secure with glue and two 1-1/4" nails or screws per cleat as illustrated above.

Glue/nail sides to top and bottom boards, offsetting nails slightly to avoid splitting the wood.

MATERIALS LIST FOR DEEP MODULE

Material for two or more basic rectangles plus boards for back

Nailing cleats:
(4) 1x2 or 1x1, 13¾" long
  (¾" square molding stock)
Yellow glue
1½" finishing nails for corners
1½" finishing nails for cleats
1¼" flathead screws

BASIC UNIT

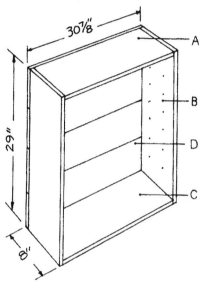

The basic modular unit starts with a square or rectangle of 1x8s (A, B, C). Apply a bead of carpenter's glue where boards meet at the corner and secure the joint with two 1-1/2 inch finishing nails or screws per board. Glue/nail back in place with two nails per board, each end. Countersink nails and fill for a more finished appearance.

For a more finished appearance, corner joints may be mitered, then assembled as above.

MATERIALS LIST FOR BASIC UNIT

A — **Top:** (1) 1x8, 29⅜" long
B — **Sides:** (2) 1x8, 29" long
C — **Bottom:** (1) 1x8, 29⅜" long
D — **Back:** (4) 1x8, 30⅞" long
Yellow Glue
1½" finishing nails or 1¼" screws

DOORS

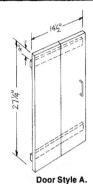

Door Style A.

Cut four lengths of 1x8s, each 27-1/4 inches long. Glue and screw 1x2 wood cleats to back of door, using four 1-1/4 inch screws per cleat. Position cleats 2 inches from top and bottom of door. If doors are more than 36 inches high, use three cleats per door.

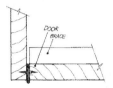

Mount two hinges on outside edge of door, 2 inches from upper and lower edges. Pre-drill holes for

screws to avoid splitting wood. If doors are more than 48 inches high, use three hinges per door.

To install doors, allow 1/8 inch clearance top and bottom. Clearance of 1/8 inch is also allowed along each side and between the doors (3/8 inch total). Be sure doors are flush with face of unit before setting screws.

Install purchased door pulls plus door catches top and bottom.

MATERIALS LIST FOR DOORS STYLE A
Door face: (4) 1x8, 27¼" long
Door cleats: (4) 1x2, 13⅝" long
Yellow glue
1¼" flathead screws
2 sets of hinges
Door pulls and catches

For other module sizes

Storage units with doors may be made any size. However, to avoid ripping boards lengthwise for door panels, it's best to plan your design using standard size lumber for the doors. (See standard lumber sizes, above.)

For example, to build a narrower unit, 1x6s may be used for the door panels (instead of 1x8s,) making the overall width of the storage module 24-1/4 inches (instead of 30-7/8). Greater widths may be achieved by using three lengths of lumber per door instead of two.

To determine width of finished unit, measure total width of doors and add 1-7/8 inches (1-1/2 inches

for sides of unit and 3/8 inches for door clearance.) To determine height of finished unit, add a total of 1-3/4 inches to height of doors.

If you've already decided what height and width you want the finished unit to be, it's easy to calculate the size of the doors:

Height After establishing height of finished unit, subtract 1-3/4 inches. (This allows 1-1/2 inches for top and bottom of unit and 1/4 inch for door clearance.)

Width Determine width of finished unit and subtract 1-7/8 inches (1-1/2 inches for sides plus 3/8 inch clearance.)

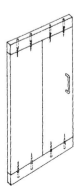

Door Style B

A different look may be achieved by finishing the top and bottom of door with 1x2s, as shown. (Wood cleats are eliminated.) Countersink 1 inch and predrill for 1-1/4 inch wood screws or use 2-1/4 inch self-threading type of screw.

MATERIALS LIST FOR DOORS STYLE B
Door face: (4) 1x8, 25¾" long
Door band: (4) 1x2, 14½" long
Yellow glue
1¼" flathead screws, or
2¼" self threading screws

Desk Unit

A handy desk or hinged shelf may be constructed by installing Door Style B on the basic module, as shown. Attach hinges on the bottom edge of door and to the inside of the module.

Purchase drop leaf table supports or use two lengths of chain to support door when in the open position. Install purchased door pull and door catches.

MATERIALS LIST FOR DESK UNIT
Basic Unit
Door Style B
1 set of hinges
Drop leaf table supports
Door pull and door catches

Any of the Western softwood species may be used for these projects. For maximum economy, choose common grade boards such as #3 or #2 & Better, Common. Most units illustrated in this Plan Sheet are designed to be cut from 8-foot stock for minimum waste. In order to minimize shrinking and swelling, make sure the lumber you buy has been properly seasoned, then store it for a week to ten days in the room where it will be used.

top with a plastic laminate, like Formica. Melamine is a particle board that has already been covered with a plastic laminate. Many clothes closet storage systems use Melamine exclusively. It is strong and easy to clean. In addition, you can buy thin rolls of plastic laminate that are attached to the bare edges of Melamine boards with a regular clothes iron. These strips are used to finish the appearance of Melamine boards that are cut from full 4x8 sheets to fit shelves, cabinets, or counters.

When working with solid wood, plywood, particle board or Melamine, plan to use wood glue and drywall screws to secure panels together. Although nails will work fine in most cases, drywall screws will provide stronger and more permanent joint connections.

Floor Level Counters

Much the same as a workbench, floor level counters offer loads of storage space under worktops. Counters do not have to be big. In fact, you can build them from 12 to 24-inches deep to fit along garage side walls. At narrow depths, counters provide secure storage and small worktops for jobs that do not require much workspace. A narrow countertop will also make an ideal spot to place supplies upon while preparing to store them inside upper cabinets.

SHELVES

For a simple shelf support, glue/nail 1x1 or 1x2 cleats to inside of units. Or purchase shelf clips from your lumber dealer or hardware store.

Shelves are 29-3/8" long.

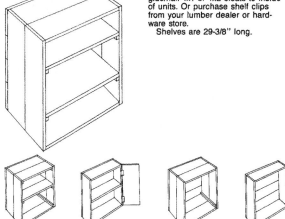

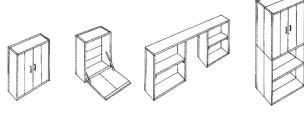

In addition to the previous plans, you can also build similar units using 3/4-inch AC plywood. These are two units from Brian Lord's garage/workshop. They are supported on top of a 2x4 base and feature 3/4-inch AC plywood for the top, bottom, sides and shelves. Rails and stiles were made from clear Douglas fir and the doors are birch hardwood plywood. The units will be positioned against the wall behind, shimmed level and secured to wall studs with 3-inch drywall screws.

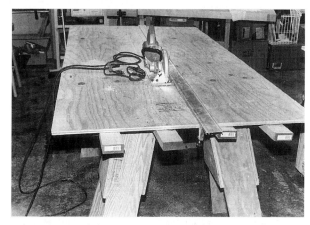

Instead of a super table saw set up, cutting full sheets of plywood is easiest and safest when done on top of sawhorses and 2x4s. Notice that this plywood sheet rests on top of four 8-foot 2x4s; two on each side of the lengthwise cut. A saw guide is secured in position to ensure a straight cut. When the cut is complete, both sides of the plywood will remain equally supported on top of their own two 2x4s. Note that the good "A" side of this 3/4-inch AC plywood sheet faces down. This will result in a clean cut on the good side because saw blade teeth will cut through the good side first and then rip out of the other side causing slight splintering.

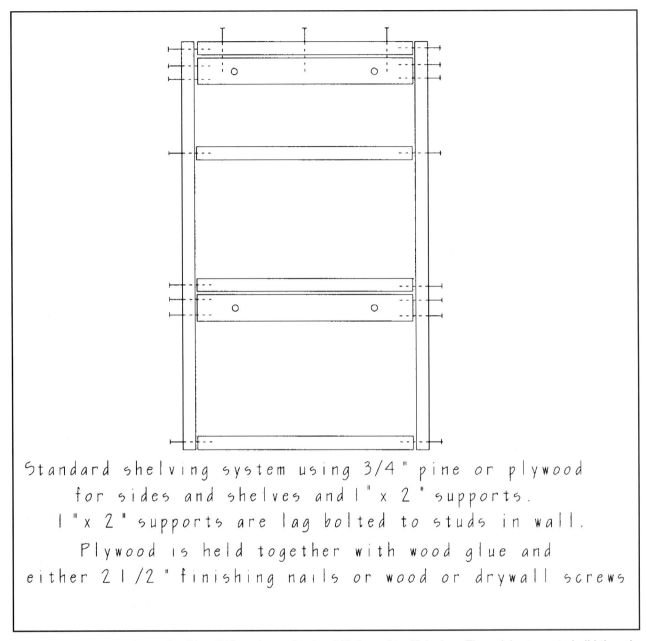

Standard shelving system using 3/4" pine or plywood
for sides and shelves and 1" x 2" supports.
1" x 2" supports are lag bolted to studs in wall.
Plywood is held together with wood glue and
either 2 1/2" finishing nails or wood or drywall screws

Simple shelf units may be made with solid boards ranging in width from 4 to 12 inches. The quickest way to build them is to just glue and nail shelves to side panels. Use clamps to hold 1x2-inch cleats while they are nailed in place. Plan to use 3/4-inch wood and 2 1/2 to 3-inch finishing nails. Shelves should be no longer than 36 inches to prevent sagging.

Counters can be made to any comfortable height. Doors may be made to swing out on hinges or slide back and forth on guides, like clothes closet doors. Sliding counter doors may be best for small workshops, as you will be able to gain access to counter storage while a car or pickup truck is parked alongside. Sliding counter doors will always result in at least half of the storage area being closed off at any one time. On the other hand, hinged doors may not have enough room to open when a vehicle is parked in the workspace.

Of greatest importance for counters is the toe-kick space. This is the area at the base of the counter where your feet will be while working at the counter-top. Counters built flush along the front from the top down to the floor make it most uncomfortable while standing and working at them. Equipped with a 3-1/2-inch high by 4-inch deep toe-kick at the floor level, room is made for a person's feet while standing at the counter. This small attribute is worth its weight in gold and must be factored into any counter you intend to build. Counters are generally built on top of

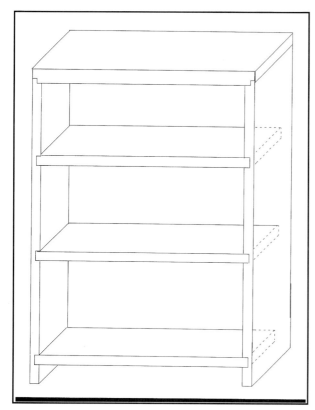
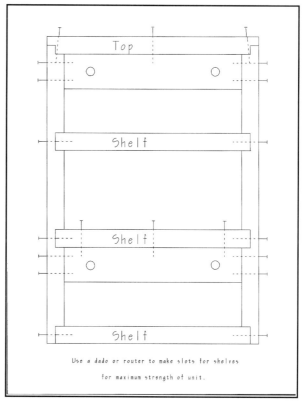

Use a dado or router to make slots for shelves
for maximum strength of unit.

For maximum strength and stability, build shelf and cupboard units with dadoes cut for the shelves and rabbets for the top. This system of interlocking shelves and panels through dadoes and rabbets, along with wood glue and nails or screws, will result in heavy duty storage accessories capable of supporting almost anything. If each shelf and the top will be required to support heavy loads, place a cleat under each one and secure all the cleats to wall studs with 3-inch drywall screws

a 2x4 frame. This framing is the part that actually rests on the floor. In cases where you may want to occasionally wash down the workshop floor with water from a garden hose, you should consider placing the counter on top of a layer of roofing felt or asphalt shingle material. This will keep the 2x4 framing off the floor to prevent moisture from wicking its way into the wood. In addition, you should install plastic cove molding along the base of the counter to help keep water from creeping under the counter unit.

Wall mounted storage units

Almost any kind of storage unit can be mounted to a garage or workshop wall. It is imperative that lag bolts and other fasteners be driven into wall studs to maximize support and ensure units will not pull away from walls when loaded with tools, materials or supplies. In basements with concrete or block walls, storage units are secured to walls using special fasteners designed for such applications. Most require holes that are bored into the concrete or block wall first. Special threaded inserts are then tapped into the holes. Bolts are fed through holes in the storage unit cleats and screwed into the inserts.

Placement of wall mounted storage units is important. Since they will stick out from the wall from 9 to possibly 24 inches, you must be certain they will not interfere with other workshop activities. In addition, be sure that wall mounted storage units are positioned in such a way that the bottoms do not become a head bumping hazard. In a one-car garage for example, design side wall mounted storage units so that the bottoms are more than 6-feet off the floor. This way, you can walk and work under them without fear of bumping your head.

Open Shelves

A host of shelf brackets in all sorts of designs are available at home improvement centers and hardware stores. Most are very easy to install. Use 3/4-inch thick wood, plywood, particle board or Melamine for shelves. Brackets should be spaced no more than 32 inches apart for most applications. If you plan to store heavy objects on shelves, install brackets no more than 16 inches apart; the distance between normal wood framed wall studs. In unfinished garages with open studs, you can build shelf brackets out of plywood and nail or screw them to the studs. Notch out sections of the shelves so they slide over studs to make for a full fit. Open shelves

Automobiles parked in garages or workshops after being driven in rain or snow will cause water to drip and puddle on garage or workshop floors. To help prevent water from wicking its way up wood counters and floor cabinets, cover their bottom edges with glue-on plastic cove molding. This material is available in rolls. Special pieces are made for outside corners, as shown here.

These workbenches and storage units were constructed with materials from the Simpson Strong-Tie Connector Company. The extensive use of Simpson connectors makes jobs like this quick and easy. Storage is neat and orderly and the workbenches are capable of supporting large amounts of weight and rugged abuse.

provide good storage and make it easy to locate the things stored on them. However, being out in the open makes those things stored on shelves susceptible to the accumulation of dust and other airborne debris created in the workshop. If you anticipate creating large amounts of dust and airborne debris, you should consider cabinets and cupboards rather than open shelves.

Cupboards and Cabinets

Generally, cupboards are narrow cabinets 4 to 12-inches deep located on the upper parts of walls. Cabinets, on the other hand, are mostly deeper than 12 inches and rest on the floor or take up space along the lower parts of walls. Both cupboards and cabinets offer secure storage and protect objects inside from dust and other debris. Cabinets will also do a much better job of keeping things inside and on shelves when bumped by tools or large auto parts.

Cupboards and cabinets are fundamentally boxes mounted on walls or set on floors and equipped with doors. You can build them out of solid wood, plywood or Melamine. The difference between a simple shelf unit built with sides and a cupboard or cabinet is that the cupboard and cabinet will have a face frame of rails and stiles attached to the front edges of the top, bottom and side walls. The rails and stiles dress up the front of the unit and provide solid wood to which door hinges are secured. To best envision this system of rails and stiles, look at your home's kitchen cabinets. (6-19)

Workshop cupboard and cabinet doors may be made from 3/4-inch AC plywood, although birch or another hardwood plywood will take paint and stain much better than general grade plywood. Cut doors 1/2 to 5/8 inch longer and wider than the openings and rabbet the edges with a 3/8-inch router bit. This way, the doors will close into their openings and the lip created

by the rabbet edge will help to keep dust and debris out of the storage space. You will need to use door hinges designed for 3/8-inch rabbeted doors. You could make cupboard or cabinet doors out of Melamine, especially if the rest of the unit is made from that material. With Melamine, you will not be able to rabbet door edges and should use European hinges for the doors. European hinges require a shallow hole be drilled in the doors for the base of hinges to fit into. These types of hinges are very strong and perfect for doors made with Melamine or particle board.

Pegboard

Pegboard works very well for all kinds of light-weight storage needs, especially in small workshops where maneuvering room is at a premium. In tight workshops, consider installing shelves or cupboards high on the wall and filling in the space underneath with pegboard. This arrangement will offer you a convenient storage system without taking up much working room.

Many auto enthusiasts prefer to paint pegboard in red, white or other hues. This helps to dress up their shop area and make it look tidy, crisp and bright. Use a felt tip marker to outline the items stored on pegboard to make it easier to return things to their proper places.

In some cases, auto workshops are enhanced with pegboard panels placed between shop stalls. Use 1x4 or 2x2 lumber to build a frame and then cover each side with pegboard. Suspend the panel from ceiling joists with heavy-duty hooks. Then secure it to the floor with turnbuckles or heavy chain. Outfit each side of the pegboard panel with the tools and accessories needed for whatever type of work is conducted in the related stalls.

SHELVES

These easy-to-build shelves will help you to get organized. The sizes shown here are standard but can be customized to meet your particular needs. They can be easily finished with paint to match the decor of your home. These shelves are ideal for the garage, basement, office or playroom. For heavy-duty requirements, use the 2x4 shelving materials for either the 4' or 8' long versions.

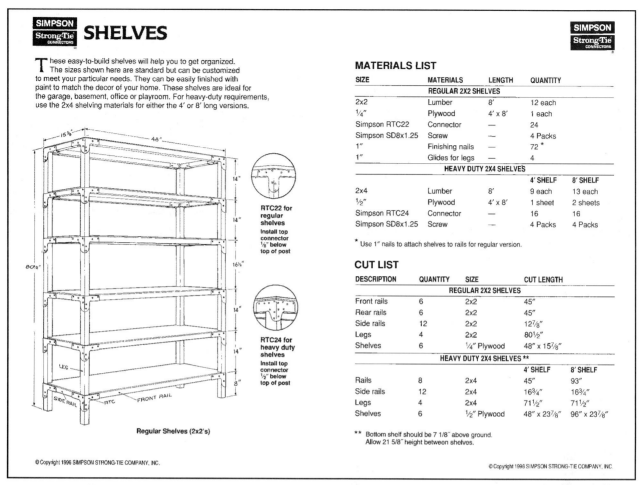

RTC22 for regular shelves
Install top connector ⅛" below top of post

RTC24 for heavy duty shelves
Install top connector ½" below top of post

Regular Shelves (2x2's)

MATERIALS LIST

SIZE	MATERIALS	LENGTH	QUANTITY	
REGULAR 2X2 SHELVES				
2x2	Lumber	8'	12 each	
¼"	Plywood	4' x 8'	1 each	
Simpson RTC22	Connector	—	24	
Simpson SD8x1.25	Screw	—	4 Packs	
1"	Finishing nails	—	72 *	
1"	Glides for legs	—	4	
HEAVY DUTY 2X4 SHELVES				
			4' SHELF	8' SHELF
2x4	Lumber	8'	9 each	13 each
½"	Plywood	4' x 8'	1 sheet	2 sheets
Simpson RTC24	Connector	—	16	16
Simpson SD8x1.25	Screw	—	4 Packs	4 Packs

* Use 1" nails to attach shelves to rails for regular version.

CUT LIST

DESCRIPTION	QUANTITY	SIZE	CUT LENGTH	
REGULAR 2X2 SHELVES				
Front rails	6	2x2	45"	
Rear rails	6	2x2	45"	
Side rails	12	2x2	12⅞"	
Legs	4	2x2	80½"	
Shelves	6	¼" Plywood	48" x 15⅞"	
HEAVY DUTY 2X4 SHELVES **				
			4' SHELF	8' SHELF
Rails	8	2x4	45"	93"
Side rails	12	2x4	16¾"	16¾"
Legs	4	2x4	71½"	71½"
Shelves	6	½" Plywood	48" x 23⅞"	96" x 23⅞"

** Bottom shelf should be 7 1/8" above ground. Allow 21 5/8" height between shelves.

The Simpson Strong-Tie Connector plans, materials list and cut list make building quality storage units quick and simple.

Pegboard can be placed on walls, between workshop stalls, on the inside of cabinet or cupboard doors, from other doors and on the sides of workbenches or mobile carts. 1/4-inch pegboard is recommended and you have to ensure pegboard rests at least 1/4 inch away from walls and doors to make room for inserting the hooks. If you have had bad luck using pegboard in the past because hooks seemed to fall off the board each time you retrieved a tool, try using the newly developed Sta-Put Color Pegs. These handy hooks are equipped with an extra part that snaps into pegboard holes and prevents them from ever coming loose unless you physically grab on and pull them out.

This cabinet was made according to plans provided by the Simpson Strong-Tie Connector Company. Equipped with door locks, a unit like this would be ideal for the secure storage of expensive tools.

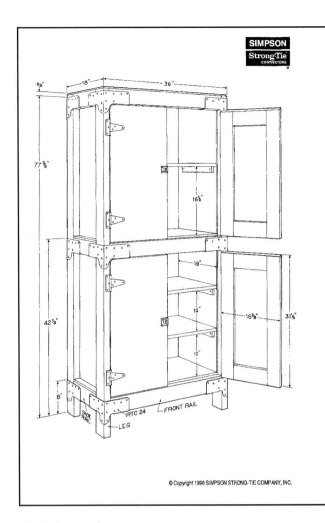

© Copyright 1996 SIMPSON STRONG-TIE COMPANY, INC.

 **CABINET**

MATERIALS LIST

SIZE	MATERIALS	LENGTH	QUANTITY
2x4	Lumber	8'	7 each
1x4	Lumber	8'	4 each
1x2	Lumber	8'	1 each
3/8"	Plywood	4' x 8'	2 each
1/2"	Plywood	4' x 8'	1 each
1/4"	Hardboard	4' x 8'	1 each
Simpson RTC24	Connector	—	12
Simpson SD8x1.25	Screw	—	2 Packs
2"	Finishing nails	—	40
1"	Glides for legs	—	4
4"	T-hinges	—	8
3"	Barrel bolt	—	2
4"	Door handles or hasps	—	4
	Wood glue	—	1 tube

CUT LIST

DESCRIPTION	QUANTITY	SIZE	CUT LENGTH
Legs	4	2x4	78"
Front & back rails	6	2x4	33"
Side rails	6	2x4	11¼"
Door frames (vertical)	8	1x4	31¼"
Door frames (horizontal)	8	1x4	9¼"
Doors *	4	3/8" Plywood	16⅜" x 31⅛"
Side panels **	4	3/8" Plywood	16⅜" x 31⅛"
Cabinet top	1	3/8" Plywood	18" x 36"
Cabinet floors ***	2	1/2" Plywood	17" x 36"
Shelf supports	6	1x2	14"
Shelves	3	1/2" Plywood	16" x 32¼"
Backing	2	1/4" Hardboard	34⅛" x 33⅞"

* Measure door openings after frame is built. See installation tips, page 26.
** Notch top corners so panel does not cover inside of RTC's.
*** Notch corners for pass-through of 2x4 legs.

© Copyright 1996 SIMPSON STRONG-TIE COMPANY, INC.

Attic Space Storage

Most garages and workshops offer plenty of open space in the attic or area of the roof above the workspace. Roof assemblies are built with separate rafters or installed as part of a truss system. With either, you must understand that this area is not generally designed to support a great amount of storage weight. Rafters and trusses are designed to support roofs and the materials that make up outer roof systems. Lower members are built into the roofing system to support the top of the roof. Therefore, you must be keep in mind that too much storage along the bottom of rafter or truss systems could cause entire roof assemblies to collapse.

Sometimes, lower roofing members can be beefed up to support some auto workspace storage. This reinforcing may entail the installation of wider joist members that span across garage or workshop spaces or the construction of a Glu-Lam and post support system. In any case, it is highly recommended that you contact a truss or roofing engineer to determine just what is needed to enhance your workshop's attic space so that it can handle the amount of storage you would like to put in there.

A truss engineer can easily determine how much

 **CABINET**

This attractive cabinet unit has shelves for handy storage and organization. The doors allow for a neat appearance and security if necessary. The number and height of shelves can be adjusted to meet your particular requirements.

Installation Tips:

1. Assemble cabinet frame with 2x4's and RTC24s.
2. Check the squareness of frame.
3. Install top and floors with two finishing nails.
4. Install side panels from the inside with SD8x1.25 screws. Notch top of side panels to avoid interference with inside of RTC connector.
5. Measure the door openings, leaving ⅛" space around the doors for a proper fit.
6. Use a sander around the upper outside door corners to conform with the RTC24.
7. Fasten hinges to doors, attach doors to cabinet, and install barrel bolts and door handles or hasps.
8. In the interior, fasten shelf supports. Glue shelves to the supports or leave loose for adjustable shelving.

See page 28 for Cabinet Materials and Cut Lists.

These plans from the Simpson Strong-Tie Connector Company will help you build quality storage cabinets.

Most home based garages and workshops will eventually become home to many household items. Be forewarned and plan for this dilemma. Ron Hoffer has made good use of two 1/4inch pegboard sheets by securing them high on a wall and outfitting them with enough pegboard hooks to support most all of his landscaping tools and a few other things.

1x6 clear Douglas fir boards were cut to 1 1/4-inch and 2 1/4-inch widths. Each was then run through a jointer to mill them down to 1-inch and 2-inch widths respectively and to ensure the edges were perfectly flat. The 1-inch wide boards were used for outer perimeter rails and stiles and shelf edge faces. The 2-inch boards were used for the center stiles that will separate doors on each side. Another section was milled to a 3/4-inch width for the bottom panel face. Nails were countersunk and the resulting holes filled with wood putty.

The rabbeted edges on this counter door help to protect the inner space from the accumulation of workshop dust and other debris. When planning to install rabbeted doors, be certain to cut doors 1/2 to 5/8 inch longer and wider than door openings. This allows the door lip to shut against the rails and stiles, while the other part of the door fits inside the opening.

weight the lower members of a roof system are capable of supporting. They have access to charts and graphs that explain what loads specific sizes of lumber and truss designs can handle. Once they have all the information, they can design a support system that will allow you to make a viable storage space out of the otherwise wasted space above your workshop area. Plans should also include a solid floor made of 1/2- or 3/4-inch plywood or 1x4 boards.

Realistic Attic Storage

Thoughts of having abundant storage in an attic space must be combined with logistical reality. Do you really think you can fit fenders and quarter panels in the attic? How big is the attic opening? How easy will it be to get parts up and down from that space? How will you be able to see what is stored in there? Before storing anything in your beefed up attic space, be sure to install lights.

During a full blown auto restoration, you will have boxes and boxes of parts to store. These will most likely be filled with small assemblies. Package each related assembly in a separate box and be certain to label them clearly. Be realistic with the big parts. Can you really get a fender into the attic

access opening? How much weight can you actually carry up a ladder? If it takes two or three people to get a heavy part into the attic, it will most certainly take that many to get the part out. Do you want to rely upon getting help when you want to retrieve that heavy part or would you rather have the independence of knowing you can retrieve parts whenever you want?

Save attic storage for those parts and boxes of stuff you can safely handle by yourself. Plan a storage system so you can quickly find the things you want when you need them. Interior parts in one corner; engine accessory parts in another; trim in another, etc.

Chapter 7
CREATIVE STORAGE

The need for additional storage increases as automotive endeavors become more complicated. At this point, auto enthusiasts have to take a closer look at their work areas to find new storage space.

Locating Space

Stand in the middle of your workspace and look around. Are there clear wall areas that may support a set of shelves or a narrow cupboard? Space on upper walls near ceilings may serve well for storing things needed only occasionally. The inconvenience of having to use a ladder may be offset by the benefits of clearing out other more usable storage or work spaces.

Are some storage spots awkwardly filled with oddly shaped tools or other things that result in empty areas? If so, you should try to rearrange things so spaces are filled and storage is more compact. You may need to move oddly shaped tools to different locations or remove seldom used handles or projecting parts.

Tool boxes make excellent storage units for groups of related items. You might improve your workshop's overall storage by using different storage boxes to group tools together, like spray painting tools and supplies, bodywork dollies and hammers, etc. Label and stack boxes to take maximum advantage of shelf and cabinet space.

Large storage areas under workbenches are great, but are you actually using this space? Maybe you could rearrange things a bit differently and install a short shelf on one side or back of the space for storing smaller supplies, like spray paint cans, cans of oil, filters, etc.

Organized workshop storage takes advantage of every square inch of open space. It also requires thoughtful placement of items so they are easy to recognize and retrieve. Use a wide felt pen to mark the contents of storage boxes. Store related items close to each other, like the box of spray painting tools next to the box of bodywork tools.

Do the same for supplies. Every workshop has an inventory of fresh motor oil, auto filters, lubricating grease, tune up parts, spare light bulbs, auto polish and wax, shop towels, etc. Designate a particular locker or cabinet for just these types of materials. If you wish, make up an inventory sheet for each shelf

with minimum and maximum supply amounts listed. Using this method, you can quickly determine which supplies are running low. Simply reorganizing cabinet shelf space so all the tall items are on the bottom and the shorter ones toward the top can be useful. Adjusting things this way may even make room for a new shelf.

Above Garage Doors

An often overlooked storage space is the area just above garage door openings. Depending upon the ceiling height and the configuration of the garage door, you may be able to install a wide shelf above the opening. Secure a ledger board across the top of the opening, run 2x4s down from the ceiling joists or rafters and join those with 2x4 cross members to support a 3/4-inch plywood shelf. This will make an ideal spot for storing all kinds of things.

Home garages set up as auto workshops are not always immune from the effects of typical family storage. You may have camping gear, outdoor summer furniture and other things that could easily fit above the garage door. Other household items may also have to be stored in home garages, such as garden and landscaping tools, bicycles, sporting goods, etc. If the space above your garage door opening is limited, perhaps you can install sections of 3 or 4-inch plastic pipe against the ceiling to hold long-handled tools like shovels and rakes. Simply determine the spacing of ceiling joists or rafters and drill 3/4-inch holes in one side of the pipe at those measurements; drill smaller holes opposite the large ones. The big holes provide access for a screwdriver that will be used to drive screws through the little holes and into the joists or rafters. Hang bicycles from sturdy hooks secured to ceiling joists or rafters. Perhaps one entire wall of the garage could be designated for just family storage and the rest for automotive storage. Keeping family and automotive storage separate works out best for everyone.

Between Ceiling Joists

Many home designs feature bedrooms built above attached garages. These floor plans eliminate all attic space above garages and the storage space that the area could have provided. However, you may be able to take advantage of some of the space

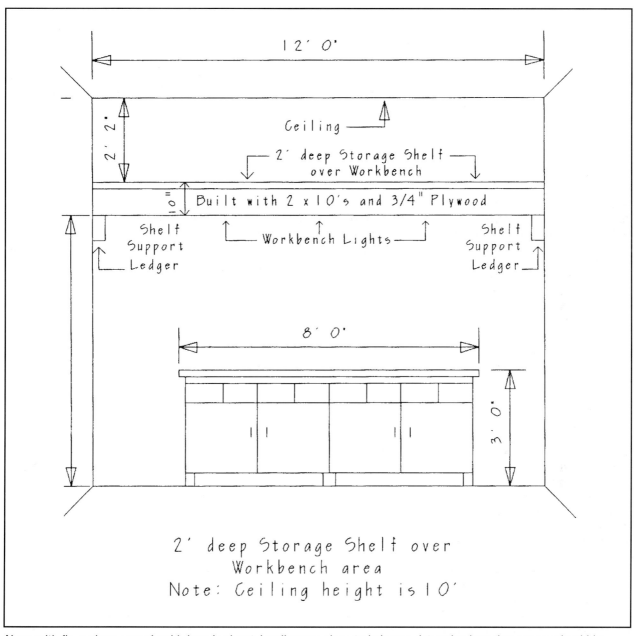

2' deep Storage Shelf over
Workbench area
Note: Ceiling height is 10'

Along with floor plans, you should draw horizontal wall space plans to help you determine how these areas should be outfitted. Consider installing a heavy duty rack above workbench areas for the storage of large auto parts and assemblies. Here, a 10-foot ceiling makes room for a large storage rack above a workbench area.

between the garage's ceiling joists. This opportunity also exists in basement workshops.

In most cases, garage and basement ceiling joists consist of 2x10 or larger dimension lumber. In reality, 2x10 boards measure 1 1/2 inches by 9 1/4 inches. Truss joists, a newer style of prefabricated joists, will measure 1 1/2 inches by 9 1/2 inches. Spaced at 12 to 16 inches apart, the area between joists may offer storage room for numerous lightweight items.

Keep in mind that, heating ducts, electrical wires, plumbing pipes and other utility lines or parts may

be located between some ceiling joists. Scout the locations of these things by determining where bathrooms and heat registers are arranged upstairs. Take measurements from an outside wall that is common to both the upstairs living areas and the garage or basement to the bathrooms and heat registers above. This should help you estimate where pipes and ducts are located between the garage and basement ceiling joists and hidden by the ceiling's drywall cover.

Once you have determined where the openings between ceiling joists should be clear, carefully

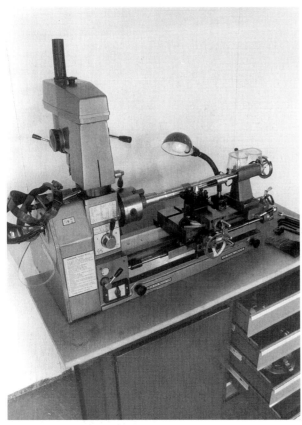

The Smithy is a lathe, mill, drill all wrapped up in one piece of equipment. Instead of a simple table or workbench, this unit is mounted on top of a combination tool chest and cabinet. This arrangement works very well, as all the accessories and tools used with the Smithy are conveniently stored within easy reach. A similar set up may prove useful for other benchtop units; like sandblast cabinets, drill presses and so on.

To make the doors, Saydan made frames using 1x4 boards. Each joint is secured with a plywood gusset. 1/4-inch paneling was then nailed to the frame and the door hinged on one of the closet's studs. The doors do an excellent job of hiding all the stuff in the closet but because of their lightweight construction should not be expected to provide much security.

remove drywall from the garage or basement ceiling. Wear safety goggles and a dust mask for protection against the abundant amount of drywall dust and debris that will be created by its removal. In addition, you must be extremely careful to avoid cutting into any electrical wires! To ensure your safety, cut the power to all electrical lines at the main circuit breaker(s) at the electrical service panel.

The job of removing drywall will be messy, so be prepared. You will also have to arrange to haul off the old drywall. Satisfied that you have opened up all the joist spaces you desire for storage, begin the task of cleaning up before going any further. This will help to clear the atmosphere of drywall dust and remove the tripping hazards created by piles of old drywall stashed around the workspace.

Home living spaces must be separated from attached garages and basement workshops by 5/8-inch drywall secured to the common walls and ceiling or floor. This is a fire safety requirement found in the Building and Fire Codes. Therefore, each open

storage space between joists must be lined with 5/8-inch drywall on the sides and top. Drywall mud must be applied over nail or screw heads and each seam must be coated with drywall mud and tape. Finish the process with coats of primer and paint.

Open joist spaces may be outfitted with boxes that are hinged at one end and secured at the other with hooks or hasps. Boxes can then be filled with lightweight objects for storage. Instead of boxes, install 2x4 boards, closet dowels or pipe across the bottoms of the openings to support fishing poles, long handled landscaping tools, auto trim and so on. Carefully calculate the spacing between bottom braces to ensure you have enough room to get storage objects in and out of the space. For maximum support and convenience, consider using clothes closet dowels and the brackets designed for them. One bracket will fully encircle the end of a dowel while the other features an open space at the top so dowels are easily lifted up for removal.

This is a set of plans from the Western Wood Products Association that explains how to build a modular storage system. Units like this may prove most valuable for those auto enthusiasts who must share workshop space with other family members and their household storage needs.

EASY WEEKEND PROJECT

The modular storage unit shown here is easy to adjust to whatever length and height you need. 1 x 6 boards are spaced 1 inch apart over 2 x 4 supports. The 1-inch slots let you insert shelves, drawers or bins as needed. When additional storage space is required, the units can be expanded by simply adding another upright or two.

It's portable

Uprights slip into 1 x 4 retainers on the ceiling and floor. No nails required. So if you decide to move, just pack up the parts and take them along.

Modular Storage Unit
Fig. 1

27³/₄" wide x 22" deep x 93" high (or height of ceiling)

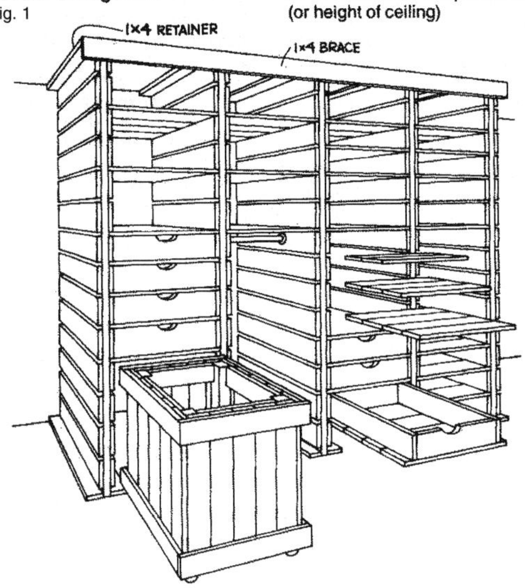

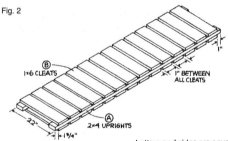

4—Nail two 1 x 4 retainers (C) to ceiling joists. (Fig. 3) Toggle bolts may be used if ceiling is drywalled. Space retainers 1¹/₂" apart, making sure they're parallel. Install second set of retainers on the ceiling, parallel to the first, 25¹/₂" on center. Continue to add retainers as needed, 25¹/₂" on center.

5—Slip 2 x 4 uprights of one module between the retainers. Using a level, make certain module is plumb, then install second set of retainers on floor. (Fig 3) Use 8d nails if floor is wood; use concrete nails and/or adhesive if floor is concrete. Repeat with additional modules.

6—For added stability, nail a continuous 1 x 4 brace to front of modules, flush with ceiling. (See Fig. 1.) Use glue and (2) 6d or 8d nails at each upright.

7—Cut 1 x 6 lumber 23³/₄" long for shelving (D). Slip boards into the slots to form shelf. You can use up to four boards per slot, depending on the depth of shelf you need.

Fig. 3

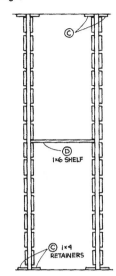

Materials List for Modules

(Material required for one shelving module, 27¾" wide)
(A) Uprights: (4) 2 x 4, 93" (or wall height)
(B) Cleats: (56) 1 x 6, 22"
(C) Retainers: (8) 1 x 4, 22"

(D) Shelves: (1-4 per shelf) 1 x 6, 23¾"
Front brace: (1) 1 x 4, cut to total width of modules
Nails: 4d, 6d and 8d nails
Yellow glue

MODULES / SHELVING

Fig. 2

1—Measure height from floor to ceiling and cut 2 x 4 uprights (A) to length. (For ease of installation, trim 1/4" off upright length.) Cut 1 x 6 cleats (B) to length (22").

2—Lay the 2 x 4s on the floor (Fig. 2), with outside edges spaced 22" apart. Glue/nail the first 1 x 6 cleat to the 2 x 4 uprights, positioning it 1³/₄" from the bottom. Make certain bottom and sides are square and fasten with (3) 4d (1¹/₂") nails at each end.

3—Glue/nail remaining cleats to one side, allowing a 1" space between cleats, keeping sides and cleats square. Position top cleat so it is 1" down from the top of 2 x 4 uprights. Turn the unit over and add cleats to other side. (Fig. 2)

TIP—A 1-inch wide board used as a spacer will speed installation and ensure accuracy.

DRAWERS

Fig. 4

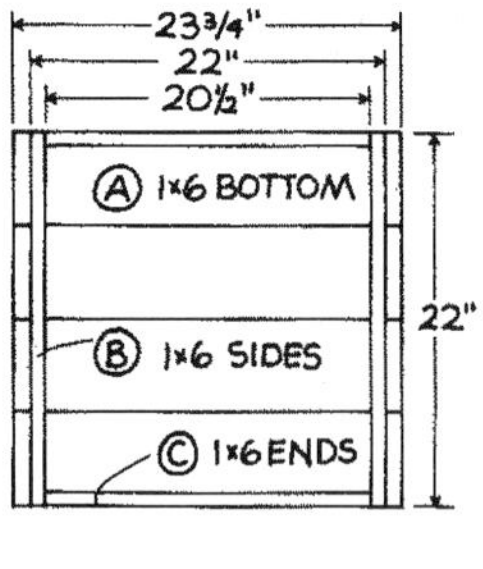

Fig. 5

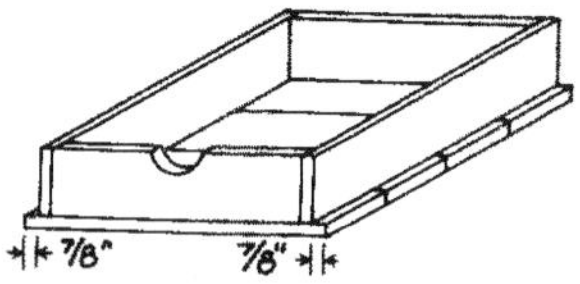

1—Cut 1 x 6 sides (B) and ends (C) to length. Glue/nail corners to form a square. (Fig. 4) Center four 23³/₄ shelf boards over the square, overhanging drawer frame 7/8" on each side. (Fig. 5) Glue/nail in place, using 6d nails. Cut handhold in front, or install drawer pull. Use additional 1 x 6 lumber to create drawer dividers.

2—Slip drawer into the slots between cleats. Shelf boards act as drawer runners. Waxing runners will help drawers slide easily.

3—For deeper drawers, use 1 x 8, 1 x 10 or 1 x 12 lumber for sides, instead of 1 x 6s.

Materials List for Drawer

(A) Bottom: (4) 1 x 6, 23³/₄
(B) Sides: (2) 1 x 6, 22"
(C) Ends: (2) 1 x 6, 20¹/₂"
Nails: 6d common
Yellow glue

BIN

Fig. 6

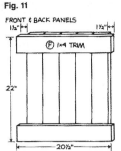

20½" wide x 19" deep x 22" high (plus casters)

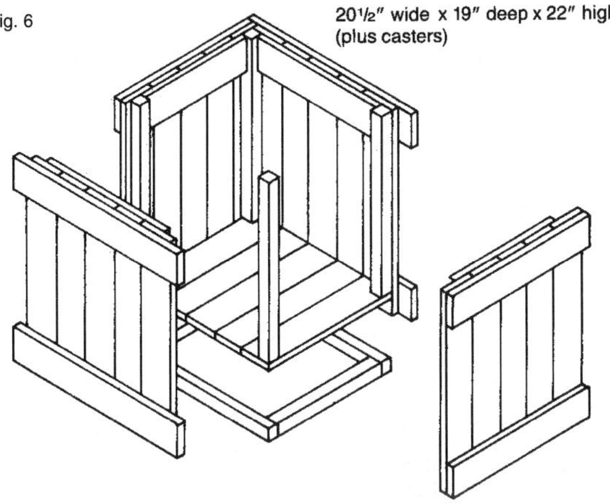

Fig. 7

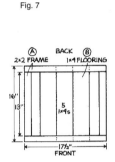

Ⓐ BACK Ⓑ
2×2 FRAME   1×4 FLOORING
16"
13"   5
          1×4s
17½"
FRONT

Fig. 8

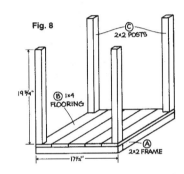

Ⓒ
2×2 POSTS
19¾"
Ⓑ 1×4
FLOORING
Ⓐ
2×2 FRAME
17½"

1—Base: Glue/nail 2 x 2 frame (A) together, using (2) 8d (2½") nails per corner. (Fig. 7) Cut 1 x 4 flooring (B) to length and glue/nail to frame, using (2) 4d nails each end.

2—Posts: Attach posts (C) to base, keeping sides square with base. (Fig. 8)
TIP—Before applying 1 x 4 flooring, glue/nail the four 2 x 2 corner posts to outside corners of two 1 x 4 bottom boards. Nail from the bottom, using (2) 6d nails per post. Or toenail post to base.

Fig. 9

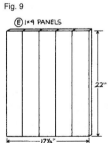

Ⓔ 1×4 PANELS
22"
17½"

Fig. 10

SIDE PANELS
Ⓓ 1×4 TRIM
22"
17½"

3—Bin Sides: Cut (20) 1 x 4 sides (E) to length and assemble the four side panels. (Fig. 9) Each side uses (5) 1 x 4s, 22" long. (For tighter joints and a more finished appearance, edge-glue and clamp 1 x 4s until glue sets.)

For side panels: Glue/nail 1 x 4 trim (D) to top and bottom of panel, flush with edges. Use 3d (1¼") nails. (Fig. 10)

Fig. 11

FRONT & BACK PANELS
1½"   1½"
Ⓕ 1×4 TRIM
22"
20½"

Fig. 12

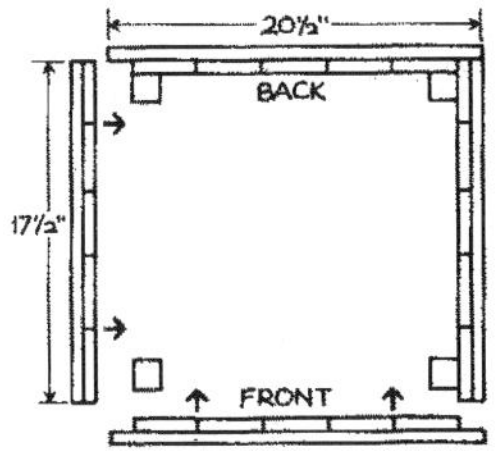

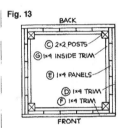

20½"
BACK
17½"
FRONT

For front and back panels: Glue/ nail 1 x 4 trim (F) to panel, flush with top and bottom edges. (Fig. 11) Trim extends 1½" on either side of panel. Attach with 1¼" nails.
4—Position front and back panels on frame so base of panel is flush with bottom of frame and top is even with top of posts. Outside edges of vertical 1 x 4 panels are flush with posts. (Fig. 12) Turn bin on side and glue/nail posts to panel, using 8d nails. Glue/nail base to frame.
5—Position side panels so base is flush with frame and outside edges are covered by front and back panels. Glue/nail to posts and base; nail corners where front and back panels overlap sides. (Fig. 12)
6—Inside trim (G): Before cutting boards, check actual measurement between posts to ensure accuracy. (Fig. 13) Glue/nail trim to inside, flush with top, using 6d (2") nails. Toenail to posts.
7—Install purchased casters on 2 x 2 frame.

Materials List for Bin

Frame: (2) 2 x 2, 17½" (front and back)
(2) 2 x 2, 13" (sides)

Floor: (5) 1 x 4, 16"
Posts: (4) 2 x 2, 19¾"
Side panels: (20) 1 x 4, 22"
Front/back panel trim: (4) 1 x 4, 20½"
Side panel trim: (4) 1 x 4, 17½"
Inside trim: (2) 1 x 4, 14½" (front/back)
(2) 1 x 4, 13" (sides)
Nails: 8d, 6d, 4d, 3d
Yellow glue
(4) 2" casters

Fig. 13

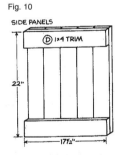

BACK
Ⓒ 2×2 POSTS
Ⓖ 1×4 INSIDE TRIM
Ⓔ 1×4 PANELS
Ⓓ 1×4 TRIM
Ⓕ 1×4 TRIM
FRONT

CLOTHES POLE/WIDE STORAGE AREAS

Fig. 14

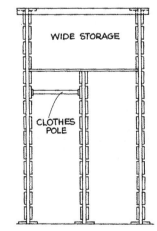

WIDE STORAGE
CLOTHES POLE

Omit shelving. (Fig. 14) Install clothes pole brackets in center of cleats approximately 40" above floor for shirts, 64" for longer items. Cut pole to length and install.

Build (or cut down) one module to desired height. (Fig. 14) Install four 1 x 6 shelves, 49½" long. Secure short module by nailing down through shelves into cleats and 2 x 4 uprights with 8d nails.

Caution: Be certain that you review and understand all steps of construction and verify all dimensions before cutting your material. While every effort has been made to insure accuracy in the design and drawings of all WWPA plans, the possibility of error always exists and WWPA cannot accept responsibility for lumber improperly used or designs not first verified.

STURDY BICYCLE RACK

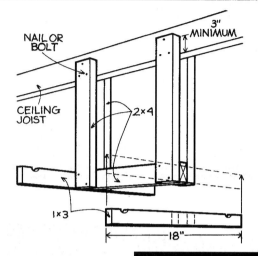

About 12 ft. of 2 x 4 and 3 ft. of 1 x 3 is all it takes to build this sturdy rack for two boys-style bikes.
1—Assemble the rack by nailing or bolting the 24" 2 x 4 between the two pairs of upright 2 x 4s. (Adjust the dimensions to fit the space and your bikes. Uprights should overlap joists by a minimum of 3".)
2—Cut a 1" notch in both ends of the 1 x 3s, 2" to 3" from the end of the boards. Nail or screw to end of rack, as illustrated.
3—Slip top of 2 x 4 uprights over ceiling joist and nail or bolt in place.

Materials List for Bicycle Rack

Materials List
Uprights: (4) 2 x 4, 28" (approx.)
Brace: (1) 2 x 4, 24" (approx.)
Hangers: (2) 1 x 3, 18"
Nails: 10d
Bolts/screws: (Optional) ¼" (minimum diameter) machine or carriage bolts

NOTE: Be certain that you review and understand all steps of construction and verify all dimensions before cutting your material. While every effort has been made to insure accuracy in the design and drawing of all WWPA plans, the possibility of error always exists and WWPA cannot accept responsibility for lumber improperly used or designs not first verified.

These Western Wood Product Association plans show you how to build a number of different specialty-type garage storage units. Any of them should help you better organize your garage/workshop to make more room available for your auto endeavors.

OVERHEAD STORAGE

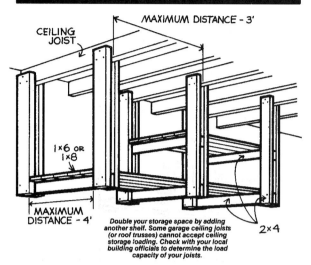

Double your storage space by adding another shelf. Some garage ceiling joists (or roof trusses) cannot accept ceiling storage loading. Check with your local building officials to determine the load capacity of your joists.

You may think your garage can't hold another thing. But have you looked at all that unused space overhead? Here's a suspended storage unit that takes advantage of that space to store lightweight, bulky items, such as sleeping bags, holiday ornaments and empty luggage.
1—Assemble two or more shelf support units, following directions given in Step 1 for "Bike Rack." (Omit 1 x 3s.) Distance between uprights should not exceed 4'.

2—Attach to ceiling joist, as directed. Distance between vertical support units should not exceed 3'.
3—Nail or bolt 1 x 6 or 1 x 8 boards to base, as shown.

Materials List for Overhead Storage

Shelf support: Each pair of supports uses approximately 12' of 2 x 4. Adjust dimensions to fit space. Shelving: 1 x 6 or 1 x 8, as needed

NOTE: Maximum spans for 2 x 4s are based on the use of Standard or Better grade lumber.

RAIN AND SNOW GEAR HANG-UP

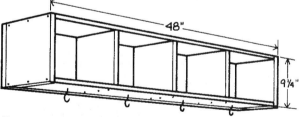

Now you can put an end to wet, muddy clothes in the house. This handy "closet," with shelves for shoes, boots and gloves, makes it easy to shed soggy outdoor gear in the garage. Mount it low enough so the kids can reach it too.
1—Glue/nail ends to shelves, using 6d nails. Glue and nail or screw back to shelves and ends, using 6d nails or 1½" screws.
2—Glue and nail dividers in place, as illustrated, using 6d nails on top,

bottom and back. Install coat hooks under bottom shelf.
3—Locate studs and attach unit to wall, using two 2½" screws per stud.

Materials List for Hang-Up

Shelves: (2) 1 x 10, 46½"
Ends: (2) 1 x 10, 9¼"
Back: (1) 1 x 10, 4'
Dividers: (3) 1 x 10, 7¾"
4 coat hooks
Construction glue
Fasteners: 6d nails

BETWEEN-STUDS STORAGE

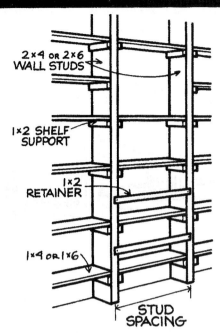

2×4 or 2×6 WALL STUDS

1×2 SHELF SUPPORT

1×2 RETAINER

1×4 or 1×6

STUD SPACING

If the wall studs in your garage are not covered, you already have a built-in shelf system. All you have to do is add 1 × 4 or 1 × 6 shelving.

Use 1 × 2s the depth of the stud for shelf supports, then nail the shelves in place. A 1 × 2 retainer may be added for small items.

FLIP-TOP SHELF

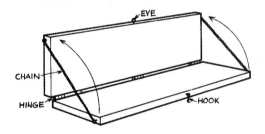

EYE

CHAIN

HINGE

HOOK

Tired of wrestling with an armload of groceries while you fumble for the house keys? Install this fold-away shelf in the garage near the back door to make unloading the car a lot easier.

1—Shelf must be long enough to extend over two studs (usually 16" apart), but that is the only length restriction.

2—Cut shelf board and back board same length. Install hinges along edges of boards, as illustrated, not more than 24" apart. Locate studs and nail or screw backboard to

studs with 10d nails or 1½" screws.

3—Install a chain at both ends of shelf to support shelf in open position. Install hook and eye or magnetic catch to keep shelf in closed position when not in use.

Materials List for Flip-Top Shelf

(2) 1 × 8 or 1 × 10 boards
Hinges
Fasteners, 10d nails or 2½" screws
Chain
Hook & eye

EASY SKI RACK

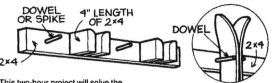

DOWEL OR SPIKE   4" LENGTH OF 2×4

2×4

DOWEL   2×4

VARIATION: Dowels may also be used to support skis.

This two-hour project will solve the ski storage problem forever. It's all done with 2 × 4s.

1—Cut two 4" lengths of 2 × 4 for each pair of skis. Round inside corners, as illustrated.

2—From the back, glue/nail or screw blocks to horizontal 2 × 4, using two 12d nails or 2½" screws per block. Space blocks 1" to 1½" apart. (Check your skis for exact

spacing.) Allow about 12" between skis.

3—Locate studs and attach rack with two 12d nails per stud.

4—Install a 4" dowel (or 12d nail) for poles. To install dowel, drill a hole the diameter of the dowel and ¾" deep, glue dowel in place.

UTILITY SHELVES

(Plans courtesy Georgia-Pacific)

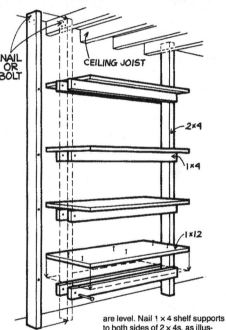

NAIL OR BOLT

CEILING JOIST

2×4

1×4

1×12

Here's a handy shelf unit that's exceptionally easy to build. Because of the sturdy T-style design of the shelf support, shelves may be up to 8' long.

1—To determine length of 2 × 4s, measure distance between floor and ceiling joist and add at least 3" for overlap.

2—Temporarily nail 2 × 4s in place and check with a level to make sure they are vertical. Finish nailing 2 × 4s to joists, using (3) nails per 2 × 4.

3—Mark location of shelves on vertical 2 × 4s, making sure shelves

are level. Nail 1 × 4 shelf supports to both sides of 2 × 4s, as illustrated. (If unit is too close to wall to nail shelf supports, drill ¼" holes through all thicknesses and secure with 5½" carriage bolts.) Nail shelves to 1 × 4 supports with 8d nails.

Materials List for Utility Shelves

Uprights: (2) 2 × 4s
Shelf supports: (2) 1 × 4s per shelf
Shelves: 1 × 10 or 1 × 12, up to 8' long
Nails: 6d, 8d
Bolts: (optional) 5½" carriage bolts

Garages and workshops with living areas or offices above are unable to provide any type of attic storage space. However, it is reasonable to expect that the joists above these attic-less areas are at least 9 to 10 inches deep. Thus, you may be able to take advantage of the open space between joists. Since these spaces separate garage/workshop areas from actual home living spaces, the top and sides must be covered with 5/8-inch thick drywall or a comparable fire resistive material.

Taking full advantage of the entire open space between garage and basement ceiling joists eliminates the opportunity to insulate the ceiling between the garage and basement and the floor above. Consider using insulating foam board if insulation is an important concern, either for temperature control or soundproofing. This material is available in different widths and corresponding R-values. At a 1-1/2- or 2-inch thickness, insulating foam board will help to insulate and soundproof, while taking up only minimal space.

Out of the way areas

Searching for out of the way storage areas in a basement, garage or detached auto workshop can be enlightening. This is especially true when conducting a full frame-off auto restoration. In their assembled state, automobiles take up a specific amount of room, namely one parking stall. However, once you start dismantling a project vehicle, it may

seem that nothing short of an aircraft hangar will be big enough to handle all the parts.

This is where you must take time to straighten up and organize all storage areas. Leave no empty spaces in cabinets or on shelves. Install shelves above doorways and maybe on the backsides of solid core doors. If a workbench was pulled away from the wall a few inches, would there be room to slide in a deck lid, hood or door? What if some of the wheeled equipment pieces were moved away from the wall a few inches? Would this make room for some of the larger dismantled auto parts?

Many avid and experienced auto enthusiasts solved their dismantled auto parts storage problems early on by constructing small sheds in their homes' back or side yards. Maybe a simple lean-to built on the side of your garage or workshop would suffice?

Economical metal and plastic sheds can be purchased in kit form from home improvement centers and other retail stores. *Hemmings Motor News* and other auto magazines frequently carry ads from mail order companies that manufacture and sell tent-like storage structures that are easy to put together. If your garage, basement or detached workshop is simply overflowing you may have to just bite the bullet and make plans for a storage shed.

Crates and Drums

Milk crates can be great sources for storing many things. They are sturdy and their open design makes it easy to see the objects stored in them. One or two crates just placed on the floor may work well for temporary storage, but why waste valuable floor space for just a couple of crates? Instead, build a platform on wheels that can support four milk crates placed next to each other in a square. Then stack crates on top of the first tier for added storage. You may find that this system will safely handle 24 crates; four tiers with six crates to a tier.

Empty drums may also prove useful as storage containers. Fifty-five-gallon drums are heavy and difficult to move around easily, but smaller ones might be perfect for storing clean rags, spare upholstery parts (like arm rests and console pieces), floor mats, hoses, belts, rolls of masking paper or paper towels, and so on. Outfit the tops of drums with plywood and cover those lids with cushions to turn the drums into dual purpose storage units and handy stools.

A large heavy duty storage rack in the corner of a garage or workshop next to a garage door opening might be perfect for storing dismantled auto parts, especially for frame-off restorations. The top illustration shows a horizontal view of a 2-foot wide, 4-foot long and 8-foot high rack made with 2x4s and 3/4-inch plywood. The bottom illustration is a vertical view looking down. It shows how 2x4 shelf frames are constructed and lag bolted to wall studs.

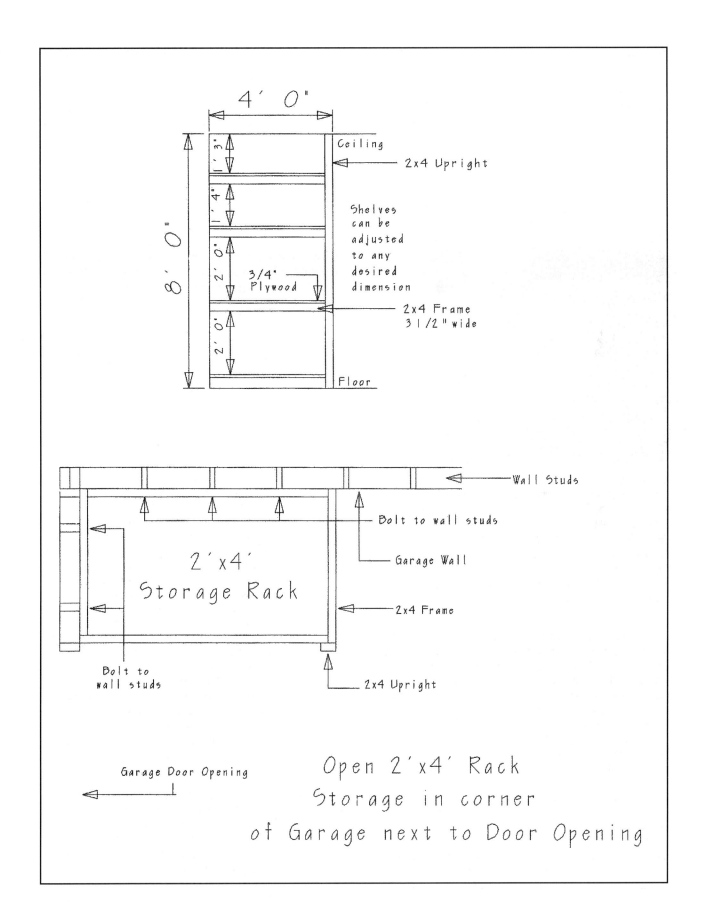

4' 0"

8' 0"

1' 3"

1' 4"

2' 0"

2' 0"

Ceiling

2x4 Upright

Shelves
can be
adjusted
to any
desired
dimension

3/4"
Plywood

2x4 Frame
3 1/2 " wide

Floor

Wall Studs

Bolt to wall studs

Garage Wall

2' x 4'
Storage Rack

2x4 Frame

Bolt to
wall studs

2x4 Upright

Garage Door Opening

Open 2' x 4' Rack
Storage in corner
of Garage next to Door Opening

133

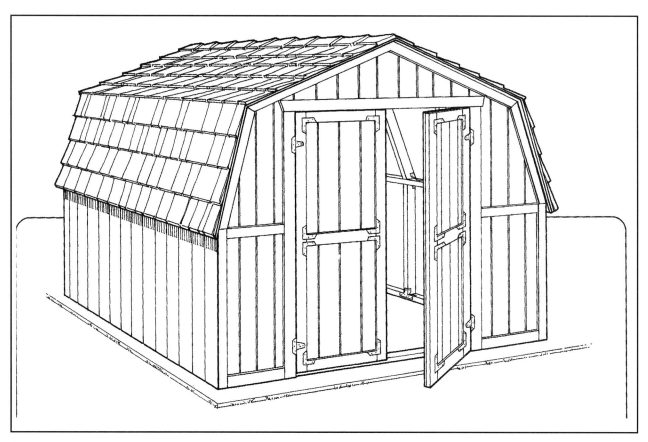

Sheds make ideal storage for household items and dismantled auto parts. The Simpson Strong-Tie Connector Company offers kits for its Utility Shed design. Kits include easy-to-follow plans and all the hardware needed to build this attractive unit.

Cupboard and Cabinet doors

The inside faces of cupboard and cabinet doors make great spots for pegboard. In addition, you can outfit most doors with small shelves. Shelves must be equipped with fronts to keep items from falling off of them each time doors are opened or closed. Small door shelves are great for storing boxes of screws, rivets and other fasteners. You could also design larger shelves to hold sandpaper, magazines, notebooks with information about project vehicles and operating instructions for power tools and equipment.

Hooks with threaded shanks could be installed on the inside faces of solid doors to hold power tool accessories, rolls of tape, wrenches, sanding discs, etc. When outfitting cupboard or cabinet doors, be certain that screws are driven into solid wood. If your cupboards or cabinets are equipped with panel or hollow core doors, like many kitchen units, you must ensure that screws are driven into the door edges only, as panels will not support screws or hooks nor the loads placed on them.

Mobile Carts

Almost all professional auto repair shops use mobile carts. Most are made of metal and have a shelf at the bottom and a lip around the work top to keep screws and other things from falling off. Heavy-duty locking wheels make them easy to roll around and secure once positioned for the work at hand. Work carts can be simple, as just described, or they can be designed to serve as combination workbenches and storage units.

Large combination mobile work carts and storage units may prove most useful for those auto enthusiasts with limited floor space. Tools and supplies are easy to roll out to carports and driveways when one-car garages are full and work needs to be done on other vehicles. Equipped with a vise, a multiple outlet electrical extension cord and pegboard for hand tool storage, mobile work carts may prove most convenient. The lower portions of mobile work carts could be left open for transporting auto parts to and from main workshop areas. This can be useful for those who have parts cars outdoors or large workshop areas.

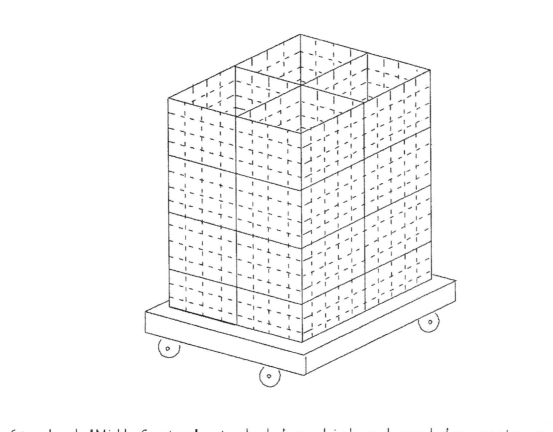

Standard "Milk Crates" stacked four high and used for parts or other storage. Crates are stacked on top of a wood or metal base equipped with casters. Each crate is independent for easy removal.

Another simple means of creative storage involves the use of common milk crates. A wood frame and plywood floor equipped with casters can support a number of milk crates stacked on top of each other. Openings on the sides of crates make it easy to see what is stored in them. Simply lift one off of the other to get to those crates that store the things needed. On casters, this unit is easily moved from place to place around workshops.

Other Storage Solutions

A quick inspection of the workshops, homes and surrounding yards belonging to many avid auto enthusiasts and restorers will quickly reveal their inventive nature. Some have installed patio covers between their homes and workshops to create new storage spaces. Lean-to covers have been built to extend from just under the eaves of workshops to the tops of fences a few feet away. Parts cars with windows intact have served as satisfactory storage depots, as have barn lofts, under-house crawl spaces, vacated bedrooms, and home attic spaces.

Remember that storing dismantled greasy car parts in vacant bedrooms will probably not be welcomed by your spouse or significant other. However, rejuvenated parts freshly painted and crisply detailed might be kept in such otherwise empty household spaces.

For dirty parts, consider laying out a sheet of plastic with a piece of plywood on top in the crawl space under your house. Moisture in this area may be a problem, so be sure to protect unpainted parts and those that might be susceptible to rust. If the crawl space is big enough, like under homes built on the sides of hills, you may be able to set up a storage room with a concrete floor and walls. Plan to install lights, too.

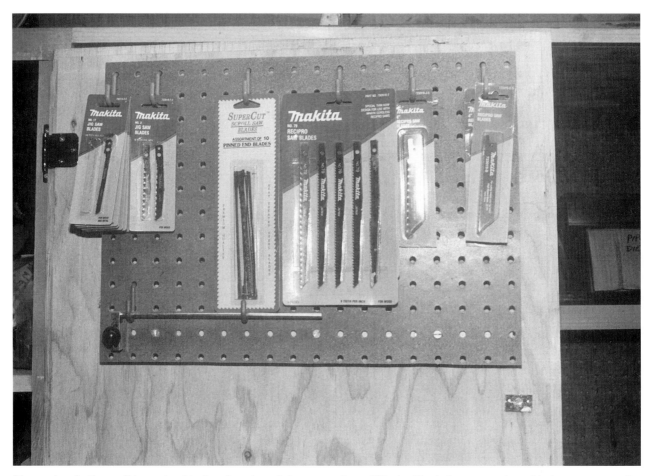

Plywood and other solid wood cabinet and cupboard doors may be outfitted with shelves or pegboard to increase overall storage capacity. Be sure to mount pegboard on runners to make room for the hooks to fit behind. Be careful when driving screws into doors to ensure they are not driven through the front faces.

Overview

Try as they may, most auto enthusiasts have never come up with a perfect set of workshop storage plans the first time around. Most have remodeled, added onto or built new shops that incorporated the numerous new ideas they discovered through trial and error or by visiting other shops. Working room and storage space always seem to be major concerns. Therefore, try to envision the type of work you expect to undertake in your workshop area and the real needs for storage of all kinds.

Planning now for the future should help you prepare for what's ahead. If you hope to complete a frame off restoration of a 1958 Oldsmobile or other large automobile in a year or two, you had better start thinking about some major storage concerns for big auto parts and assemblies. A storage shed might be perfect for all the household stuff currently housed in your garage or workshop, as you'll need the entire garage for your auto project. Planning for that situation ahead of time should help you prepare for the storage shed regarding both budget and design.

Generally, creative storage for normal auto tools and supplies and the parts that come off project vehicles can be safe and convenient. This is as long as you understand that storage units must be sturdy enough to support the loads placed on them and secured strongly enough to walls to prevent them from falling down. Look through auto magazines and visit auto workshops that belong to relatives, friends and fellow car club members. New ideas for storing workshop items are developed every day. As you use your workshop more and more, you'll soon discover your own methods for creating and developing creative workshop storage.

The ROW-503 from Stack-On Products is like a workbench on wheels. It features tool drawers and plenty of space to store parts and supplies. In addition, the top surface could be outfitted with a small vise and be used as a mini-workbench. Large wheels make this unit very easy to move around.

Dave Bowes, a product development person for The Eastwood Company, says, "Auto workshops are much more than just work spaces for car guys, they are meeting places, too!" He regards his shop as a spot where those with auto interests can gather to talk about new car stuff, old stuff and everything in between. Bowes takes special pride in making his shop look good—not just clean, but decorated, in a sense. He likes pegboard painted red and neat car posters on the walls. His workbench is covered with a stainless steel cap that is rolled under at the front and folded up at the back to create a back splash. He says that the stainless steel cap cost a little over $100, but is bulletproof. He can mix body filler on it, hammer on it and do most anything else and the cap cleans up to look great.

Workshop extras can mean anything from custom sheet metal workbench caps and bathrooms to auto lifts and television sets. It all depends on your budget, preferred creature comforts and available workshop space.

Special Accessories

The basics of any auto workshop focus on maneuvering room, tools and equipment. Beyond that, plan to outfit your workshop with special accessories to help make it a more enjoyable place to hang out. Simple creature comforts, such as a radio, a television, a comfortable chair, a refrigerator, etc., will help make the time you spend in your shop more enjoyable.

One of the most convenient workshop accessories you should consider is a sink with hot and cold water. Working on automobiles is frequently dirty work. Having a sink near by to wash greasy hands will be greatly appreciated when you need to thumb through a service manual, install new parts, put together small assemblies, eat lunch or get something out of your eye. In fact, a sink with running water may be looked upon as a safety device for rinsing eyes, cleaning wounds and so on. A large slop sink will offer more than just convenience, as its large size can accommodate car parts, tools and other objects.

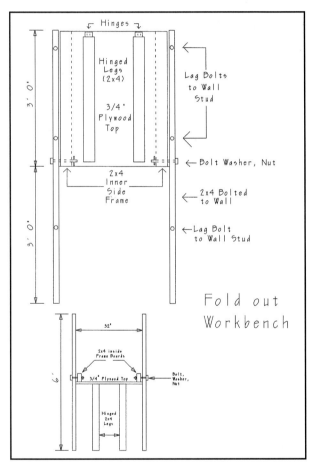

Fold-out workbenches may be required for small one-car garage workshops but can also prove useful in larger facilities. Outfitted with special tools for specific projects, a fold-out workbench might be a perfect accessory that can fold out of the way when not needed. This simple design features two 6-foot 2x4s lag bolted to wall studs through their width to provide a 3 1/2-inch wide frame. Two 3-foot 2x4s are secured to the top of a piece of 3/4-inch plywood to serve as a worktop frame and pivots. Bolts are run through both the outer frame and worktop frame members to make a pivot point. Two other 3-foot 2x4s are then hinged to the outer edge of the worktop to become support legs when the unit is pulled out.

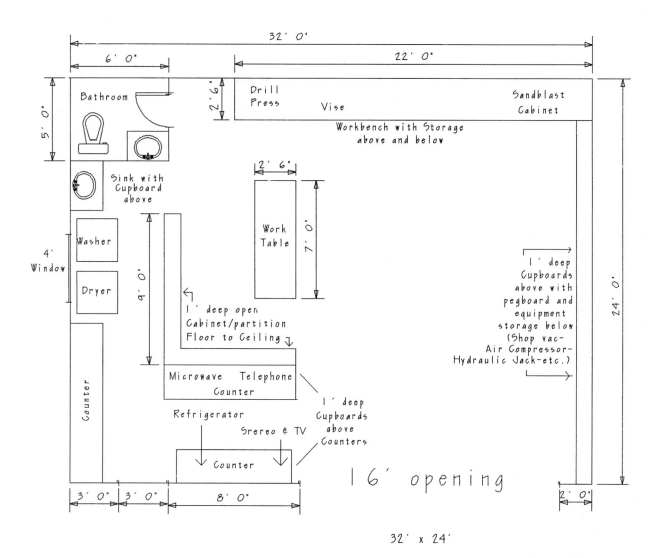

32' 0'

6' 0'   22' 0'

5' 0'

2' 6"

Bathroom   Drill Press   Vise   Sandblast Cabinet

Workbench with Storage above and below

Sink with Cupboard above

2' 6'

Work Table

7' 0'

4' Window

Washer

Dryer

9' 0'

1' deep open Cabinet/partition Floor to Ceiling

1' deep Cupboards above with pegboard and equipment storage below (Shop vac- Air Compressor- Hydraulic Jack-etc.)

24' 0'

Counter

Microwave   Telephone Counter

Refrigerator

Stereo & TV

1' deep Cupboards above Counters

Counter

16' opening

3' 0'   3' 0'   8' 0'

2' 0'

32' x 24'

Jeff Myer likes to spend time in his detached garage/workshop because most of his hobbies involve cars, trucks, boats and other motor vehicles. Therefore, he has outfitted his shop with creature comforts; like a refrigerator, microwave oven, television, sound system, a cupboard full of snacks and plenty of tools.

Workshops should be provided with some form of heat, especially in regions with cold winters. Ceiling mount natural gas and electric units work well, as do pot bellied wood stoves, hot water heating systems, etc. Of greatest concern with any workshop heater is its potential to become a fire's ignition source. This is a grave concern whenever gasoline vapors are present from a spill or leak, when conducting any type of painting and when cleaning parts with a petroleum solvent. Should any of these situations occur, make absolutely certain that all pilot lights are extinguished and natural gas lines turned off, and power to electrical heaters is switched off at the circuit breaker.

Electrical extension cords strung out over workshop floors are a hazard and a nuisance. Cords on retractable reels are really the only way to go. This model is equipped with a drop light and is located between two stalls in Chuck Saydan's workshop. Positioned near the garage doors, it comes in handy when working on rear end assemblies and when cars are parked on the driveway and need emergency repairs at night.

A cordless telephone is very handy. You can stand over your project vehicle and look at the assemblies you are describing to an auto parts person. A telephone conversation may be carried on without having to completely stop what work you might be doing. A cordless phone may be a lifesaver should you need to call for help in an emergency. An intercom between your workshop and house might also prove to be a handy and useful step saver.

A heating system will be greatly appreciated, especially by those who live in areas with harsh winters. Air conditioners, on the other hand, may be worth their weight in gold for workshops located in warmer climates.

Many auto professionals and enthusiasts have found excellent uses for file cabinets. Along with automotive records and journals, file cabinets are used to store books, service manuals, auto magazines, operating manuals for power tools and equipment, auto parts manuals, and other things—even sheets of sandpaper. A desk and chair may prove useful while conducting research work, especially for those interested in concours quality auto restorations.

Jeff Myer is an avid auto do-it-yourselfer. He enjoys spending time in his detached garage workshop. Over time, he has set up the shop with a sound system, a television, a refrigerator, a microwave oven, a cupboard full of snacks, an easy chair and a bathroom. The clothes washer and dryer along one wall are separated from the workshop area by a 12-inch deep floor to ceiling partition that doubles as a huge open storage cabinet.

Moving car bodies and frames around workshops is made much easier and safer with use of special dollies. A number of different brands are frequently advertised in *Hemmings Motor News* and other auto related magazines. Some are capable of supporting full size cars in a 360-degree rotation. This makes it easy to complete undercarriage work and other special restoration endeavors.

Special workshop accessories may include almost anything that makes the time you spend in your shop more convenient, comfortable and safe. A paper towel dispenser, a hand cleaner dispenser, a coat rack for coveralls, extra compressed air outlets, a ceiling mounted air hose reel, a portable light on a stand, a tire changing machine, and anything else that can save you time and energy may be considered a special accessory. Nothing is really taboo, as long as the item or piece of equipment is operated safely and according to manufacturer's instructions.

Specific Processes

Many auto repair, alteration or restoration projects require the use of special equipment or processes. Most of this equipment is available from The Eastwood Company, Harbor Freight Tools, other auto and tool related mail order outlets, local retail tool outlets and autobody supply houses. To customize the use of your process equipment, you might be able to build specialty centers around your workshop so systems can be up and running in a matter of minutes.

Sandblast Cabinet

Auto restorers rely on sandblasting as a way to prepare various parts and assemblies for refinishing. While portable sandblasters work well, they can create quite a mess. This is where a sandblast cabinet may prove most efficient. Units are available in benchtop or larger stand-alone models. Sandblast cabinets maintain media inside units so workshops remain clean and media can be recycled. Sandblast cabinets are outfitted with heavy-duty rubber gloves. Many users extend the life of these gloves by putting a set of leather gloves over them.

Welding Center

Welders employ numerous means for securing metal parts. Some use portions of their car lifts as welding stands. Others rely mostly on clamps. For many smaller welding chores, consider setting up a benchtop welding center. You will need a ventilation system, like the exhaust hoods used for kitchen stoves. Be sure to install the proper type of ducting through walls and to the outside. This material should be insulated to protect walls from the heat that will pass through the ducts. Material is available at home improvement centers and wood stove outlets that sell exhaust ducting for heating systems.

The welding center should also be equipped with metal walls to keep sparks confined. Sand and fire bricks in the base will serve as a way to secure parts for welding. The welder can rest on a shelf below the center and all welding clamps and tools maintained close by for convenience. Be sure a fire extinguisher is close at hand.

Parts Cleaning

Cleaning greasy auto parts is never a pleasant job. However, this task is made easier with use of a parts washer. These tubs are equipped with pumps that circulate solvent or degreasing fluid through units and out small nozzles. Racks and shelves are handy for storing parts during cleaning episodes and for parts drying. Parts cleaning tubs feature lids that are supported in open positions with fusible link assemblies. If fire occurs in a tub, the fusible link will melt and the lid will close to smother the fire. Instead of solvent, many auto enthusiasts have had good results using biodegradable and nonflammable degreasing fluids.

Spray Painting

Because of environmental concerns and rules and regulations, painting automobiles in home workshops or garages has become a major concern. Adding to those concerns are the harmful respiratory effects posed by some materials now used extensively in newer paint products. In addition to the use of fresh air respiratory systems, home based auto painters must also be concerned about paint overspray and the pollution caused by solvents in paint products. It may not be long before automobiles may only be painted in approved spray paint booths to help eliminate the air pollution caused by paint overspray.

If you are able to paint cars in your workshop or garage, you should insist upon using a full face fresh air respirator. Units are available through The Eastwood Company, local autobody and paint supply stores and outlets that sell safety equipment. In addition, you should wear painter's coveralls and latex gloves. To help reduce overspray, and save paint, use a High Volume Low Pressure (HVLP) paint system.

Painting stalls can be created in workshops or garages with the use of heavy mil plastic. Secure a strong cable from the ceiling around the stall and attach plastic with shower curtain hooks. Clean the floor and wet it down with water to help reduce paint overspray from sticking to it. With a workshop or garage door open, and the outside ground or driveway wet down with water to keep dust at bay, place a fan at the other end of the stall so it blows air out. This will give you a mini paint booth with ventilation.

Workshop lighting is vital for safe and efficient working. Be inventive with the lighting in your shop and install extra fixtures in special places where they will do you the most good. Chuck Saydan installed a 4-foot fluorescent light on the side wall of his shop to help illuminate the area under vehicles while they were raised on his lift. Autobody repair technicians also like to install lights on side walls to help them spot defects on body side panels.

Overview

Home workshops and garages are places where do-it-yourselfer's accomplish, or try to accomplish, a wide variety of projects. As an auto enthusiast, chances are you also have interests in home improvement and woodworking. This brings up another area of concern—where do you store and operate woodworking machines? After all, sawdust and precision engine parts are not necessarily compatible.

One way to solve the mixture of an auto workshop and woodworking shop is to keep the areas separated. One side of the workshop could be outfitted with auto tools and equipment, while the other is set up with woodworking machines. Secure a cable across the ceiling in the middle of the shop and hang a plastic curtain from it to help keep sawdust away from dismantled engines, transmissions and other auto parts. Invest in a quality sawdust vacuum control system, too. (8-9)

Once you begin to use your workshop on a regular basis, you will soon discover that some alterations may work to serve you better. This always happens. It is doubtful that any workshop owner has ever set up his or her shop perfectly the first time. Those who spend time in home workshops relish opportunities to improve upon what they already have. It is fun to install new pieces of equipment and set up new creature comforts. Do the best you can during the planning and creative stages of your new workshop area. Should you come across a new idea while setting up the space, put it into effect. Always keep personal and overall workshop safety at the forefront of your installations and have fun. Look upon your new workshop as a place where you will accomplish many tasks, have a good time teaching others the things you have learned and enjoy yourself doing the things you like to do.

SOURCES

Products, diagrams, information and photos from a number of different companies have appeared throughout this book. For your convenience, the following is a list of these companies, complete with their addresses and telephone numbers. You are encouraged to contact them for additional information, product literature, catalogs, and the like.

Adjustable Clamp Company
417 North Ashland Avenue
Chicago, IL 60622-6397
(312) 666-0640
Jorgensen, Pony, and Adjustable Clamps

American Plywood Association (APA)
PO Box 11700
Tacoma, WA 98411
(206) 565-6600
Information and Building Plans for Plywood

American Tool Companies, Inc.
PO Box 337
De Witt, NE 68341
(402) 683-2315
Vise-Grip, Quick-Grip, Prosnip, CHESCO, and more tools

Behr Process Corporation
3400 West Segerstrom Avenue
Santa Ana, CA 92704
(800) 854-0133
Paint, stain, varnish, sealers, and more

Campbell Hausfeld
100 Production Drive
Harrison, OH 45030
(513) 367-4811
Air compressors, pneumatic tools, pressure washers, and more

Crush-Proof Tubing Company
100 North Street
McComb, OH 45858
(800) 654-6858
Vehicle exhaust tubing for workshops

Eagle Windows and Doors
375 East Ninth Street
Dubuque, IA 52004
(319) 556-2270
High-quality wood windows and doors

The Eastwood Company
580 Lancaster Avenue, Box 3014
Malvern, PA 19355-0714
(800) 345-1178
Automotive restoration tools, equipment and supplies

Harbor Freight Tools (Central Purchasing, Inc.)
3491 Mission Oaks Boulevard
Camarillo, CA 93011
(800) 423-2567
Automotive tools, equipment and supplies

Kohler Company
444 Highland Drive
Kohler, WI 53044
(414) 457-4441
Bathroom fixtures and accessories

Lasko Metal Products, Inc.
820 Lincoln Avenue
West Chester, PA 19380
(800) 394-3267
Power Toolbox, fans and more

Makita USA, Inc.
14930 Northam Street
La Miranda, CA 90638-5753
(714) 522-8088
Power and cordless tools and equipment

Plano Molding Company
431 East South Street
Plano, IL 60545-1601
(800) 874-6905
Plastic toolboxes, storage units and shelves

Power Products Company (SIMKAR)
Cayuga and Ramona Streets
Philadelphia, PA 19120
(800) 346-7833
Fluorescent lighting

Quality Doors
603 Big Stone Gap Road
Duncanville, TX 75137
(800) 950-3667
Cabinet doors and refacing materials

Rotary Lift (A Dover Industries Company)
2700 Lanier Drive
PO Box 1560
Madison, IN 47250-0560
(800) 445-5438
Automotive lifts

Simpson Strong-Tie Connector Company, Inc.
4637 Chabot Drive, Suite 200
Pleasanton, CA 94588
(800) 999-5099
Metal connectors, shed kit, and construction supplies

Smithy Company
3023 East 2nd Street
The Dalles, OR 97058
(800) 345-6342
Multi-purpose lathe, drill, mill

Stack-on Products
Box 489
Wauconda, IL 60084
(847) 526-1611 Fax: (847) 526-6599
Metal storage cabinets

The Stanley Works
1000 Stanley Drive
New Britain, CT 06053
(800) 551-5936
Hand tools, hardware and more

Sta-Put Color Pegs
23504-29th Avenue West
Lynnwood, WA 98036-8318
(206) 483-9694
Pegboard hooks that stay in place

Western Wood Products Association
522 SW Fifth Avenue
Portland, OR 97204-2122
(503) 224-3930
Information and building plans for wood

WoodsmithShop Catalog
2200 Grand Avenue
Des Moines, IA 50312
(800) 444-7002
*Fold-Down Work Center, woodworking tools, plans
    and supplies*

INDEX